ST. MARY'S COLLEGE
LIBRARY

EthniCity

EthniCity

Geographic Perspectives on Ethnic Change in Modern Cities

Edited by
Curtis C. Roseman
Hans Dieter Laux
and
Günter Thieme

ROWMAN & LITTLEFIELD PUBLISHERS, INC.

ROWMAN & LITTLEFIELD PUBLISHERS, INC.

Published in the United States of America
by Rowman & Littlefield Publishers, Inc.
4720 Boston Way, Lanham, Maryland 20706

3 Henrietta Street
London WC2E 8LU, England

British Cataloging in Publication Information Available

Library of Congress Cataloging-in-Publication Data

EthniCity : geographic perspectives on ethnic change in modern cities
/ edited by Curtis C. Roseman, Hans Dieter Laux, and Günter Thieme.
p.   cm.
Includes bibliographical references and index.
1. Cities and towns.   2. Emigration and immigration—Social
aspects.   3. Ethnic relations.   I. Roseman, Curtis C.   II.   Laux,
Hans Dieter.   III. Thieme, Günter.
HT215.E74   1996   307.2'16—dc20   95-30780   CIP

ISBN 0-8476-8032-0 (cloth: alk. paper)
ISBN 0-8476-8033-9 (pbk.: alk. paper)

Printed in the United States of America

∞ ™ The paper used in this publication meets the minimum requirements of
American National Standard for Information Sciences—Permanence of Paper
for Printed Library Materials, ANSI Z39.48–1984.

Contents

Figures

Tables

xi

Acknowledgments

We gratefully acknowledge the assistance of many others in preparing this volume. We thank the Commission on Population Geography of the International Geographical Union, Professor Daniel Noin, president, for sponsorship of the symposium and support for the book cartography. The Department of Geography, University of Southern California, provided additional support for the symposium. Among several individuals who assisted in the organization of the symposium and subsequent preparation of the book are Elizabeth Roseman, James Tyner, Estella Tilley, Jennifer Gaston, and Darlene Warr. Eugene Turner and Patricia Neumann provided help with the production of maps. Our final thank you goes to Professor Diego Vigil of the University of Southern California from whom we borrowed the name for this book, *EthniCity*.

Introduction

Modern EthniCities

Curtis C. Roseman, Hans Dieter Laux, and Günter Thieme

In the waning years of the twentieth century, fundamental changes in global political, economic, social, and cultural systems are occurring. Such changes are intimately linked to shifts in migration systems that have carried diverse sets of people on a variety of paths. Among the most prominent of these paths are migration flows from third world countries to more-developed countries. Many urban areas in the developed world are experiencing ethnic diversity in their populations that is of recent origin. These, along with cities that have a longer history of ethnic diversity, contain varieties of peoples having distinctive cultures and origins. We call these cities EthniCities.

In EthniCities, various combinations of ethnic groups often compete for housing, employment, educational resources, and political representation. Frequently, urban ethnic groups are also confronted by residential segregation, discrimination, xenophobia, and conflict. Ethnic diversity, however, has contributed to the cultural enrichment of many urban places, including the diversification of language and religion, and the emergence of new cultural activities such as ethnic businesses, restaurants, and festivals.

This book focuses on geographical processes and concomitant socioeconomic and political issues associated with ethnic diversity in a variety of urban areas in eleven countries. Although varying in size, complexity, and historical background, each of these urban areas contains ethnic diversity that is of crucial importance to fundamental issues facing their respective societies. In some cases the population size and residential spatial distribution of some or all ethnic groups has been relatively stable; in many other cases these dimensions have changed very rapidly in the last few years.

In this volume, both the broader geographic context and more specific analyses of ethnicity are presented for each EthniCity. Each urban chapter first reviews aspects of the roots of ethnic diversity in its urban area, thereby linking each city to broader migration processes. Each also presents analyses and interpretations of recent intraurban ethnic patterns, with particular emphasis on spatial processes and related issues.

Among our collection of EthniCities are the very large "world cities," such as Los Angeles, London, and Paris, which are central nodes in global systems of trade, communications, and migration (Sassen 1991). In addition, several smaller urban areas are included. Owing to location or economic base, they have been incorporated into new systems of migration and become more ethnically diverse in recent decades. The unique contribution of this volume, therefore, is the juxtaposition of geographic analysis and interpretation of ethnic change across a variety of urban areas that exist within a range of locational and societal contexts.

Most of the chapters in this volume began as papers presented at the International Geographical Union (IGU) Population Geography Symposium held in Los Angeles at the University of Southern California in August 1992. A primary purpose of the symposium was the comparison of urban ethnic change from a geographic viewpoint. The focus of this volume is on urban areas in eleven countries: Los Angeles and Chicago (USA), Sydney/ Melbourne (Australia), Paris (France), London (UK), Amsterdam (The Netherlands), the Ruhr conurbation (Germany), Vienna (Austria), Milan (Italy), Madrid (Spain), Johannesburg/Durban (South Africa), and Singapore.

Changing Migration Systems

Recent global political and economic restructuring has resulted in increasing and diversifying forms of labor and capital mobility (Sassen 1988; Kritz, Lim, and Zlotnik 1992; Massey et al. 1993). Migration flows are impacting urban places worldwide. The following description of major migration systems is important to understanding the emergence of EthniCities. The five general types are (1) internal migration, (2) regional international migration, (3) global migration, (4) illegal migration, and (5) refugee migration.

First, *internal migration* has contributed to ethnic diversity in urban areas within some countries. The significant migration of African-Americans to most large cities in the United States, and the migration of African Blacks to the urban regions of South Africa are among the most important. Expanded labor needs in the urban industrial sector have been a primary basis for such movements (Sassen 1988). Smaller numbers of native populations have urbanized within the United States, Canada, and Australia.

Second, *regional international migration* has supplied labor to many industrialized countries from nearby "peripheral" locations. Two of the largest in recent decades focus on the United States and Western Europe. Very large numbers of Mexicans have migrated to the United States over the last thirty years, a system that developed because of significant wage differentials coupled with spatial proximity. Although this system has a long history, the maintenance of a guest worker program—the Bracero Program—by the United States in the 1950s played an important role in the perpetuation of the system. It established strong connections between many Mexican people and places in the United States, thus establishing a familiarity with the destination country that eased later migration (Massey et al. 1987).

Guest worker programs in the industrialized countries of western Europe, established in the 1950s and 1960s, contributed to the evolution of another large regional system with origins mainly in southern Europe and Turkey. Most of these labor migrants had rural backgrounds, little education, and few job skills. Over time, as labor needs subsided, temporary migrants became permanent residents who were often joined by kin through family reunification permits (Castles and Miller 1993). Important additional regional systems include the flows in the late 1980s and early 1990s of Eastern Europeans to Western Europe due to rapid political change, of labor migration to several Southern European countries from neighboring areas of North Africa, and of migration from the Caribbean area to the United States and Canada. Some regional migration flows have evolved from previous colonial or geopolitical connections between origin and destination countries, including flows of North Africans to France, Cubans to the United States, and Pacific Islanders to New Zealand. Other regional migration systems are emerging because of regional alliances among neighboring countries. New high-skill migrants recently have been moving among the countries of the European Union, and in the future, similar flows may be stimulated by the North American Free Trade Agreement (NAFTA).

Third, longer distance *global migration streams* have been important in recent years. Changing immigration policies in the largest of the traditional immigration countries—Australia, Canada, and the United States—have stimulated much long distance settlement migration. Australia and Canada have been the destinations for a variety of European-origin migrants since World War II and, more recently, migrants from Asia. The United States has received large numbers of migrants from several Asian and Latin American countries. These and other long distance flows of settlement and labor migrants include persons with wide-ranging occupational skill levels. Many are highly educated and favored for their expertise, especially in high-technology and medical professions (Fawcett and Carino 1987; Gould 1988). Included also are entrepreneurial migrants (Portes and Rumbaut 1990) who become middleman minorities in destination countries. As with regional systems, some global migration relates to special relationships or former colonial ties, including the Philippines with the United States, Indonesia and Surinam with the Netherlands, and the Caribbean and the Indian subcontinent with the United Kingdom.

Fourth, large flows of undocumented or *illegal migrants* are imbedded within both regional and global migration systems. Most relatively developed countries are destinations for illegal immigrants who either cross borders or overstay non-immigrant visas. Illegal immigrants are especially numerous in the United States, but are found in significant numbers in Australia, New Zealand, and western and southern European countries as well.

Finally, a variety of *refugee migrations* have made significant contributions to ethnic change in many countries. These include refugees moving within Europe just after World War II, Cuban refugees moving to the United States at various points in time since 1960, people emigrating to Germany and other European countries after the breakup of the former Yugoslavia since 1991, and Southeast Asian refugees moving to the United States and many other countries in the 1970s and 1980s after the end of the Vietnam War.

All of the current international migration systems are evolving in an era of high-speed international travel and instant global communication. Frequent contact among ethnic group members in widely separated places is possible through telecommunication, travel, and even cyclical migration. The result is the ability to maintain international systems of identity among kin and even more broadly within ethnic groups (Alonso 1987). Thus, as EthniCities and other multiethnic places have emerged, so too have multiplace ethnic identity groups. Considerable return migration and periodic circulation back to the home country characterize many immigrant groups in EthniCities. Parallel to these ideas are the concepts of the "multistate nation" and "multination state," which place the idea of ethnic diversity and global ethnic connections into the context of the state (Mikesell, 1983).

Migration Systems and EthniCities

The impact of changing migration systems on many EthniCities has changed significantly over the last four decades. Strong urbanward internal migration streams, which persisted for decades until the 1960s in many developed countries, have declined as contributors to urban growth (White

1984). Instead, numerous cities in North America, Europe, and Australia have received large flows of immigrants, who have brought with them not only their labor but also their languages, religions, and other ethnic attributes that are new to their destinations.

Coupled with these new migration patterns, fertility differentials also contribute to increasing ethnic diversity. In many EthniCities, the population of the host society has experienced significantly lowered birth rates since the 1960s and a concomitant aging process. In contrast, many immigrant groups have maintained higher birth rates (White 1984; Ogden, 1984; O'Hare 1992). The result is that many EthniCities have ethnic populations of recent arrival that are growing rapidly, and whose children populate the schools and playgrounds in urban neighborhoods. The role of fertility in the differential growth of ethnic populations is particularly important in several European countries where the birth rates of the dominant populations are below replacement levels.

The EthniCities examined in this volume have emerged within countries that have experienced contrasting ethnic and migration histories. In Europe sometime in the last five decades, most countries have shifted from emigration societies to immigration societies (Sassen 1988). The migration of guest workers to many northern and western European countries in the 1950s and 1960s began a trend toward ethnic diversity in many of their cities (King 1993). Some cities, especially in the United Kingdom and France, drew immigrants mostly from former colonial origins, whereas others drew workers predominantly from southern Europe. More recently, urban areas in several southern and eastern European countries have also been receiving migrants (Castles and Miller 1993). In some European countries, including Germany, immigrants and their children often continue to be "foreigners" for an undetermined period of time due to legal restrictions on gaining citizenship. Nonetheless, the population growth of foreign groups and their establishment of communities in major cities have had a substantial impact within most European societies.

In contrast to the cities of Europe, some EthniCities have emerged within countries that have a much longer history of immigration, and whose policies permit naturalization of most immigrants. In the United States and Australia, the roots of modern ethnic diversity stem from colonists joining native populations in past centuries. Further diversity in the United States came from the importation of slaves from Africa. In these cases, however, discrimination policies and practices prevented viable communities of non-European–origin populations.

Over the last 150 years in the United States, and since World War II for Australia, additional ethnic diversity has come from massive immigration of ethnic groups mainly of European origin. EthniCities emerged with large numbers of different European ethnic neighborhoods. In the United States, most large cities also received numerous rural to urban African-American migrants in the first half of the twentieth century, adding to their ethnic diversity. Since the late 1960s ethnic change in Australian and American cities has been caused by substantial increases in immigrants from new origins as the result of revised immigration policies.

South Africa and Singapore represent contrasting cases. In South Africa, the ruling White minority, mainly of Dutch and British origin, created the apartheid system. This system, which remained in place until 1991, resulted in strict residential separation between the White minority on the one hand, and the African native population as well as the Indian and Colored population groups on the other hand. In Singapore of the nineteenth century, the native Malay population group was outnumbered by Chinese immigrants who were recruited as cheap labor by the British colonial government. Although the Chinese make up about 75 percent of Singapore's population, followed by Malays and Indians, the official ethnic policy is one of distinct multiculturalism and equal opportunities among the ethnic groups.

A range of ethnic community types is revealed in the analyses contained in this EthniCity volume. Settlement forms range from spatially distinct ethnic enclaves that contain a rich ethnic identity to scattered settlements with little localized identity within the urban area. Some ethnic groups are hidden in the urban landscape and others are quite visible as the result of particular occupational niches or community forms (Portes and Manning 1986). Numerous individual ethnic communities in EthniCities are quite new and rapidly expanding, whereas others have been in place for generations. Indeed, many have evolved from temporary settlements of guest workers (Castles and Miller 1993). Finally, some ethnic communities are severely marginalized within their broader urban and national societies, suffering from poverty, lack of access to resources, and constrainment to undesirable locations. Yet others are thriving economically and stay together largely as the result of choice.

Concepts and Measurement of Ethnicity

The meaning of ethnicity and the delineation of ethnic groups varies among different societies and, indeed, across the eleven countries covered here. A detailed discussion of the subtle, as well as dramatic, ways in which various societies construct and modify ethnic group identifications and boundaries is beyond the scope of this introduction. However, it is important to briefly introduce some ways in which ethnicity is conceptualized and how these lead to the measurement of ethnicity as the basis for aggregate analyses of ethnic communities.

Much research has taken place on ethnic identity and the identification of ethnic groups (e.g., Thernstrom 1980; Jabbra 1987; Allen and Turner 1988; Waters 1990). Some common ground in the general conceptualization of ethnicity can be gained by considering four aspects of ethnic group identification (Jabbra 1987): First, and at a minimum, most observers agree that an ethnic group has cultural characteristics that are shared. They include language, religion, and various customs. Second, ethnic groups typically have some sort of common origin, identifiable history, or self-identification. Third, structural attributes also may be important, including social interaction, demographic characteristics, and locational clustering. Finally, many ethnic groups are identified on the basis of physical characteristics, most commonly race, but also grooming, dress, and/or proxemic behaviors that have been passed on through generations.

The aggregate measurement of some ethnic characteristics is difficult using most quantitive data, including census materials. However, measures that represent broad surrogates for cultural characteristics, origin, and race are common, although their availablility varies from country to country (as is illustrated in this volume). Language spoken is a cultural measure used in the Sydney/Melbourne study (see chap. 3). Origin measures are more common and include birthplace (see chaps. 3, 5, and 8: Sydney, London, and Vienna); nationality (see chaps. 4, 6, 7, 8, 9, and 10: Paris, Amsterdam, Ruhr, Vienna, Milan, and Madrid); and foreign stock (foreign parentage), which is used in the Los Angeles analysis (chap. 1). Race measures are used in Los Angeles, Chicago (chap. 2), and South Africa (chap. 11). Finally, broader self-identified concepts of ethnicity include "ethnicity" (see chaps. 5, 6, and 12: London, Amsterdam, and Singapore) and "ancestry" (see chap. 1, Los Angeles).

What Is Ahead

The first three case studies are from two countries having long-standing immigration policies, the United States and Australia. The in-depth treatment of ethnic change in Los Angeles in chapter 1, by James P. Allen and Eugene Turner, is an appropriate beginning, not only because Los Angeles was the site of the Population Symposium upon which this volume is based, but also because Los Angeles has become one of the most ethnically diverse metropolitan areas in the world. Allen and Turner link rapid ethnic population change to the internationalization of the Los Angeles economy and the nexus of migration streams converging there. Using measures of race, Hispanic origin, and foreign stock, they track the evolution of ethnic diversity that has led to a complex set of residential segregation patterns.

Chapter 2, written by Erick Howenstine, focuses on recent changes in residential segregation in Chicago using alternative statistical measures. Howenstine shows that the long-standing strong segregation between African-American and White, European-origin populations has been modified by the presence of immigrants from Asia and Latin America. He demonstrates that White suburbanization has contributed substantially to the concentration of ethnic groups in the inner city, a phenomenon that also had a strong impact on the more complex patterns of ethnic change in Los Angeles.

In chapter 3, Graeme Hugo examines the major ethnic transformations that have occurred in recent decades in Sydney and Melbourne, Australia. A primary force underlying these transformations has been immigration from Europe since World War II, superseded more recently by Asian immigration. Hugo utilizes race, birthplace, and language as measures of ethnicity and demonstrates the emergence of a great variety of settlement forms, ranging from rapidly dispersing ethnic groups to maintenance of strong ethnic enclaves.

Chapters 4 through 10 focus on European cities. Two are very large world cities, Paris and London, whose ethnic variety derives importantly from colonial linkages. In chapter 4, Michelle Guillon and Daniel Noin analyze the development in Paris of several foreign populations whose demographic characteristics vary considerably. Early dependence on manual labor and more recent entrance into the service sector is documented. Inequalities in the employment and housing sectors persist. Unlike many other cities clear ethnic residential concentrations or enclaves have rarely developed in Paris. This may be due to the long-standing tradition of egalitarianism in France. Guillon and Noin argue that residential segregation is primarily based on socioeconomic status, rather than ethnicity.

David McEvoy, in chapter 5, analyzes data for London based on ethnic self-identification, which became available for the first time in the 1991 British census. Immigration from the Commonwealth since World War II has led to the formation of several large ethnic groups in London with Indians ranking first in number followed by Black Caribbeans. Using segregation indices, various levels of ethnic community clusters are shown to exist. McEvoy concludes that ethnic minorities are concentrated, though in a differential manner, in those parts of London's society and space that are no longer desirable to the White majority.

Like Paris and London, Amsterdam, the subject of chapter 6, has received immigrants from colonial origins. It also has received guest workers from Turkey and other Mediterranean countries. Sako Musterd and Wim Ostendorf show how the occupational and social mobility of these groups have benefited from the Netherlands' welfare-state policies. Further, the groups are not highly segregated residentially. High unemployment, exacerbated by low educational achievement, however, continues to be a major disadvantage to immigrant communities.

The Ruhr conurbation in Germany, chapter 7, is representative of traditionally heavy manufacturing areas that have experienced significant industrial restructuring over the last two decades. Hans Dieter Laux and Günter Thieme document the growth and composition of foreign populations in the region, with particular emphasis on Turks as the largest group among the guest-worker populations. Analyses of demographic structures, labor-force characteristics, and education demonstrate the position of the various groups of foreigners between marginalization and integration into the German society.

Chapter 8, by Heinz Fassmann and Rainer Münz, depicts a rich history of immigration to Vienna involving migrants from its regional hinterland and more recently labor migrants from other parts of central and southeastern Europe. As in the case of Paris, Amsterdam, and the Ruhr, many temporary labor migrants have settled permanently in Vienna. Residential and labor-market segregation significantly affect these groups. Similar to the situation in Germany, lack of citizenship and associated privileges, such as voting rights, for foreigners are important issues in Vienna.

Milan, the subject of chapter 9, has received significant numbers of immigrants only in recent years. Felicitas Hillmann documents a recent pattern of female migrants who move to Milan alone. Because many are employed as domestics, they are not concentrated spatially but distributed in very different ways than other immigrants. Existing assistance programs do not serve female immigrants adequately. Hillmann's examination of three female immigrant groups from diverse origins (Philippines, Peru, and Somalia) shows also that transnational household strategies initiate female migration to Milan.

Similar to Milan, immigration to Madrid, analyzed in chapter 10, is a relatively new phenomenon. The authors, a group of Spanish scholars, show that the origins of recent migrants to Madrid include southern Europe, North Africa, and South America. As in other cities, especially those in which immigration is of only recent origin, employment and housing opportunities are limited for foreign populations. However, major residential clusters have not yet developed. Attitudinal surveys show that social tensions between

Spaniards and immigrants are minimal, partly because of the relatively small number of immigrants.

Cities in South Africa, discussed in chapter 11, are experiencing rapid change as the result of the abolition of apartheid in 1991. Jürgen Bähr and Ulrich Jürgens focus on Johannesburg and Durban in their analysis of the forces that are shaping residential patterns. Here it is not immigration from abroad, but instead firmly institutionalized racial categories of the past, accompanied by rural to urban migration and strict residental separation, that sets the context for current changes. A variety of new settlement processes in urban and suburban areas is examined.

In the urban case study of chapter 12, Warwick Neville discusses and documents the major significance of ethnicity to a variety of government policies in Singapore. Ethnic categories—the largest being Chinese, Malay, and Indian—are based on origin and correlated highly with religion. In striking contrast to South Africa, ethnic categories have been used in Singapore as the basis for residental integration, not segregation. No ethnic enclaves or concentrations have been allowed to develop. Neville shows how ethnic management has led to the perpetualization of ethnic and cultural pluralism in Singapore.

The final chapter, "Immigration and Ethnicity in the Urban Milieu," Frederick Boal weaves together the stories of migration and urban ethnic communities that are told in the preceding chapters. Boal frames his analysis in terms of several general concepts, including Castles and Miller's (1993) immigrant settlement model and Esping-Andersen's (1991) typology of welfare states. Boal discusses contrasting forces that influence the variations in urban experience of immigrant and ethnic groups, including immigration policies, welfare structures, immigrant adjustment processes, residential segregation, societal responses to immigrants, and historical/cultural contexts. In addition, he carefully considers common threads, including some ethnic community-forming processes and roles that are played by ethnic and immigrants groups in the labor market at both low and high ends of the labor spectrum. Boal also reflects on perceptions of ethnic and immigrant groups held by "majority" or "host" societies. He does so not only by reviewing the evidence contained in the chapters, but also by summarzing the perspectives and interpretations made by chapter authors and, especially, by analyzing the language used by these authors. Boal concludes that the "rich harvest both of similarity and of contrast in urban ethnic experience" represented in the chapters of this book calls for additional, broader comparative research.

References

Allen, James P., and Eugene J. Turner. 1988. *We the People: An Atlas of America's Ethnic Diversity.* New York: Macmillan.

Alonso, William. 1987. "Identity and Population." In *Population in an Interacting World*, ed. William Alonso, Cambridge, MA: Harvard University Press.

Castles, Stephen, and Mark J. Miller. 1993. *The Age of Migration: International Population Movements in the Modern World*. New York: Guilford Press.

Esping-Andersen, Göspa. 1991. *The Three Worlds of Welfare Capitalism*. Cambridge: Polity Press.

Fawcett, James T., and Benjamin V. Cariño, eds. 1987. *Pacific Bridges: The New Immigration from Asia and the Pacific Islands*. Staten Island, NY: Center for Migration Studies.

Gould, W. T. S. 1988. "Skilled International Labor Migration: An Introduction." *Geoform* 19 (4):381–85.

Jabbra, Nancy W. 1987. "Toward a Definition of Ethnicity." *Immigration Research Report*. 1(1):5–12.

King, Russell, ed. 1993. *Mass Migrations in Europe. The Legacy and the Future*. London: Belhaven.

Kritz, Mary M., Lin Lean Lim, and Hania Zlotnik, eds. 1992. *International Migration Systems, A Global Approach*. Oxford: Clarendon Press.

Massey, Douglas S., Rafael Alarcón, Humberto Gonzáles, and Jorge Durand. 1987. *Return to Atzlan: The Social Process of International Migration from Western Mexico*. Berkeley and Los Angeles: University of California Press.

Massey, Douglas S., et al. 1993. "Theories of International Migration: A Review and Appraisal." *Population and Development Review* 19(3): 431–66.

Mikesell, Marvin W. 1983. "The Myth of the Nation State." *Journal of Geography* 82(6):257–60.

Ogden, Philip. 1984. *Migration and Geographical Change*. Cambridge: Cambridge University Press.

O'Hare, William P. 1992. "America's Minorities—The Demographics of Diversity." *Population Bulletin* 47(4). Washington, D.C.: Population Reference Bureau.

Portes, Alejandro, and Robert D. Manning. 1986. "The Immigrant Enclave: Theory and Empirical Examples." In *Competetive Ethnic Relations*, ed. Susan Olzak and Joane Nagel. Orlando, FL: Academic Press.

Portes, Alejandro, and Ruben G. Rumbaut. 1990. *Immigrant America: A Portrait*. Berkeley, Los Angeles, and Oxford: University of California Press.

Sassen, Saskia. 1988. *The Mobility of Labor and Capital*. Cambridge: Cambridge University Press.

———. 1991. *The Global City: New York, London, Tokyo*. Princeton, N. J.: Princeton University Press.

Thernstrom, S. 1980. *Harvard Encyclopedia of American Ethnic Groups*. Cambridge, MA: Harvard University Press.

Waters, Mary C. 1990. *Ethnic Options: Choosing Identities in America*. Berkeley: University of California Press.

White, Paul. 1984. *The West European City: A Social Geography*. London and New York: Longman

Chapter 1

Ethnic Diversity and Segregation in the New Los Angeles

James P. Allen and Eugene Turner

The nature of Los Angeles has undergone a major shift in just three decades. In the early 1960s, its people were mostly transplants from eastern and midwestern states, and the majority were of European ancestry. By the 1970s, many of these Americans and their children were moving outward from Los Angeles. Typically, their places were taken by immigrants from Mexico, Central America, and numerous Asian countries. As a result of these changing patterns of net migration, the social fabric of many parts of Los Angeles was substantially transformed.

In this chapter we investigate this change and the residential patterning of the new ethnic diversity. First, we examine the range of ethnic populations residing in Los Angeles in 1990 compared to 1960 and explain the reasons behind the dramatic shift in composition. Second, we map 1990 ethnic concentrations and measure residential segregation for 1960, 1980, and 1990. These provide important clues as to how and where the newcomers have fitted into Los Angeles and have, in turn, remolded parts of it. The degree of residential segregation between ethnic groups is an indirect geographical measure of assimilation between groups or, conversely, their cultural, social, or economic differences. Although the causes of segregation between any two groups are complex and are the subject of much debate, we assume in this chapter that the degree of spatial separation is a key indicator of the degree of socioeconomic difference. Our study focuses on the 8.9 million people of Los Angeles County, which includes the city of Los Angeles and numerous suburbs.

1

Ethnic Populations in 1960

The continued significance of racial appearance in American society means that the categories of White, Black, and Asian will be basic to our analysis of change. However, it is ethnicity—the shared sense of common heritage and identity—rather than physical appearance that distinguishes the various Asian peoples as well as those of Mexican origin and other Latinos, who range widely in their physical appearance. For this reason we use race, country of origin, first reported ancestry, and foreign stock data from U.S. censuses to define compositional changes, although we will refer to all such groupings as *ethnic* and all except Whites as minorities.

The ethnic composition of Los Angeles County in 1960 was the product of varying rates of fertility, mortality, net migration, and assimilation operating over the previous century (table 1.1). Although a few Los Angeles residents traced their Mexican family lineage back to the pre-1848 period of Mexican control and some Asian immigrants and American Blacks began to make their homes here in the late nineteenth century, it was the much larger in-migrations of Blacks, Asians, and Mexicans during the first three decades of the twentieth century that laid the foundations for those communities. Nevertheless, these groups were dwarfed by the massive twentieth-century arrival of English-speaking White Americans, resulting in overwhelming White dominance numerically in addition to earlier established White political and economic hegemony.

Non-Hispanic Whites

The category of non-Hispanic Whites, to be referred to simply as Whites, comprises people of some European ancestry, as well as nearly all Canadians, Australians, and people from the Middle East. Those of European origin are not identified by specific nationality or religion. This is because most of them were, to a large extent, culturally and socially assimilated into the broader society of White Americans and because the focus of our chapter is on the new, non-European immigrants.

Whites came to southern California from all parts of the United States but particularly from the farm areas of the Midwest, from Ohio west to Kansas and Oklahoma. These newcomers brought to Los Angeles the conservative attitudes and agrarian Protestant Christian culture that came to characterize Los Angeles at midcentury (McWilliams 1946). Nevertheless, the White population was not culturally homogeneous. The attractiveness of southern California's climate and potential for riches lured a wide range of people, including urban American Catholics and Jews from Germany and Eastern

Table 1.1 Los Angeles County: Ethnic Composition, 1960 and 1990

Group (1960)	Number of persons	% of tot. pop.	Group (1990)	Number of persons	% of tot. pop.
Total population	6,038,771	100.0	Total population	8,863,164	100.0
White (non-Spanish surname)	4,877,850	80.8	White (non-Hispanic)	3,618,850	40.8
Spanish-surname White	576,716	9.6	Hispanic origin	3,351,242	37.8
Black	461,546	7.6	Black (African-American)	992,974	11.2
American Indian	8,109	0.1	American Indian[a]	45,508	0.5
Asian and other non-White	115,250	1.9	Asian and Pacific Islander	954,485	10.8

Sources: U.S. Bureau of the Census, 1961, 1962b, 1963c, and 1991.
Notes: In 1990 persons of mixed racial parentage were classified by the person in the household completing the questionnaire. In 1960 persons of mixed racial parentage were classified according to the race of the non-White parent and mixtures of non-White races were classified according to the race of the father. Approximately 97.5% of the Spanish-surname population was classified as White; American Indians and Filipinos constituted over half the non-Whites of Spanish surname.
[a]Includes Eskimos and Aleuts, totaling 1,609 in 1990.

Europe. People born in Europe constituted an important 9 percent of the White population of Los Angeles in 1960. More cosmopolitan than most White Angelinos, they and American transplants from eastern and midwestern cities were often leavening agents in the dominant culture.

American Indians

The original American Indian inhabitants of Los Angeles, their numbers decimated during the Spanish and Mexican periods, left very few descendants who remained here and retained a primary Indian identity. Not until the 1950s did that many Indians leave their reservations and, encouraged and subsidized by the federal government, come to southern California for work. Nevertheless, their numbers have remained very small relative to the other major ethnic groupings.

Latinos

The well-known and convenient label, *Latino*, refers to the aggregation of Spanish-speaking nationalities from Latin America, although most Latinos identify more strongly with their specific national heritage than with *Latino* or any other inclusive term. The methodology for measuring this group changed between 1960 and 1990 so that data for 1960 are expressed in terms of the group's distinctive Spanish surnames and data for 1990 refer to the population of Spanish or Hispanic origin (table 1.1). However, the effects of the change are minor and comparison of the 1960 and 1990 numbers is appropriate.

People of Mexican heritage have always dominated the Latino population of Los Angeles, but by 1960 Mexicanos whose families first arrived in Los Angeles in the twentieth century far outnumbered those whose ancestors had lived here during the period of Mexican territorial control (before 1848). During the early decades of this century, Mexicans were able to cross into the United States with little difficulty because the U.S. government encouraged their migration as a source of cheap labor, particularly in railroad work and agriculture. Many migrant farmworkers later settled in Los Angeles during the winter and took manufacturing and construction jobs.

The importance of Mexican immigration during the early twentieth century shows in the fact that, as of 1960, 80 percent of the people with Spanish surnames in the Los Angeles area had been born in the United States. In other words, the 1960 equivalent of today's Latino population could certainly not be described as predominantly immigrant.

About 16 percent of the foreign-born population of Spanish surname was not from Mexico (table 1.2). Latinos from more distant countries have typically been more educated and wealthier than immigrants from Mexico because transportation costs preclude the migration of poor people. Many had light skins and spoke English before arriving, easing their assimilation into White society and making them often invisible to both Whites and people of Mexican origin.

People from Asia and the Middle East

Despite deep-seated prejudice and later discriminatory laws against Asians, the 1870s found Chinese laborers working in Los Angeles, to be followed two decades later by Japanese. In the early years, many were farmers who had developed other business operations when possible. Between 1941 and 1945 the Japanese were forcibly removed from West Coast locations like Los Angeles, but by 1950 returning Japanese had reestablished homes and businesses. Beginning in the 1920s, Filipinos who arrived here as students often got jobs in Los Angeles as houseboys, and laborers who worked seasonally on San Joaquin Valley farms frequently used Los Angeles as a winter home.

Through most of the period from the 1880s to 1965, Asian immigration was severely restricted, but in the 1950s many Asians found they could reside in the United States under other laws. In 1960, there were twice as many Japanese, Chinese, and Filipinos in Los Angeles County as there had been in 1950, and in 1960 Los Angeles was the largest mainland Japanese settlement in the United States (table 1.3). However, like the people of Mexican heritage, the Asians living here in 1960 were not primarily immigrants: 79 percent of the Japanese and 62 percent of the Chinese had been born in the United States. The likelihood of much acculturation despite discrimination and restrictions by Whites is further suggested by the fact that 23 percent of the Chinese and 32 percent of the Japanese in Los Angeles were third-generation Americans and thus not even counted as foreign stock (U.S. Bureau of the Census 1962b).

The beginnings of several other ethnic communities may be discerned as of 1960, many originating from students attending universities. In the Turkish foreign stock group are large numbers who are not ethnically Turkish but who remember that they were born in some part of the Ottoman Empire.

Blacks

In the 1890s, Black Americans, many of whom first came to Los Angeles as railroad porters, began to settle in larger numbers. At first, Los Angeles

Table 1.2 Los Angeles-Long Beach Metropolitan Area: Population of Latin American and Caribbean Origin, 1960 and 1990

Nationality	1960 foreign stock	1990 population	% Change 1960-90	Nationality	1960 foreign stock	1990 population	% Change 1960-90
Mexican[a]	579,732	2,527,160	336	Jamaican[b]	1,335	7,992	499
Salvadoran	1,112	253,068	22,660	Costa Rican	1,915	7,811	308
Guatemalan	1,774	125,091	6,951	Argentinean	2,660	6,697	152
Cuban	4,144	45,887	1,007	Chilean	1,114	6,080	446
Puerto Rican	NA	40,082		Panamanian	2,099	5,281	152
Nicaraguan	2,992	33,846	1,058	Brazilian[b]	1,490	3,428	130
Honduran	860	22,968	2,571	Bolivian	408	2,800	586
Peruvian	1,310	21,902	1,572	Dominican	457	2,202	382
Columbian	1,763	21,678	1,130	Haitian[b]	233	1,799	672
Ecuadoran	1,591	18,958	1,092	Trinidadian[b]	NA	1,472	
Belizean[b]	308	9,551	3,001	Guyanese[b]	NA	1,162	
				Venezuelan	477	1,095	130

Sources: U.S. Bureau of the Census, 1962b, 1991, 1992a, 1992b.
Note: Most 1990 Hispanic-origin figures are either complete count or 12.7% sample data. Figures for smaller and non-Hispanic populations represent first reported ancestry from summary tape file (STF4) (12.7% sample), where possible, or public use micro sample (PUMS)(5% sample). Data for 1960 are based on a 25% sample. The foreign stock comprises the foreign-born plus the U.S.-born of foreign parentage. In 1990 the metropolitan area was equivalent to L.A. County, but in 1960 it also included Orange County.
NA indicates figures for 1960 are not available by individual countries of origin.
[a] Because Mexican settlement is so much older than that of other groups, the Mexican figure for 1960 includes the 326,694 foreign stock population plus an estimated 253,038 U.S.-born people of Mexican origin whose parents were also U.S.-born.
[b] Population not of Hispanic origin.

Table 1.3 Los Angeles-Long Beach Metropolitan Area: Population of African, Middle Eastern, Asian, and Pacific Island Origin, 1990 and 1960

Nationality	1960 foreign stock	1990 race/ancestry	% change 1960-90	Nationality	1960 foreign stock	1990 race/ancestry	% change 1960-90
Chinese[a]	19,286	245,033	1,171	Pakistani	151	4,500	2,880
Filipino[a]	12,122	219,653	1,712	Laotian	NA	4,101	
Korean	2,587	145,431	5,522	Nigerian	NA	4,091	
Japanese[a]	77,314	129,736	68	Turkish	9,583	3,942	-41
Armenian	(4,675)	100,647	2,053	Assyrian	NA	2,905	
Vietnamese	NA	62,549		Ethiopian	NA	2,897	
Iranian	(671)	51,764	7,614	Palestinian	NA	2,591	
Asian Indian	1,945	43,829	2,153	Australian	5,490	2,304	-42
Cambodian	NA	27,819		Sri Lankan	NA	2,304	
Thai	(118)	19,106	16,092	Afghan	NA	1,922	
Lebanese	2,981	17,055	472	Jordanian	NA	1,720	
Samoan	—[b]	11,934		Iraqi	5,490	1,706	-74
Israeli	2,807	11,627	314	Tongan	—[b]	1,546	
Hawaiian	NA	8,009		Malaysian	NA	1,494	
Guamanian	—[b]	5,632		South African	1,283	1,362	6
Indonesian	—[b]	5,107		Bangladeshi	(in Pak.)	1,060	

Sources: U.S. Bureau of the Census, 1962b, 1963a, 1963c, 1991, 1992b.
Note: Figures represent first reported ancestry from summary tape file 4 (12.7% sample), where possible, or public use micro sample (5% sample). Parentheses denote substitution of data on mother tongue of the foreign-born where foreign stock data not available. In 1990 the total of first reported Arab ancestries was 49,406 (summary tape file 3).
[a]Because of an older settlement, 1960 figures represent racial identity rather than foreign stock.
[b]1960 data show 1,523 foreign stock for all Pacific Islands other than Australia and New Zealand.

seemed to provide more opportunities for success than other places, but by
the 1920s the early optimism was waning. Whites established restrictions on
Blacks concerning employment, use of public facilities, and residence.
Nevertheless, Los Angeles attracted many Blacks, and between 1940 and
1960 employment opportunities related to the defense buildup and the
booming postwar economy meant that Los Angeles's Black population increased by 500 percent.

Although most Los Angeles residents who had originated in African or
Caribbean countries were White, non-Whites (nearly all Blacks) did constitute 70 percent of the Jamaican foreign stock and half of those from other
former British colonies in the Caribbean (U.S. Bureau of the Census 1962b).

Minority Invisibility in 1960

Although in the four decades before 1960 Whites had constituted over 85
percent of Los Angeles County's population, they still comprised over 80
percent of the total in 1960. They had increased their numbers by over 1.29
million during the 1950s and continued to exercise ultimate economic and
political control. Because most of the larger minority populations were U.S.-
born, minority assimilation of the culture of the Whites was widespread.
Nevertheless, White dominance together with the fact of residential segregation between Whites and larger minorities, meant that most Whites were
little aware of the presence of people of color and Mexicanos except as
sources of cheap labor or as troublemakers or criminals. For the most part,
minorities were invisible in the world of the Whites.

Factors Underlying Ethnic Change, 1960–1990

Ethnic change in Los Angeles during these three decades of 1960–1990
was driven by five broad factors: changes in U.S. immigration laws, economic
opportunity differentials between Los Angeles and less-developed countries,
the increasing internationalization of the world economy, political changes
that created new groups of refugees, and the massive net movement of Whites
to new suburbs beyond the bounds of Los Angeles County. Existing foreign-
stock populations became facilitators of post-1960 immigration to Los
Angeles. Networks of personal contacts are an important means by which
immigrants implement preferences based on perceived opportunities. Many
migration choices depend on personal contacts in potential destinations—
friends or relatives who can help find housing and a job. Because networks
of personal contact expand over time and reduce difficulties for later migrants,

they tend to increase the flows of immigration over time (Massey et al. 1993) and so become an additional factor in their own right.

Changes in Immigration Law

In 1965, the U.S. Congress enacted major changes in immigration laws that opened the doors to much greater immigration from many more countries. The old national-origins quota system, which had been so strongly biased to the advantage of northern and western European countries, was eliminated and replaced by annual quotas of twenty thousand immigrants per country. The new law, stressing family reunification, allotted most immigrant visas to close relatives of people already living in the United States. However, a limited number of professionals and others with occupational skills in demand could immigrate without such family connections.

The first people to take advantage of the new law were previous immigrants already residing here in 1960, averaging approximately a third of the foreign-stock population (tables 1.2 and 1.3). Those who wished could usually sponsor the immigration of close family members right away. Over time more and more people qualified as immigrants and many later became citizens, permitting the entry of others in ever-expanding networks of families in numerous countries.

Immigration from Latin America displayed special characteristics. Mexico, the West Indies, and other Western Hemisphere countries, as important suppliers of farm labor, were exempted from quotas in the 1965 immigration legislation as they had been in earlier years. In 1976, all Western Hemisphere countries were given the same annual quota of twenty thousand persons.

Economic Opportunity Differentials

Reduced immigration from Europe and Japan since 1960, compared to the years before 1920, occurred primarily because most economic opportunity differentials between those areas and the United States were eliminated. On the other hand, the role of contrasting opportunities is especially evident in the case of Mexico. Throughout this century less-educated Mexicans have made great economic gains by coming to the United States to work. Although Mexico's economy has modernized in the last decades and new jobs have been created, the more rapid growth of Mexico's population because of the decline in the death rate has meant that an increasing number of Mexicans could find little work within their own country. During most of the 1980s, the effect of the large wage differential for unskilled labor was exacerbated by increased difficulties in the Mexican economy (Cornelius 1989), prompting still more migrants, including many families, to try to enter the United States illegally.

Internationalization of the Economy

According to world systems theory, international migration is the result of capitalism's inevitably increasing penetration of poorer countries (periphery and semiperiphery) from its base in the richer core countries, epitomized during the last half century by the United States (Wallerstein 1974). The greatly increased immigration to the United States since 1960 is compatible with this theory. The international flows of managers, technical experts, labor, and capital have exceeded anything known in the past and have made economic opportunities in Los Angeles and elsewhere more easily known by potential migrants. One indication of these changes is the 1400 percent growth of estimated total direct foreign investment in the world between 1960 and 1987 (Sassen 1991). At the U.S. end of these links, corporations in Los Angeles County were second only to New York City in employment in the high-end service sector—in services such as banking, finance, insurance, real estate, and business services.

Employment by U.S. corporations or the U.S. government (including the military) often initiated the personal ties that began new migration chains. The United States and Los Angeles became much more closely tied to Asian countries, and the trade connections developed by Asian and Asian-American entrepreneurs often made immigration easier. In the case of Mexico, personal contact networks between Mexican villages and Los Angeles have existed for many decades, but new migrations are probably developing as a result of the post-1985 import liberalization, privatization, and deregulation of the Mexican economy (Rubio and Trejo 1993). In other cases, such as in Korea, dislocations associated with economic developments triggered migrations (Light and Bonacich 1988).

Refugees

The countries from which the United States has accepted refugees since about 1960 reflect the government's policies and the internationalization of American political and military influence. Because policies have been strongly geared to the defeat or containment of communist governments, most refugees have been either escapees from communist countries or people who supported the U.S.-backed side during wars and revolutions.

Waves of anti-Castro Cubans were the first large refugee group, but in 1975—after the fall of Saigon and American defeat in Vietnam—tens of thousands of refugees from Southeast Asian countries entered the United States, many later settling in Los Angeles. Escapees from Eastern Europe countries, Jews and Armenians from the former Soviet Union, and others who fled revolutions in Ethiopia and Iran or war in Afghanistan and Central America swelled the refugee numbers here.

Because of the forced and rapid nature of their migration decision, refugees usually tend to settle among friends, relatives, and compatriots for mutual support—more so than do economic migrants. This is why in Los Angeles County there are particularly large refugee communities of Iranians, Armenians, Russian Jews, and Cambodians, but hardly any Hmong.

Out-migration of Whites

The drop in proportions of Whites in Los Angeles County between 1960 and 1990 (table 1.1) was due not only to the growth of non-White and Latino populations, but also to net out-migration. Most of the decline was the result of suburbanization (Allen 1990). Thousands of families bought homes in newly built suburbs in adjacent counties. Others, fewer in number, left southern California completely, migrating to towns and suburbs in nearby states including Oregon, Washington, Nevada, and Arizona.

In addition to its role in directly changing ethnic proportions, this deconcentration by Whites opened up already established housing, employment, and business opportunities in Los Angeles for many new immigrants. If there had been no net White exodus during the last three decades, the relative economic opportunities in Los Angeles compared to other U.S. places and countries of origin would have been different and some immigrants, particularly those bringing money and skills, might not have settled in Los Angeles.

Recent Migration and Ethnic Composition

Immigration into Los Angeles County has been so massive that by 1990 the county contained 45 percent of the entire foreign-born population of California (U.S. Bureau of the Census 1992a). Moreover, the recency of immigration is evident in the fact that 53 percent of all the foreign-born in Los Angeles County in 1990 entered the United States in the 1980s.

Apart from the White population decline, the most significant characteristic of the county's ethnic transformation since 1960 has been the growth of the Latino population from about 10 percent to nearly 40 percent of the total county population (table 1.1). Immigration from Mexico accounted for most of the growth, but the high birth rate of Mexican immigrants and their youthful age structure were important factors also. A projection of the 1990 Latino population from a 1980 base shows that natural increase accounted for over 40 percent of Latino population increase compared to net in-migration.

Although Mexico has been the largest supplier of legal immigrants to the United States since 1960, the motivation to migrate has been so strong that hundreds of thousands have crossed the border illegally and settled in Los Angeles County. Although people from many countries are residing in the region illegally, the vast majority of the 800,000 residents of Los Angeles County who submitted applications for amnesty under the Immigration Reform and Control Act (IRCA) of 1986 were from Mexico (U.S. Immigration and Naturalization Service 1992). Although people of Mexican origin still comprise 75 percent of Latinos in Los Angeles, the comparable figure in 1960 was about 85 percent. This greater diversity within the Latino population is primarily due to the growth of large populations from several Central and South American countries (table 1.2). Salvadorans and Guatemalans arrived in the greatest numbers, especially during the 1980s, when so many were fleeing violence.

The Black population of Los Angeles County has doubled since 1960, but in-migration slowed during the 1970s and, in the 1980s, was less than out-migration. Many Blacks left Los Angeles for suburban and other destinations. Although the Black population grew during the 1980s, Blacks in Los Angeles constituted a slightly lower percentage of the total population than they did in 1980.

The group that grew most rapidly after 1960 was Asians and Pacific Islanders (tables 1.1 and 1.3). As a result of net immigration, their numbers quadrupled between 1970 and 1990. The Chinese population (with varied origins in Taiwan, Hong Kong, Southeast Asian countries, and the People's Republic of China) grew during the 1980s by 161 percent to surpass the numbers of Japanese and Filipinos. Perhaps the most important feature of the new ethnic diversity is the great range of nationalities present: ten different Asian and Pacific Islander groups number at least five thousand people. Los Angeles County has more Filipinos, Koreans, Cambodians, Thais, and Guamanians than any other county in the United States and ranks second in numbers of Japanese, Vietnamese, and Samoans.

Some Middle Eastern ethnic groups have also grown rapidly since 1960, particularly the Armenians and Iranians, many of whom arrived as refugees. Because Armenians, the largest of these, have lived as a minority within several different countries, the cultures that these immigrants have brought to Los Angeles vary somewhat. The largest number were from the former

Soviet Union, but other Armenians came from Iran and Arabic countries, particularly Lebanon (U.S. Bureau of the Census 1992b).

Ethnic Concentrations in 1990

The foregoing background information sets the stage for examining geographical patterns of the new ethnic diversity within Los Angeles County. Ethnic settlement and adaptation processes have occurred in specific places within Los Angeles and other destination cities. As a first step toward understanding the new ethnic diversity, we will focus on the spatial distribution of residence of major ethnic groups.

Mapping Methodology

Our maps cover the more densely populated southern half of the county and are designed to emphasize the larger ethnic concentrations. In each tract with a population of twenty-five or more we identified and mapped the largest ethnic population (fig. 1.1) and the second largest (fig. 1.2) from 1990 U.S. census data.

Because the maps had to accommodate many ethnic groups of different sizes, in some respects the patterns may be misleading. First, it is impossible to tell from the map what percentage of the total population in any area is held by the predominant and second leading ethnic groups. Toward the center of the very large areas on figure 1.1 where either Whites, Blacks, or people of Mexican origin are shown as predominant, the ethnic group is represented in very high proportions—often over 80 or 90 percent of the total population. In such cases, the second leading group is weakly represented. Zones of greater heterogeneity occur on the fringes of these large areas, such as in Koreatown, Gardena, and Carson. Second, the sheer numbers of Whites and people of Mexican origin mean that the maps understate many Asian concentrations. For example, despite the large size of the Cambodian settlement in Long Beach, Cambodians are nowhere the most numerous group and are only the second leading group in two tracts. Similarly, most tracts in Koreatown contain more people of Mexican origin than Koreans. Last, although not easily seen on these maps, there is some ethnic diversity in all tracts. Ethnic proportions for the four basic groups have been mapped elsewhere (Turner and Allen 1991) and the degree of residential mixing between specific groups is assessed statistically in the next section on residential segregation.

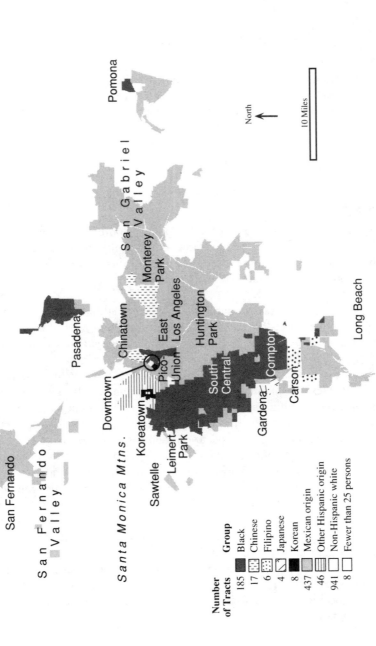

Fig. 1.1 Predominant Ethnic Group by Census Tract, Metropolitan Los Angeles County, 1990

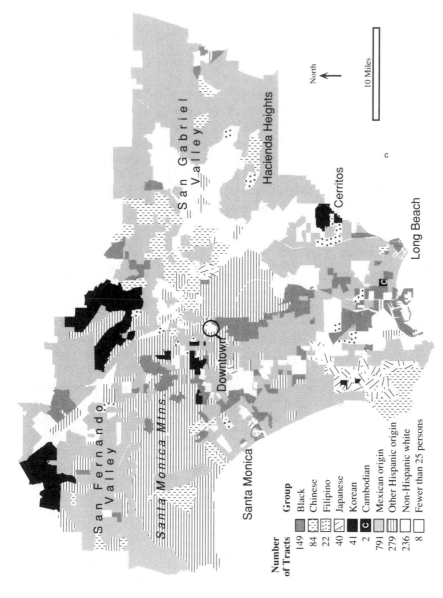

Number of Tracts | **Group**
149 | Black
84 | Chinese
22 | Filipino
40 | Japanese
41 | Korean
2 | Cambodian
791 | Mexican origin
279 | Other Hispanic origin
236 | Non-Hispanic white
8 | Fewer than 25 persons

San Fernando Valley

Santa Monica Mtns.

Santa Monica

Downtown

San Gabriel Valley

Hacienda Heights

Cerritos

Long Beach

North

10 Miles

Fig. 1.2 Second Leading Ethnic Group by Census Tract, Metropolitan Los Angeles, 1990

General Interpretations

Ethnic residential concentrations within Los Angeles County result, in general, from four factors: (1) the history of earlier ethnic settlements, which often developed near major centers of employment; (2) the relative sizes of different groups, with larger groups typically expanding their settlement area into areas formerly dominated by other groups; (3) ethnic differences in economic resources, with poorer people living in more centrally located housing in inner cities; and (4) widespread tendencies for living among members of the same ethnic group.

People are generally aware of the ethnic character of the neighborhood in which they live, and the neighborhoods people move to reflect patterns of ethnic preferences and avoidances (Clark 1992). Although residents usually appear to accept and in some cases welcome ethnic diversity and change in their neighborhood, an underlying interethnic tension is widespread. Because this is found particularly in the meeting zones between different groups and in zones where groups differ in economic resources or population growth rates, these maps suggest patterns of possible tension.

Central Locations of Poorer Groups

Because Whites and Asians have median household incomes that are about 50 percent higher than Blacks and Latinos, the poorer sections of the county are most likely to be occupied by Blacks and Latinos. The least-expensive housing is usually found in the older parts of both Los Angeles and Long Beach, often near their downtowns. The oldest part of Long Beach appears as predominantly Mexican but with two tracts that are more heavily Black.

The area near downtown Los Angeles has a more complex ethnic geography. Latinos comprise most of the surrounding population, with Salvadorans and Guatemalans particularly concentrated in the Pico-Union barrio west of downtown. Chinatown and Koreatown represent the lowest-cost Chinese and Korean settlements in the county. Within the downtown are two tracts where Whites and Koreans predominate; most of these are elderly people who live in federally subsidized apartments. The tracts to the east (shown as Black) are dominated by the populations of two prisons and skid row (fig. 1.1).

Other Latino Concentrations

Mexican settlement east of downtown Los Angeles began in the first two decades of this century, but it now extends over a large area eastward from downtown and south central into the older suburbs of the San Gabriel Valley. The oldest and cheapest housing in this area, such as in East Los Angeles and Huntington Park, is close to railroad lines and industrial areas, sources of past and present employment. Geographically separated outlying settlements of Mexicanos, such as San Fernando, show the locations of early farm labor and manufacturing jobs.

The large "Other Hispanic" area on the left side of fig. 1.2, between the San Fernando Valley and Santa Monica, is characterized by very expensive homes. The area is about 90 percent White but is designated here as Other Hispanic because it contains live-in Latina maids and child caregivers, most commonly from El Salvador, as well as some wealthy families from Central and South America.

Changes in Black Concentrations

Black residential areas have all changed under the impact of recent Mexican immigration. During the 1980s, many Mexican immigrants, often sharing the cost of housing among two or more families, settled in areas having relatively inexpensive dwellings, including some predominantly Black areas. In particular, the eastern portion of the largest Black settlement (south central Los Angeles) became roughly half Black and half Latino. This is an example of ethnic invasion and succession, the widely observed process by which housing in Los Angeles and other places is filtered down from one ethnic group to a more recently arrived and poorer group. Meanwhile, the largest Black concentration has shifted westward to higher income areas in Leimert Park and nearby Crenshaw Boulevard.

Asian Concentrations

Asians concentrations other than those in the newer suburbs have ties to the past. For example, Chinatown's current location stems from urban planning and renewal decisions in the 1930s that forced a displacement from earlier Chinese concentrations. The Japanese concentration in Gardena has its roots in the first decade of this century, when Japanese families from Hawaii bought farm land in the area (Hirabayashi and Tanaka 1988). Japanese dispersal south of Gardena (fig. 1.2) is rooted in Japanese farming in this area before World War II and 1950s suburban developments. The tiny Sawtelle settlement originated with Japanese nurserymen who landscaped and maintained the grounds of wealthy Whites in nearby areas (Nishi 1958).

Monterey Park represents a prosperous suburban Chinese settlement, quite in contrast to Chinatown. Because the population of individual Asian groups is so much less than that of the other groups mapped, most of its suburban concentrations appear only on figure 1.2. For instance, the large Chinese influx is evident in a large area northeast of Chinatown and near Monterey Park, where Chinese-oriented services and shopping are easily accessible by car. Many high-income Koreans live in new suburbs, such as those in the northern edge of the San Fernando Valley, Glendale-La Crescenta (north of downtown), and Cerritos.

Residential Segregation: Group Differences and Change

It is often assumed that immigrants and minorities tend to become less segregated from the White population as they become economically success-ful and more assimilated to the dominant culture and society. This associa-tion between geographic patterns and socioeconomic structure has strong theoretical underpinnings and has generally been confirmed in research, although Black Americans do constitute a major exception (Massey 1985). In this section we measure segregation among major ethnic groups in Los Angeles. We consider both changes in segregation levels over time and recent levels as measured in the 1990 census.

Data and Method

Although there are several different concepts of segregation and many ways to measure these (Massey and Denton 1989; White 1986), the index of dissimilarity, or D, is the single most widely used statistic and thus the one permitting easier comparison with the results of other studies. This index basically compares two groups as to the sum of the differences in their proportional representations in each tract. It ranges between zero and one, with low values indicating a low degree of segregation. The value of D can be interpreted as the percentage of the smaller group that would have to move to a different tract in order for the group to comprise the same percentage of the total population in all tracts. It is useful to describe index values below .30 as low, those between .30 and .60 as moderate, and those above .60 as high, as suggested by Massey and Denton (1993). Recognizing that the index of dissimilarity is not strictly comparable when the group being measured constitutes a very small percentage of the total population (Cortese, Falk, and Cohen 1976), no groups with fewer than twenty-five thousand are included. Indices are calculated for 1,652 census tracts in Los Angeles County in 1990, and fewer numbers of tracts in preceding years.

Historical Levels of Segregation

The years 1910 and 1960 provide benchmarks against which segregation in 1980 and 1990 can be compared. In the interest of precise comparisons, calculations for both of these years were based on numbers of Whites without Spanish surnames rather than the total White population. Although the nature of 1960 tract data made it impossible to measure the segregation of individual Asian groups, 63 percent of the aggregated Asian and American Indian population was Japanese and another 16 percent Chinese.

Measures of segregation for 1910 are available only for the city of Los Angeles, but they provide some basis of comparison, at least between groups. Indices of dissimilarity, based on data from unpublished census schedules, were calculated for the 242 enumeration districts in the city (Bruce forthcoming). The results indicate that the Chinese were the most segregated of all minority groups (D = .73), but Black-White segregation was next highest (D = .65).

Over the next few decades the Black population of Los Angeles grew rapidly through in-migration, and segregation increased substantially, primarily because of efforts by Whites to contain the Black population within sharply defined ghettos. For most of the period since 1920, Blacks were the most segregated group in Los Angeles. By 1960, the segregation between Blacks and non-Hispanic Whites in Los Angeles County was extremely high (D = .90) according to our calculations. Previous measurement of D for metropolitan areas in 1960 compared only Whites (including those of Spanish surname) to non-Whites (including Asians), resulting in a slightly lower segregation value of .89 for Los Angeles (van Valey, Roof, and Wilcox 1977). Los Angeles was one of the three most highly segregated large metropolitan areas in the country. Among the twenty-four metropolitan areas with populations over one million in 1960, segregation between Blacks and non-Hispanic Whites was greatest in Chicago, but ranked next and equal in segregation were Los Angeles and Milwaukee.

In Los Angeles, the Asian and American Indian group was much less segregated (D = .64), and segregation of the Spanish surname population from Whites without Spanish surnames was still lower and moderate (D = .55). In comparison with thirty-five other cities in the Southwest, the city of Los Angeles was about average, with the Spanish surname group most segregated in Texas cities (Moore and Mittelbach 1966).

White-Minority Segregation, 1980 and 1990

During the last three decades, levels of Black-White segregation dropped across most of America, but Los Angeles County experienced a greater than average reduction of 20 percent. As a result, Los Angeles changed from being one of the most highly segregated large metropolitan areas in 1960 to being about average in 1990, with a D value of .73 (Harrison and Weinberg 1992b). As in Los Angeles, the decline in Black-White segregation during the 1980s was generally greater in those metropolitan areas with large Latino populations (Frey and Farley 1993).

The reduction in segregation was due to a dispersal out of all the areas of Black concentration, including "suburban ghettos" in such places as Pasadena and Pomona (Turner and Allen 1991), and the absolute decline of the county's White population. Although many Whites believe that social class has replaced race as the source of Black-White differences (Bullard and Feagin 1991), it has been demonstrated that the remaining and still substantial residential segregation between Blacks and Whites is not essentially the result of differences in the incomes of the groups. Black-White segregation levels in thirty metropolitan areas across the country in 1980 varied little by income level (Massey and Denton 1993). Our own calculations for Los Angeles in 1990 show this also. Low-income (<$25,000) Black and White households were only slightly more segregated from each other (D = .75) than were Black and White households with $25–50,000 incomes (D = .70) or those with incomes over $50,000 (D = .71).

The concentrated settlement in Los Angeles of new and relatively unassimilated immigrant groups, together with the decline in Black-White segregation, has meant that Blacks are no longer the group most segregated from Whites. Cambodians, Salvadorans, and Guatemalans appeared more highly segregated than Blacks in 1990 (fig. 1.3). However, because these groups are much smaller in number than Blacks, we could not be confident in any statement concerning the relative segregation levels of these groups until we eliminated the extraneous effect of population-size differences. To do this, we estimated the size effect by the binomial approximation formula and subtracted this from the D values (Cortese, Falk, and Cohen 1976; Winship 1977). Adjusted D values were as follows: Blacks, .71; Cambodians, .76; Salvadorans, .71, and Guatemalans, .68. The adjusted values make it clear that Cambodians are indeed more segregated than Blacks, Salvadorans are equally as segregated as Blacks, but Guatemalans are less segregated.

Trends in Asian and Latino segregation since 1960 are compatible with the theoretical basis of segregation research. Japanese in 1990 were much less segregated than they apparently were in 1960, presumably the result of continuing socioeconomic assimilation and little immigration. The opposite trend occurred for people of Mexican origin, whose segregation increased since 1960 due to the arrival of so many poor and unassimilated immigrants. Similarly, values of D increased over the 1980s for Chinese and Koreans

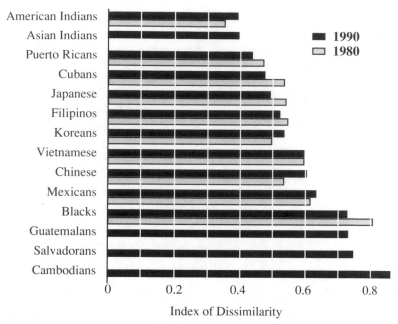

Index of Dissimilarity

The absence of a bar indicates unavailability of data
or a group with fewer than 25,000 persons.

Fig. 1.3   Segregation from Non-Hispanic Whites, Los Angeles County, 1980 and
1990

because the settlement of so many immigrants near family and friends
outweighed the effects of the deconcentrating tendencies associated with
assimilation and improved economic status. These small increases in Asian
and Latino segregation are similar to the general trend in large metropolitan
areas (Harrison and Weinberg 1992a).

Reduced Filipino segregation in 1990 (fig. 1.3) relates to continuing
assimilation and the fact that immigrants from the Philippines are often well
educated and fluent in English, permitting many of them access to middle-
class housing in suburban areas, many of which are predominantly White.
Similarly, the Cuban and Puerto Rican populations showed reduced levels of
segregation in 1990. Both grew by less than 10 percent during the 1980s and
are, on the average, more assimilated than people of Mexican origin.

22   James P. Allen and Eugene Turner

In contrast to the high degree of segregation of the poor and relatively unassimilated Cambodians and Salvadorans, many of whom were refugees, the lowest degree of segregation among new immigrants was found for Asian Indians. Their high levels of education and English-language skills and, in some cases, the wealth they brought with them have made it possible for them to disperse widely into many White-dominated areas.

In general, Asians and Latinos are more segregated in Los Angeles than in most other large metropolitan areas. The index for Asian-White segregation in Los Angeles was .46 compared to the average of .42, but Asians in New York, San Francisco, and San Diego are more segregated than in Los Angeles (Harrison and Weinberg 1992b). Latinos in Los Angeles (D = .61) are also more segregated than in most metropolitan areas of over one million (D = .54) although Latino segregation is still higher in New York, Chicago, and Newark.

Segregation between Race and Hispanic-origin Groups

Segregation between all the larger minority groups is moderate or high (table 1.4). The fact that all four of the Asian groups are moderately and increasingly segregated from the others is a demonstration of the impact of

Table 1.4   Los Angeles County: Segregation between Selected Groups, 1990, and Change 1980–1990

Group	Black	Mexican	Salvadoran	Chinese	Filipino	Korean	Japanese
White	.73	.64	.75	.60	.52	.54	.49
	-.08	.02	_a	.06	-.03	.04	-.05
Black		.60	.64	.80	.70	.78	.73
		-.13	_a	-.01	-.09	-.05	-.04
Mexican			.48	.66	.54	.70	.66
			_a	.04	-.02	.03	.02
Salvadoran				.78	.61	.66	.75
				_a	_a	_a	_a
Chinese					.58	.58	.49
					.06	.09	.06
Filipino						.50	.56
						.02	.02
Korean							.51
							.02

Sources: U.S. Bureau of the Census, 1981, 1991, 1992a.
Note: White indicates non-Hispanic White. Bold type indicates 1990 index of dissimilarity (D) between groups. Regular type indicates change in D between 1980 and 1990.
aData on Salvadorans not available for 1980.

recent immigration and the separateness of each group, culturally and socially. However, the differences in distribution between Latino groups (Salvadorans and Mexicans) are not as great despite their high percentage of recent immigrants because they have a common Spanish language and face common economic difficulties.

Black and Mexican-origin populations are more segregated from Chinese, Koreans, and Japanese than they are from Whites. With their higher incomes and greater choice of neighborhoods, some Asians may be demonstrating an avoidance of Blacks and Mexican-origin people that is even greater than the avoidance attributed to Whites. The largest change during the 1980s was reduced Black-Mexican segregation, the result of the arrival of so many Mexican immigrants into the poorest part of south central and similar areas that had been more exclusively Black (fig. 1.1).

Impacts of Ethnic Change

Because of the large net domestic out-migration from Los Angeles County during the last twenty years, population growth has been due to immigration and natural increase (Allen 1990). During the last half of the 1980s even net legal immigration did not balance the net domestic out-flow. By 1990, population growth in the county was primarily the result of natural increase, particularly of the Latino population.

Los Angeles now has a new international cultural diversity, widely extolled in principle but usually adopted only in the form of ethnic cuisine and festivals. Most Whites, especially those whose roots were in midwestern small towns and farming areas, which traditionally have lacked minorities, have found the adjustment difficult. Blacks, often in competition with immigrants, have also been understandably resentful (Johnson and Oliver 1989).

The economic impacts of recent immigration to America are large and involve both benefits and costs, but they are complex and difficult to measure (Bouvier 1992; Muller 1993). Technically trained engineers, computer programmers, physicians, and nurses—all representing a brain drain from their countries—have enriched the supply of skilled workers and professionals in southern California. Apart from immigration, the five-county area including Los Angeles experienced a net in-migration of college graduates from other states and counties between 1985 and 1990 (Frey 1994). This net domestic in-movement suggests that the presence of many college-educated immigrants did little to dampen the salaries of highly educated Americans in this area.

On the other hand, there has been a large domestic out-migration from this area of people with less than college educations (Frey 1994). One of the reasons for their departure may have been competition from low-skilled immigrant workers. The availability of a large supply of immigrant labor has probably kept the cost of services such as child care, lawn maintenance, food service, and car washing in Los Angeles lower than it would otherwise be. Some manufacturers, particularly in the garment and furniture industries, have taken advantage of the abundant immigrant workforce to keep production costs low. Immigrant day laborers may have reduced the costs of numerous construction, repair, and maintenance projects compared to what they would have been without such an ample supply of eager workers.

Other aspects of the impact involve such matters as the investment of immigrant wealth in Los Angeles and the sending of remittances back to relatives, the rejuvenation of some neighborhoods and the decline of others, employment in immigrant-created businesses, and ethnic differences in work skills and demand for public services. In Los Angeles County, two major studies attempted to measure the net cost of county assistance to immigrants (Los Angeles County Internal Services Department 1992; Clark and Passel 1993). Although both concluded that the taxes immigrants paid go disproportionately to the federal government resulting in a special burden on county and state taxpayers, they disagreed on the size of that deficit and were unable to measure some components of cost and benefit.

The political impact of the new ethnic populations depends on patterns of ethnic concentration. Substantial changes in the ethnic composition of cities or districts force political redistricting, efforts by established political leaders to adapt to the change, as in south central Los Angeles (Stewart 1993), and sometimes an increase in voting according to ethnicity, as in Monterey Park (Horton 1989). In addition, political conflicts within immigrants' countries of origin are often carried over to Los Angeles because immigrants residing here can be influential in those struggles (Dresser 1993).

The range of languages spoken by the immigrants has raised barriers between ethnic communities and native English speakers and immigrants. Of people who speak Spanish or both Spanish and English at home, 41 percent of those age 18 and older do not speak English at all or do not speak it well (U.S. Bureau of the Census 1992a). Among adults who use an Asian language in the home, 25 percent speak English not at all or not well. Nevertheless, most immigrants realize how important English is for success, and many make great efforts to improve their skills.

Because 32 percent of all public school students in Los Angeles County in 1990–91 did not use English as their primary language, the burden of education has become a heavy one for schools (Los Angeles County Office of Education 1992). The range of language represented (ninety languages used in the county public schools) is mostly due to the arrival of Asian and Middle Eastern immigrants. However, because Los Angeles County's Latino population increase during the 1980s was twice that of the total Asian and Middle Eastern increase, the language adjustment problem is particularly focused on Latinos. Moreover, the higher birth rate of immigrant Latinos compared to Asians has meant that Latinos are a much younger population. This is the primary reason why Spanish speakers comprise 84 percent of all public school students identified as having limited English proficiency in 1991.

Transformation of Los Angeles County

The ethnic composition of Los Angeles County has been transformed since 1960 by net immigration from Latin America and Asia and net out-migration of non-Hispanic Whites. In combination with the economic restructuring that has occurred (Soja, Morales, and Wolff 1989), a new Los Angeles has emerged. A major feature of this new city has been the creation of new ethnic communities and the rapid growth of others that were only incipient in 1960. A count of the groups in tables 1.1–1.3 shows forty different ethnic populations numbering at least one thousand without even acknowledging any diversity within either the White population of European ancestry or the Latino aggregate of seventeen Spanish-speaking nationalities. Some of the ethnic groups are themselves divided by language, religion, politics, or other identity into somewhat separate communities.

Many neighborhoods have experienced the process of ethnic invasion and succession, and a variety of new and expanded ethnic communities have appeared in both central areas of older housing and newer suburban areas. Black-White segregation, which in 1960 was the third highest of all large metropolitan areas, is now about average. However, Asians and Latinos are substantially more segregated from Whites in Los Angeles County than in the average large metropolitan area. Within Los Angeles County, segregation between the major minority groups showed moderate and high levels, and the large scale of immigration has meant that Mexicans, Chinese, and Koreans are slightly more segregated from Whites than they were in 1980. In 1990 Cambodian-White segregation was higher than Black-White segregation, and Salvadorans were equally as segregated as Blacks.

Because residential segregation mirrors the structure of society, this study has confirmed the presence of substantially separate ethnic communities. The old dichotomy of Black and White, with its terrible divisions and tensions, has probably weakened as Los Angeles has become more multiethnic. Latinos and Asians may well be acting as a buffer between Black and White societies. However, immigration has been sufficiently large to slow or even counteract the expected effects of assimilation. On balance, Los Angeles is divided ethnically at least as much as it was in earlier decades.

There is no consensus among social scientists as to how high segregation must be in order to describe a place as an aggregate of separate ethnic residential areas—an ethnic mosaic. However, the values of the dissimilarity index can suggest the relative degree of residential mixing. Because segregation values were somewhat closer to the high end of the scale than the low end, Los Angeles is certainly closer to being a mosaic of geographically separate ethnic communities than it is to being a residential melting pot.

References

Allen, James P. 1990. "Migration into and out of Los Angeles County in the 1980s." *Perspective* (California State University, Northridge) 7(2):2–6, 16.

Bouvier, Leon F. 1992. *Peaceful Invasions: Immigration and Changing America.* Lanham, Md.: University Press of America.

Bruce, Christopher. forthcoming. *Residential Segregation and Occupational Structure of Non-white Populations in Los Angeles, 1910.* Master's thesis, Geography, California State University, Northridge.

Bullard, Robert D., and Joe R. Feagin. 1991. "Racism and the City." In *Urban Life in Transition,* ed. M. Gottdiener and Chris G. Pickvance. Urban Affairs Annual Review, No. 39. Newbury Park, Calif.: Sage Publications.

Clark, Rebecca L., and Jeffrey S. Passel. 1993. "How Much Do Immigrants Pay in Taxes? Evidence from Los Angeles County." Policy Discussion Paper, Program for Research on Immigration Policy. Washington, D.C.: The Urban Institute.

Clark, William A. V. 1992. "Residential Preferences and Residential Choices in a Multiethnic Context." *Demography* 29(3):451–66.

Cornelius, Wayne. 1989. "Mexican Immigrants in California Today." UCLA Institute for Social Science Research, Working Papers in the Social Sciences 5(10).

Cortese, Charles F., R. Frank Falk, and Jack K. Cohen. 1976. "Further Considerations on the Methodological Analysis of Segregation Indices." *American Sociological Review* 41:630–37.

Dresser, Denise. 1993. "Exporting Conflict: Transboundary Consequences of Mexican Politics." In *The California-Mexico Connection*, ed. Abraham F. Lowenthal and Katrina Burgess. Stanford, Calif.: Stanford University Press.

Frey, William H. 1994. "White and Black 'Flight' from High Immigration Metro Areas: Impacts on Race and Class Structure." Paper presented at the Annual Meetings of the American Sociological Association, Los Angeles.

Frey, William H., and Reynolds Farley. 1993. "Latino, Asian, and Black Segregation in Multi-Ethnic Metro Areas: Findings from the 1990 Census." Research Report No. 93–278. Ann Arbor, Mich.: Population Studies Center, University of Michigan.

Harrison, Roderick J., and Daniel H. Weinberg. 1992a. "Changes in Racial and Ethnic Residential Segregation, 1980–1990." Paper prepared for the American Statistical Association Meetings, Boston, Mass.

———. 1992b. "Racial and Ethnic Residential Segregation in 1990." Paper prepared for the Population Association of America Meetings, Denver, Colo.

Hirabayashi, Lane R., and George Tanaka. 1988. "The Issei Community in Moneta and the Gardena Valley, 1900–1920." *Southern California Quarterly* 70(1):127–58.

Horton, John. 1989. "The Politics of Ethnic Change: Grass-Roots Responses to Economic and Demographic Restructuring in Monterey Park, California." *Urban Geography* 10(6):578–92.

Johnson, James H., Jr., and Melvin L. Oliver. 1989. "Interethnic Minority Conflict in Urban America: The Effect of Economic and Social Dislocations." *Urban Geography* 10(5):449–63.

Light, Ivan, and Edna Bonacich. 1988. *Immigrant Entrepreneurs: Koreans in Los Angeles, 1965–1982*. Berkeley: University of California Press.

Los Angeles County Internal Services Department. 1992. *Impact of Undocumented Persons and Other Immigrants on Costs, Revenues and Services in Los Angeles County*. Los Angeles: County Board of Supervisors.

Los Angeles County Office of Education. 1992. "Cultural Diversity and Growth in California's Schools." *Trends* 5(1):1–8.

McWilliams, Carey. 1946. *Southern California Country: An Island on the Land*. New York: Duell, Sloan & Pearce.

Massey, Douglas S. 1985. "Ethnic Residential Segregation: A Theoretical Synthesis and Empirical Review." *Sociology and Social Research* 69(3):315–50.

Massey, Douglas S., and Nancy A. Denton. 1989. "Hypersegregation in

U.S. Metropolitan Areas: Black and Hispanic Segregation along Five Dimensions." *Demography* 26(3):373–91.

———. 1993. *American Apartheid: Segregation and the Making of the Underclass*. Cambridge, Mass.: Harvard University Press.

Massey, Douglas S., Joaquin Arango, Graeme Hugo, Ali Kouaouci, Adela Pelegrino, and J. Edward Taylor. 1993. "Theories of International Migration: A Review and Appraisal." *Population and Development Review* 19(3):431–66.

Moore, Joan W., and Frank G. Mittelbach. 1966. *Residential Segregation in the Urban Southwest*. Mexican-American Study Project, Advance Report 4. Los Angeles: UCLA Graduate School of Business Administration.

Muller, Thomas. 1993. *Immigrants and the American City*. New York: New York University Press.

Nishi, Midori. 1958. "Japanese Settlement in the Los Angeles Area." *Yearbook of the Association of Pacific Coast Geographers* 20:35–48.

Rubio, Luis, and Guillermo Trejo. 1993. "Reform, Globalization, and Structural Independence: New Economic Ties between Mexico and California." In *The California-Mexico Connection*, ed. Abraham F. Lowenthal and Katrina Burgess. Stanford, Calif.: Stanford University Press.

Sassen, Saskia. 1991. *The Global City: New York, London, Tokyo*. Princeton, N.J.: Princeton University Press.

Soja, Edward, Rebecca Morales, and Goetz Wolff. 1989. "Urban Restructuring: An Analysis of Social and Spatial Change in Los Angeles." In *Atop the Urban Hierarchy*, ed. Robert A. Beauregard. Totowa, N.J.: Rowman & Littlefield.

Stewart, Jill. 1993. "Black Flight." *L. A. Weekly*, Oct. 29–Nov. 4,18–27.

Turner, Eugene, and James P. Allen. 1991. *An Atlas of Population Patterns in Metropolitan Los Angeles and Orange Counties, 1990*. Northridge, Calif.: Department of Geography, California State University, Northridge.

U.S. Bureau of the Census. 1961. *U.S. Census of Population, 1960. General Population Characteristics, California*. Washington, D.C.: GPO.

———. 1962a. *U.S. Censuses of Population and Housing, 1960. Census Tracts: Los Angeles-Long Beach, Calif. SMSA*. Final Report PHC(1)-82. Washington, D.C.: GPO.

———. 1962b. *U.S. Census of Population, 1960. Detailed Characteristics, California*. Washington, D.C.: GPO.

————. 1963a. *U.S. Census of Population, 1960. Mother Tongue of the Foreign-born.* Subject Report. PC(2)-1E. Washington, D.C.: GPO.

————. 1963c. *U.S. Census of Population, 1960. Persons of Spanish Surname.* Subject Report PC(2)-1B. Washington, D.C.: GPO.

————. 1963b. *U.S. Census of Population, 1960. Nonwhite Population by Race.* Subject Report PC(2)-1C. Washington, D.C.: GPO.

————. 1963d. *U.S. Census of Population, 1960. State of Birth.* Subject Report PC(2)-2A. Washington, D.C.: GPO.

————. 1981. *U.S. Census of Population and Housing, 1980. Summary Tape File 1 (California).* Washington: The Bureau.

————. 1991. *U.S. Census of Population and Housing, 1990. Summary Tape File 1 (California).* Washington: The Bureau.

————. 1992a. *U.S. Census of Population and Housing, 1990. Summary Tape File 3 (California).* Washington: The Bureau.

————. 1992b. *U.S. Census of Population and Housing, 1990. Public Use Microdata Samples.* Washington: The Bureau.

————. 1993. *U.S. Census of Population and Housing, 1990. Summary Tape File 4 (California).* Washington: The Bureau.

U.S. Immigration and Naturalization Service. 1992. *Statistical Yearbook of the Immigration and Naturalization Service, 1991.* Washington, D.C.: GPO.

Van Valey, Thomas L., Wade C. Roof, and Jerome E. Wilcox. 1977. "Trends in Residential Segregation." *American Journal of Sociology* 82(4):826–44.

Wallerstein, Immanuel. 1974. *The Modern World System, Capitalist Agriculture and the Origins of the European World Economy in the Sixteenth Century.* New York: Academic Press.

White, Michael J. 1986. "Segregation and Diversity Measures in Population Distribution." *Population Index* 52(2):198–221.

Winship, Christopher. 1977. "A Revaluation of Indexes of Residential Segregation." *Social Forces* 55:1058–66.

Chapter 2

Ethnic Change and Segregation in Chicago

Erick Howenstine

From its beginning, Chicago has been home to rich diversities of peoples and neighborhoods. Large immigration streams from Europe, in the late 1800s and early 1900s, created an ethnic mosaic that has been a favorite subject of study among social scientists including geographers and members of the "Chicago School" of sociology. When European immigration waned, beginning in the World War I era, large migration streams of Blacks from the southern United States brought to Chicago additional ethnic diversity along with stark residential segregation. During the last three decades, immigrants from Latin America and Asia further added to the ethnic composition of the Chicago urban area. Today, Chicago continues to display considerable ethnic diversity as well as segregation. Although some European-based ethnic communities do remain, the major ethnic groups involved in today's urban mosaic are Blacks and people of Hispanic and Asian origin.

In the pages ahead I will examine basic changes in Chicago's ethnic and racial residential patterns between 1980 and 1990. Using census data, I will focus on spatial patterns of residence and residential segregation. Whereas most previous analyses of segregation in the United States have been limited to Black/White separation, the analysis here includes people of Asian and Hispanic origin as well. This is particularly appropriate given the recent dramatic increases of these populations in Chicago and in many other American cities. Analyses are presented for both the city of Chicago and the larger Cook County, which encompasses the city and a large suburban area.

I start with a brief history of Chicago's ethnic settlement and residential segregation. The map analysis of ethnic groups in the city and the county is

31

next, followed by several analyses of segregation among ethnic groups within the city.

Settlement of Chicago

Rapid population growth in Chicago did not begin until the 1830s, just after treaties forced native Americans to move far west from Chicago. Through the remainder of the nineteenth and into the next century, Chicago was a major recipient of European immigrants who provided labor in its rapidly expanding industrial sector. By 1840, the Germans and Irish had established separate enclaves along the banks of the Chicago River in what is now the center of the city (Chicago Department of Development and Planning 1976). Large Swedish, Czech, and Polish communities developed, along with many others. By the turn of the century, the city's ethnic fabric contained numerous communities, each with a strong local identity; some remain today. Cutler (1982,48) wrote, "A traverse in the vicinity of Halsted Street around the turn of the century from the North Side going south would have taken one successively through Swedish, German, Polish, Greek, Italian, Jewish, Czech, Lithuanian, and Irish neighborhoods." After the turn of the century, industry flourished and so did immigration. By 1920, the major European ethnic groups were Polish (350,000), Irish (200,000), Italian (124,000), and German (112,000). By 1950, at least twenty-four major ethnic areas could be identified (Chicago Department of Development and Planning 1976).

Just after the Civil War, by about 1870, 3,500 Blacks had settled near the center of the city. As the Black community grew slowly during the next few decades, it split spatially, moving west and south toward the areas currently dominated by Blacks. It was not until the World War I era, however, that the Black population grew rapidly. Fueled by unrest in the rural South and demands for wartime labor in northern cities, the great migration of Blacks substantially increased the Black population of Chicago around 1920 (Henri 1975). By 1930, 240,000 Blacks comprised about 7 percent of the city's population (Duncan and Duncan 1957,25).

Migration from southern states after World War II nearly doubled the Black population by 1950 and again by 1960. By 1980, more than 1.2 million Blacks lived in Chicago, accounting for 39 percent of the city's total population (Cutler 1982,121). The Black percentage of Chicago's population had risen not only through its increasing numbers but also as the result of second- and third-generation European-origin populations suburbanizing in large numbers. After 1980 the Black population declined by more than

100,000 owing to decreases in in-migration from the South, decreases in birth rates, and suburbanization.

Like several other large American cities, Chicago has been the destination for numerous Hispanic immigrants from Mexico, Puerto Rico, and other origins during the last two decades. The total number of Hispanics more than doubled during the 1960s and almost doubled again during the 1970s (Cutler 1982,134). By the 1990 census, they accounted for 20 percent of the city's population. Similarly, immigration from Asia has created significant Korean, Chinese, and Filipino communities in Chicago.

The increase in the population of Hispanics to more than 500,000 and Asians to more than 100,000 by 1990 has coincided with a slowing of Black in-migration and increases in White suburbanization. The population of Whites decreased by 25 percent between 1970 and 1980 and another 17 percent by 1990. The 1990 census showed that, for the first time, Chicago's minority groups were in the majority. Chicago is 45 percent White, 39 percent Black, and 4 percent Asian. It is also 20 percent Hispanic. The total of more than 100 percent is the result of the Hispanic measure overlapping with the others, the largest overlapping group being composed of Hispanic Whites.

Segregation

Many forces influence segregation, including a variety of institutional and other processes that have been imposed upon minority groups. Indian reservations, Chinatowns, and Japanese internment during World War II are extreme examples of forced segregation in United States history. The formal and systematic exclusion of Blacks from many residential areas, once practiced blatantly (Orren 1974), is still exercised in subtle ways. Other forms of discrimination and prejudice also produce spatial marginalization of many groups. Economic forces such as differential land rents also can steer lower-income groups into greater concentrations and less-attractive locations.

Ethnic residential clusters can result also from forces internal to the minority group itself. Channelized migration toward friends and family members focuses and concentrates immigrant groups. Once a critical mass is achieved, ethnic churches, businesses, and community centers can maintain and strengthen the community (Fischer 1975, 1982). The advantages of segregation may include the provision of unique goods and services, opportunities for employment and political representation, and richer cultural, linguistic, and religious expression. Therefore, decreasing measures of segregation do not necessarily mean progress for an ethnic group, although that is a common interpretation.

However, when poverty, limited access to resources, and poor housing accompany residential separation, the results can be devastating. Galster and Keeney (1988) argue that, after observing Black ghettos, majority members associate images of poverty with blackness of skin. This results in racial discrimination in the employment and housing markets, which in turn deepens and concentrates Black poverty and leads to more prejudice and discrimination. After publishing more than a dozen papers on the subject, Massey concluded that prejudice is the main cause of segregation of Blacks (1985) and that segregation is a main contributor to Black poverty (1990).

Ethnic and Racial Data for Chicago

The Chicago metropolitan area has almost eight million people and covers six counties. The largest of these is Cook County with five million people, including virtually all of the 2.8 million residents of the city of Chicago. Most of the analyses that follow use 1980 and 1990 census data by census tracts. Tracts are spatial units that are meant to be relatively homogeneous, have visible boundaries, and contain between 2,500 and 8,000 people (U.S. Department of Commerce 1983). Although important detail may be sacrificed for areas larger than the tract, some of the city analyses use data for larger community areas. These are combinations of tracts that averaged 36,000 in population in 1990.

In the decennial census, race and Hispanic origin are asked in separate questions. The broad race categories are Black, White, Asian/Pacific Islander, and American Indian/Eskimo/Aleut. In 1990, 58 percent of Chicago's Hispanics chose the residual race category "other race" (Latino Institute 1992). Of the 218,196 people who marked both Hispanic and a specific race, 93 percent were White, 5 percent Black, 2 percent Asian, and 2 percent American Indian. Therefore, 15,524 Chicago non-White Hispanics, one half of 1 percent of the city total, were counted. Sixteen percent of Whites were also counted as Hispanics.

Ethnic Distibution within the City

Figure 2.1 shows areas that are at least 80 percent White, Black, or Hispanic within the city. Tracts with no shading have less than 80 percent of any one group or have fewer than one hundred people. Asians are not

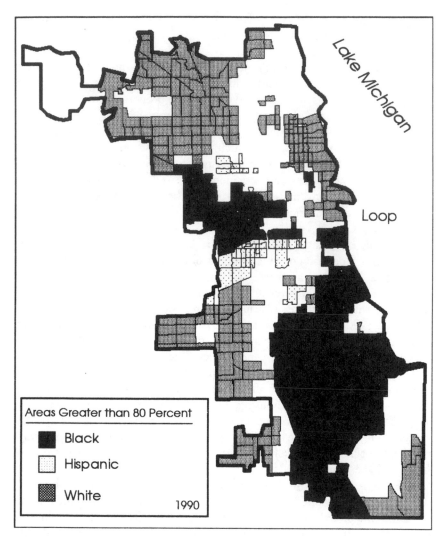

Fig. 2.1   Race and Ethnic Groups in Chicago

depicted because no tract met those criteria. Of the five areas with the greatest White concentration, all but the near north shoreline of Lake Michigan (north of the downtown "Loop") are middle-income areas that are becoming increasingly integrated with Hispanics and declining in total population. Together, these areas lost 3 percent of their population between 1980 and 1990, and fell from 98 percent to 93 percent White. The proportion Hispanic increased from 3 percent to 9 percent in the two western regions and from 6 percent to 18 percent in the extreme southeast area. There are few Blacks in any of these three areas.

In contrast, the mostly White near-north shoreline underwent gentrification in the 1980s. It is affluent, with median monthly rents of more than $1,000 for many census tracts. Whereas the proportion of Whites had declined in other parts of the city, it increased from 84 to 89 percent in the contiguous area depicted on the map, while proportions of Blacks and Hispanics there each decreased. Much of this transition occurred near the northern edge of the area shown, as a mostly White, affluent community extended northward, displacing more racially mixed and lower-income populations. Locational advantages of living near the lake include easy access to the central business district, cleaner air, vistas, and some relief from seasonal temperature extremes.

Most Chicago Blacks reside in what are known locally as the South Side and the West Side, each of which extends outward from the downtown Loop area (fig. 2.1). In the aggregate, the tracts with at least 80 percent Black population are fully 98 percent Black and have a combined population of nearly one million. These areas lost 19 percent of their population between 1980 and 1990, including most of the small Asian, White, and Hispanic populations contained therein, and also 16 percent of Blacks. Black population decline citywide was 9 percent between 1980 and 1990.

The South Side, which has nearly three times the population of the West Side, includes some relatively affluent areas and has a higher percentage (35 percent) of owner-occupied housing. Even so, 1990 monthly rents there were 11 percent below the citywide average of $360. The West Side averaged 20 percent below the average. Unlike the North Side, there is little residential development along the lakefront south of the Loop, so most Blacks do not live near Lake Michigan.

The larger integrated area visible on the map along the south shoreline (fig. 2.1) has the economic underpinning of the University of Chicago and the Museum of Science and Industry. The fifteen core tracts surrounding these two institutions were 34 percent Black in 1990 and the immediately adjacent areas were 95 percent Black.

The second largest minority group in Chicago is Hispanic and its majority is of Mexican origin (348,040; 65 percent). Smaller groups are Puerto Rican (121,209; 22 percent), Guatemalan (12,895; 2 percent), Cuban (10,475; 2 percent), and other Hispanic (42,693; 8 percent). Hispanics represent the fastest growing minority in Chicago, increasing from 7 percent of Chicago's population in 1970 to 14 percent in 1980 and 20 percent in 1990. Twenty tracts were greater than 80 percent Hispanic in 1980, increasing to 38 percent in 1990 mainly owing to a 100,000 increase in the Mexican-origin population. These figures do not include many illegal immigrants whose numbers are substantial in Chicago. Cubans were unusual because of the decrease in their population by 16 percent through both suburbanization and out-migration, particularly to Florida where the largest Cuban community in the United States resides.

In recent decades, Mexicans have settled mainly in a narrow area on the west, wedged between existing Black and White communities. What Massey called "hypersegregation" of Blacks and Mexicans (Massey and Mullan 1984; Massey and Denton 1989a, 1989b) is evident as one crosses the railway separating the Hispanic and the Black communities on the West Side. On one side of the tracks the population is 2 percent Black; on the other, 99 percent Black. One tract is 94 percent Hispanic; its neighbor, 0 percent Hispanic. Judging from median rents, however, the two sides have similar economic status; both adjoining edges are 29 percent below the city's average.

The Hispanic concentration west of downtown is comprised of two adjacent communities, both largely Mexican. The westernmost, with more than 80,000 people, is larger and faster growing having increased from 33 to 91 percent Hispanic between 1970 and 1990. Crowding in this largely Mexican community (3.5 persons per household, compared to 2.5 citywide), combined with the rapid in-migration over the past twenty years, has affected settlement patterns citywide. Resistance to spatial expansion of this community is seen on three sides: to the north by all-Black neighborhoods, to the east by gentrification, and to the south by an industrial park and a non-Hispanic White community. It did expand west into the adjacent suburb of Cicero, which gained 17,000 Hispanics between 1980 and 1990 and, incidentally, lost 11,000 non-Hispanic Whites. During the decade, some people of Mexican origin from this area also dispersed to the more distant suburbs and others overwhelmed the traditionally Puerto Rican community in the north central part of the city. Hispanics in general also moved into the narrow transition zones between the White and Black neighborhoods, and into areas left behind by Whites. Among 865 Chicago census tracts, the correlation of percentage loss of non-Hispanic Whites and percentage gain of Hispanics between 1980 and 1990 was .45.

Chicago has relatively few people of Asian descent (102,875; 4 percent of the total population), but this group experienced the highest rate of population growth (42 percent) between 1980 and 1990. No single group dominates the Asian population. In 1990, 27 percent were Filipino, 21 percent Chinese, 16 percent Asian Indian, 13 percent Korean, and 23 percent from other Asian origins. Compared to other groups, Asians are relatively dispersed. One small Chinese settlement can be found southwest of the city center (the traditional Chinatown area), and another Chinese settlement has formed on the far northeast side. Other Asian groups have developed on the north side as well. An Asian Indian community stretches along a mile-long commercial street, formally renamed Ghandi Avenue, in the far northeast. A densely Korean commercial district runs parallel to it a few miles south.

Ethnic Distribution in Cook County

The proportion of Whites in the 487 suburban Cook County census tracts decreased from 90 to 84 percent of the total population in the 1980s. Meanwhile, the Black percentage increased from 7 percent to 10 percent, and Asians and Hispanics doubled their suburban representation to 4 and 6 percent, respectively. Of these, only Asians are now suburban in proportion to their entire Cook County presence. Whites are still overrepresented and non-Asian minority groups are greatly underrepresented.

Black population settlements in suburban Chicago are primarily spatial extensions of the older South and West Side Black areas (fig. 2.2). Upward mobility often involves movement out of racial or ethnic enclaves into integrated areas (Massey 1985) and commonly into suburban areas. For Chicago's Blacks, however, suburbanization generally has not meant integration. Many of the newest, largest, and most concentrated Black suburbs lost over half of their White population between 1980 and 1990. The negative correlation of percent Black to percent White is now even stronger in suburban tracts ($-.92$) than in the city ($-.88$).

In addition to the traditional Chinatown cluster southwest of the Loop, Asians live mainly in a more dispersed pattern on Chicago's north side and have been moving into the more affluent suburbs north of the city (fig. 2.3). The relative wealth of the Asian suburban population is evident in the correlation of percent Asian with median rent in suburban tracts (.40), which is higher than the equivalent correlation for Whites (.32). Hispanics are distributed more evenly throughout the suburbs (fig. 2.4) than either Blacks or Asians.

Segregation in Chicago

Figure 2.1 alone suggests that the city of Chicago is still highly segregated. Blacks and Whites are especially separated, Hispanics are wedged between them, and Asians are dispersed throughout the northern part of the city. In

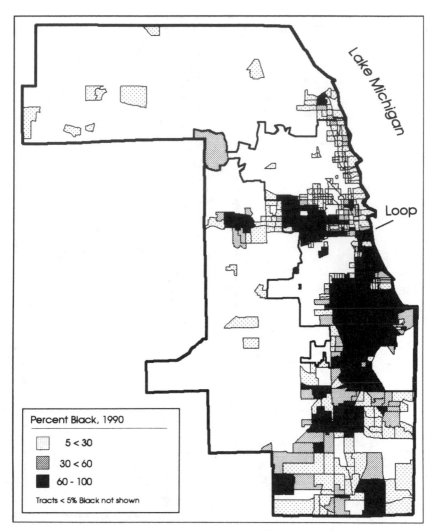

Percent Black, 1990

5 < 30

30 < 60

60 - 100

Tracts < 5% Black not shown

Fig. 2.2   Percentage Black in Chicago and Cook County

this section, degree and nature of segregation among ethnic groups will be analyzed.

Many researchers have compared measures of segregation (Duncan and Duncan 1955; James and Taeuber 1985; Massey and Denton 1988; Stearns and Logan 1986; White 1986), and all agree that the most popular among them is the index of dissimilarity (D). The index finds any group's proportion that would have to move to another area to be equally represented every-

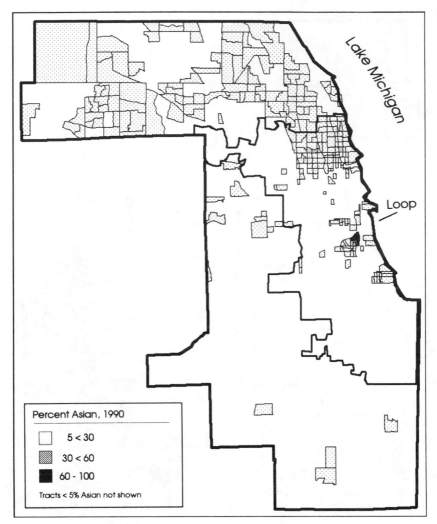

Fig. 2.3   Percentage Asian in Chicago and Cook County

where. However, it has been criticized because it can miss important
dimensions of segregation. According to Massey and Denton (1988), of five
aspects of segregation—evenness of distribution, potential for interaction with
the majority group, density of concentration, clustering, and nearness to the
urban core—dissimilarity measures only one: evenness. Therefore, it is a
common practice to accompany the dissimilarity score with other measures.
In this study I also utilize a threshold measure of segregation, Lorenz curves,

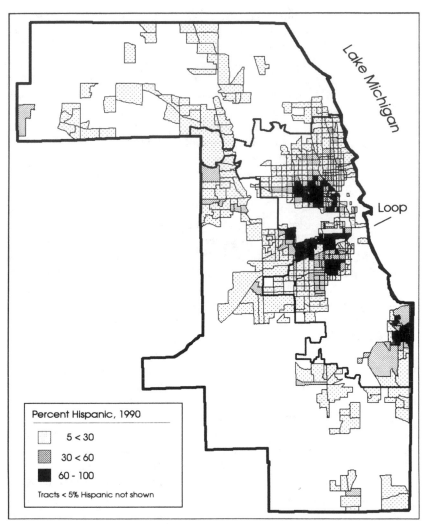

Fig. 2.4   Percentage Hispanic in Chicago and Cook County

and a measure of spatial autocorrelation in order to analyze residential segregation patterns from alternative perspectives. The analysis begins with the simplest and most general of these measures.

Arbitrary Threshold Test

The arbitrary threshold test has been used by Hayner (1991) to show crude changes in levels of segregation, and identify areas that have changed the most in their ethnic concentrations. Hayner considered a neighborhood to be integrated when no single group held at least an 80 percent majority, and relatively homogeneous if one group dominated.

This same threshold measure was applied to both 77 community areas in the city and also to the 965 smaller census tracts. Using Hayner's criterion, 48 (62 percent) of the community areas were homogeneous in 1980 and only 42 (55 percent) were homogeneous in 1990. My analysis at the tract level showed similar results, the number of homogeneous tracts decreasing from 610 (71 percent) in 1980 to 558 (65 percent) in 1990. The portion of residents living in tracts with less than 80 percent concentration increased from one-quarter to one-third during the decade.

Closer analysis of change during the decade of the 1980s shows that the 115 tracts that were homogeneous in 1980 but not in 1990 gained more than 100,000 Hispanics, Blacks, and Asians, but also lost almost as many Whites. In fact, more than half of the city's tracts lost at least 500 White residents per square mile during the last decade. If these tracts are removed from the analysis, Chicago became more segregated, not integrated, during the 1980s. In areas with a relatively stable White population, 80 percent were segregated in 1980 and 83 percent were segregated in 1990. This analysis leads to the conclusion that much of Chicago's integration can be explained by a decline in its majority group.

Whereas many tracts became integrated during the 1980s, about half as many went the other direction: they were diverse in 1980 and became homogeneous in 1990. Of these, 27 became homogeneously White, mainly through gentrification in the northernmost edge of the lakefront area. Every one of the 18 newly Black segregated tracts extended the margins of the already Black South or West sides so that, while these predominantly Black areas became less populated, they also became spatially larger. In the new Black tracts, the proportion of Whites, Hispanics, and Asians plummeted. There were also 18 new homogeneously Hispanic tracts scattered among the north central Puerto Rican zone and areas between White and Black communities.

Index of Dissimilarity

The index, D, was calculated for the relationship between broad ethnic groups (e.g., Asians) and the remainder of the population, and also for subgroups (e.g., Koreans) relative to their own broader groups (e.g., Asians). Data from 1980 and 1990 by census tracts in the city were utilized (table 2.1). One way to interpret the result is to use Kantrowitz's (1973) suggestion that values over .6 indicate relatively high segregation, and those over .3

Table 2.1 Chicago: Index of Dissimilarity, by Census Tract, 1980 and 1990

Group	1990 population	Segregation from total 1980 D	1990 D	Segregation from group 1980 D	1990 D
White	1,308,503	.749	.679		
Black	1,088,030	.893	.851		
Asian	104,681	.628	.598	Asian:	
Chinese	22,446	.772	.699	.621	.581
Filipino	27,780	.659	.558	.517	.439
Japanese	7,099	.709	.619	.538	.442
Asian Indian	16,895	.726	.659	.447	.375
Korean	14,101	.768	.711	.513	.459
Vietnamese	4,660	.909	.780	.718	.528
Hispanic	549,189	.667	.648	Hispanic:	
Mexican	355,002	.656	.629	.553	.461
Puerto Rican	120,108	.725	.649	.564	.439
Cuban	10,122	.674	.534	.660	.458

moderate segregation. Using this standard, every major group in Chicago is highly segregated, but each was less so in 1990 compared to 1980. Blacks are most segregated from non-Blacks, with D values exceeding .85 at both time periods.

All of the racial and ethnic subgroups have also become less segregated relative to their reference groups. Chinese and Vietnamese were highly segregated from other Asians in 1980, and Cubans were highly segregated from other Hispanics, but each of these groups became more integrated by 1990.

Lorenz Curves

Lorenz curves allow a visual analysis of the degree to which a particular population is concentrated or spread across tracts. A Lorenz segregation curve is constructed by ranking tracts in descending order according to the proportion of a particular group, then plotting the cumulative proportion against the corresponding accumulation of the population not in that group (James and Taeuber 1985). In the case of the Black population, with "perfect" integration, each tract would contain the same portion Black (in Chicago, 39 percent) and the curve would follow the diagonal in figure 2.5.

These curves, like D, show that Blacks, Whites, and Asians are very segregated from the remainder of the population, but less so in 1990 than a decade earlier. In 1980 and 1990, areas containing 90 percent of Chicago Blacks were also home to only 2 percent, and then 5 percent, of the city's non-Blacks. Intersection of the curve with the x- and y-axes shows the population of all-Black and zero-Black areas, respectively. In both years, fully half of Chicago's Blacks lived among less than two-tenths of 1 percent of the city's non-Blacks. However, in 1980 more than half of the non-Black population lived among zero Blacks, and a decade later only 30 percent of non-Blacks were so segregated. The corresponding statistic for the majority group shows that one-quarter of non-Whites lived in tracts without any Whites in 1980, and only 18 percent were so separated from the majority group in 1990. This indicates an increase in what Massey and Denton would call "exposure" (1988).

Hispanics remain the most ubiquitous of all groups. In both years, they were entirely absent in tracts containing only 8 percent of non-Hispanics. The corresponding figure for Asians was 15 percent, down from 32 percent in 1980.

Spatial Autocorrelation

None of the above measures of segregation distinguishes between a dispersed pattern of separate settlements and a single contiguous settlement

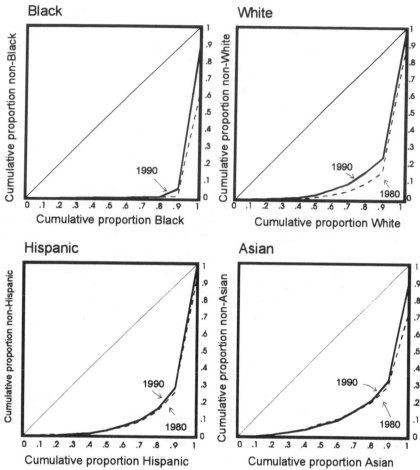

Fig. 2.5   Lorenz Segregation Curves, Chicago, 1980 and 1990

region for a particular population. This is referred to as the checkerboard problem (White 1983), or a question of clustering (Massey and Denton 1988). Several measurements of clustering have been suggested (see Dacey 1968; Geary 1954; White 1986) but are not often used because they are difficult to calculate. The measure used here is Moran's I, spatial autocorrelation. The I is the mean correlation of a population of each tract with that same population in every contiguous tract, weighted by the length of the common border. It varies from −1 (perfectly dispersed), to 0 (random), to +1 (perfectly clustered).

Tract-level autocorrelation was not possible because of software limitations, so data for Chicago's seventy-seven community areas were analyzed instead. Table 2.2 shows Moran's I for 1970, 1980, and 1990. Chicago's Black, Hispanic, and Asian areas have become more clustered during the past decade and, except for Asians, the same occurred in the 1970s. The opposite was true for the Whites, probably because of the widespread decline in the White population in the city.

The increase in spatial autocorrelation of ethnic groups between 1980 and 1990 shows that Chicago has become more regionalized. Non-White areas are now larger and better defined. The increase in autocorrelation reflects new Asian concentrations in the northeast, a stronger Hispanic presence in the west and north central areas, and spatial expansion and homogenization of Black areas. This has translated, at least for Hispanics, into political representation by way of a 1992 state congressional district that cleverly linked the Mexican population in the west with the north central Mexican/Puerto Rican area. The result was a 65 percent electoral majority for Hispanics in the district, and the election of Illinois's first Latino congressperson (Garza 1992). Voting districts that would give Asians a 27 percent concentration for city council and 24 percent concentration for state legislature are now possible, even though Asians represent only 4 percent of the county's population (Corfman 1992).

Chicago's Diversity and Integration

Chicago became more diverse in the 1980s, but it became more integrated only in terms of evenness and exposure. The arbitrary threshold measure, the

Table 2.2   Chicago: Spatial Autocorrelation of Percentage Concentration of Racial/Ethnic Groups for 77 Community Areas

	1970	1980	1990
White(%)	I=.84 (8.95)	I=.85 (9.00)	I=.82 (8.76)
Black(%)	I=.83 (8.82)	I=.86 (9.19)	I=.87 (9.27)
Hispanic(%)	I=.68 (7.22)	I=.70 (7.49)	I=.75 (8.04)
Asian(%)	I=.73 (7.79)	I=.64 (6.84)	I=.73 (7.79)

Note: I = Moran's I; t values shown in parentheses.

Lorenz curve, and the index of dissimilarity all show that the major groups were more likely to live in areas containing nonmembers in 1990 than they were previously. This appears to be related to the continued loss of White population and the influx of Hispanics rather than a large movement of Blacks. Black concentrations in the city continue to expand on the margins of existing Black communities, and suburban Blacks have extended this pattern beyond city limits. This has resulted in continued high levels of segregation of Blacks even in the surrounding areas. Yet in 1990, only about 30 percent of non-Blacks in Chicago lived in tracts with no Blacks whatsoever, whereas 50 percent did a decade earlier.

The fast-growing Asian populations in Chicago are sometimes overlooked because of their small size and their relative affluence. However, Asians are virtually absent in two-thirds of the city, so their impact in the northernmost section is magnified. Chinese, Korean, and Asian Indian centers of commerce now complement the well-established Chinatown. The northward suburbanization of Asians is remarkably rapid and affluent compared to other groups.

Eighty years ago the ethnic mosaic of Chicago was defined primarily on the basis of first- and second-generation European immigrant groups settling in inner-city neighborhoods. Thirty years ago a large population of first- and second-generation Black internal migrants from the South changed the character of that mosaic. Today the mosaic is again being changed by immigrant groups, this time from Latin America and Asia. Today's ethnic mosaic has extended to suburban territory. Details of the specific settlement and segregation patterns, as shown in these analyses, continue to change. Nonetheless, Chicago continues to be an ethnically diverse and also, to an important extent, a racially segregated urban area.

References

Chicago Department of Development and Planning. 1976. *Historic City: The Settlement of Chicago*. Chicago, Ill.: City of Chicago.

Corfman, Tom. 1992. "Asian Americans Buck the Odds in Battle for Political Power." *Chicago Reporter* 21(11):3–6.

Cutler, Irving. 1982. *Chicago: Metropolis of the Mid-Continent*. Dubuque, Ia.: Kendall/Hunt.

Dacey, Michael F. 1968. "A Review on Measures of Contiguity for Two and K-Color Maps." In *Spatial Analysis: A Reader in Statistical Geography*, ed. Brian J. L. Berry and Duane F. Marble. Englewood Cliffs, N.J.: Prentice-Hall.

Duncan, Otis D., and Beverly Duncan. 1955. "A Methodological Analysis of Segregation Indexes." *American Sociological Review* 20(2):210–17.

———. 1957. *The Negro Population of Chicago.* Chicago, Ill.: University of Chicago Press.

Fischer, Claude S. 1975. "Toward a Subcultural Theory of Urbanism." *American Journal of Sociology* 80:1319–41.

———. 1982. *To Dwell among Friends: Personal Networks in Town and City.* Chicago, Ill.: University of Chicago Press.

Galster George C., and W. Mark Keeney. 1988. "Race, Residence, Discrimination, and Economic Opportunity: Modeling the Nexus of Urban Racial Phenomena." *Urban Affairs Quarterly* 24:87–117.

Garza, Melita M. 1992. "Hispanic District Really Isn't." *Chicago Tribune.* Feb. 5(sc2),2.

Geary, R. C. 1954. "The Contiguity Ratio and Statistical Mapping." *Incorporated Statistician* 5:115–41.

Hayner, Don. 1991. "Census Finds Chicago More Diverse, Stable." *Chicago Sun Times.* Feb. 24, 1, 46.

Henri, Florette, 1975. *Black Migration: Movement North, 1900–1920.* Garden City, N.Y.: Anchor Press/Doubleday.

James, David R., and Karl E. Taeuber 1985. "Measures of Segregation." *Sociological Methodology,* ed. N. B. Tuna. San Francisco, Calif.: Jossey Bass.

Kantrowitz, N. 1973. *Ethnic and Racial Segregation in the New York Metropolis.* New York: Praeger.

Latino Institute. 1992. "Social and Economic Characteristics of the Latino Population: 1990." Unpublished report.

Massey, Douglas S. 1985. "Ethnic Residential Segregation: A Theoretical Synthesis and Empirical Review." *Sociology and Social Research* 69:315–50.

———. 1990. "American Apartheid: Segregation and the Making of the Underclass." *American Journal of Sociology* 96(2):329–57.

Massey, Douglas S., and Nancy A. Denton. 1988. "The Dimensions of Residential Segregation." *Social Forces* 67(2):281–315.

———. 1989a. "Hypersegregation in U.S. Metropolitan Areas: Black and Hispanic Segregation along Five Dimensions." *Demography* 26(3):373–91.

———. 1989b. "Residential Segregation of Mexicans, Puerto Ricans, and

Cubans in Selected U.S. Metropolitan Areas." *Sociology and Social Research* 73:73–83.

Massey, Douglas S., and Brendan P. Mullan. 1984. "Processes of Hispanic and Black Spatial Assimilation." *American Journal of Sociology* 89(4):836–73.

Orren, Karen. 1974. *Corporate Power and Social Change: The Politics of the Life Insurance Industry.* Baltimore, Md.: Johns Hopkins University Press.

Stearns, Linda B., and John R. Logan. 1986. "Measuring Trends in Segregation: Three Dimensions, Three Measures." *Urban Affairs Quarterly* 22(1):124–50.

U.S. Department of Commerce, Bureau of the Census 1983. 1980 Census of Population and Housing, Census Tracts No. 119 Chicago Pt. 4. Washington, D.C.: GPO.

White, Michael J. 1983. "The Measurement of Spatial Segregation." *American Journal of Sociology* 88:1008–19.

———. 1986. "Segregation and Diversity Measures in Population Distribution." *Population Index* 52(2):198–221.

Chapter 3

Diversity Down Under: The Changing Ethnic Mosaic of Sydney and Melbourne

Graeme J. Hugo

Postwar immigration transformed Australia from a culturally homogeneous country to one of diversity. It represented a total break with past immigration in its scale and for the first time it included large numbers of migrants of other than English/Irish origin. Between 1947 and 1991, the national population increased from 7.6 to 16.9 million and the 5.2 million new settlers arriving in Australia over that period accounted directly or indirectly (via their childbearing) for around half of that growth. The impact of postwar immigration on Australia has been greatest in the nation's two largest cities: Sydney (1991 population 3.54 million) and Melbourne (3.02 million). Their total populations have more than doubled and their share of the nation's foreign-born population increased from 46.5 percent in 1947 to 52.3 percent in 1991 while their share of the Australian-born population fell from 38.7 to 34.8 percent.

This chapter reviews the changes that have occurred in the ethnic composition of Sydney and Melbourne over the postwar period and examines the changing spatial distribution of ethnic groups within the two cities. Some of the policy implications of the changing spatial patterning of ethnic groups within the two cities are then considered, especially as they relate to access and equity and locational disadvantage issues.

The Context

Australia's space economy is characterized by a high degree of urbanization (85.1 percent of the national population lived in urban areas in 1991) and concentration in the east, the southeast and the southwest coastal zone, which comprise only 3.3 percent of the national land area but account for 80.5 percent of the total population. The proportion of the nation's population living in cities of 100,000 residents or more increased from 53.6 percent in 1954 to 62.7 percent in 1991. The nation's urban hierarchy is dominated by Sydney and Melbourne whose share of the national population has remained stable over the postwar years at around 39 percent.

There is a long-standing and well-documented rivalry between the cities (Davidson 1986) and each has its own distinctive character. Melbourne has been more conservative and traditionally a major focus of federal government activity. The headquarters of Australian based and focused companies, it was very strongly influenced by the Australian manufacturing boom of the 1950s and 1960s. Sydney, also an important government, business, and manufacturing center, has tended to be more outward looking, cosmopolitan, and trade oriented. In recent years, it has become Australia's major contact point with the booming Asia-Pacific rim economies.

Sydney and Melbourne have vied for preeminence in the Australian urban system during the last century. Melbourne was larger than Sydney over the latter half of the nineteenth century but with the gradual shift of the Commonwealth government to Canberra after Federation, Sydney's growth surpassed that of Melbourne so that in 1947 Sydney was 26 percent larger. In the "long boom" of the first two postwar decades, Melbourne's growth outpaced Sydney's, partly due to the fact that Melbourne attracted more of the rapid industrial expansion that Australia experienced during that period. Thereafter, however, Australia's economy underwent significant structural change that included a decline in manufacturing employment so that Sydney has grown faster. In 1991, it was 17 percent larger than Melbourne.

International migration has been of critical importance in the postwar growth of Sydney and Melbourne. Over the first two postwar decades, more than half of the cities' growth was attributable to net gains of overseas migrants, and net gains of people from elsewhere in Australia were minor (table 3.1).

Between 1976 and 1986, growth was lower than in the first two postwar decades; natural increase was equivalent to almost all (98.6 percent) of Melbourne's growth and 72 percent of Sydney's. However, international migration has maintained a significant role in the growth of the cities, which was counterbalanced by a net outflow of Australian-born population. The dominance of Melbourne in the early postwar decades both in terms of population growth and overseas-born settlers was reversed by 1976–1986. In the late 1980s and early 1990s, Sydney retained its dominance of the overseas

Table 3.1 Sydney and Melbourne: Estimated Components of Population Change, 1947–1966, 1976–1986, and 1986–1991

		Natural increase	Net Migration Total	Net Migration Internal	Total population increase
1947-1966					
Sydney	Number(000s)	379	457	17	836
	%	45.3	54.7	2.0	100
Melbourne	Number(000s)	366	491	6	857
	%	42.7	57.3	0.7	100
1976-1986					
Sydney	Number(000s)	237	92	-92	329
	%	72.0	28.0	-28.0	100
Melbourne	Number(000s)	205	3	-88	208
	%	98.6	1.4	-42.3	100
1986-1991					
Sydney	Number(000s)	160	16	-152	174
	%	92.0	9.2	-81.6	100
Melbourne	Number(000s)	137	53	-52	190
	%	72.1	27.9	-27.4	100

Sources: Hugo 1989,68; Australian Bureau of Statistics 1990,10; Author's estimates for 1986-1991 using Australian Bureau of Statistics Census and Vital Statistics Data.

intake. The net loss of Australian-born in Sydney has gathered pace while that in Melbourne was reduced somewhat.

This "switchover function" (Maher and McKay 1986) of Sydney and Melbourne—a net loss of migrants in exchange with other parts of Australia more than counterbalanced by an inflow of overseas migrants—is an important feature of these two cities in the postwar period and part of the phenomenon of the "turnaround" in Australia (Hugo 1989). International migration gains have directly accounted for more than half of Sydney and Melbourne's net population growth over the postwar period, and if their indirect contribution via the children they have had since settling in Australia are taken into account, that contribution is closer to two-thirds of net growth.

The growth of the overseas-born population in the two cities between 1947 and 1991 has been substantial (table 3.2). Sydney saw its overseas-born population more than double between 1947 and 1961, but the impact was less than had occurred in Melbourne. By 1961, Melbourne had surpassed Sydney in having the largest overseas-born community in the nation, but Sydney has since reasserted itself as the major focus of immigrant settlement in Australia. These shifts in the relative attractiveness of the two cities to newly arrived migrants over the postwar period have implications not only for the growth of the population but also for differences in the ethnic composition of the two cities.

Postwar immigration to Australia has occurred in a series of waves characterized by a different mix of birthplace groups as Australia's immigration

Table 3.2   Sydney and Melbourne: Overseas-Born Populations, Statistical
Divisions, 1947–1991

	Sydney		Melbourne		Australia
	Number	%	Number	%	Number
1947	191,107	25.7	125,258	16.8	744,187
1954	308,778	24.0	261,470	20.3	1,286,466
1961	434,663	24.4	444,479	25.0	1,778,780
1966	558,236	26.2	568,365	26.7	2,130,920
1971	681,313	26.4	687,266	26.6	2,579,318
1976	736,754	27.1	706,331	26.0	2,718,855
1981	834,280	27.8	754,117	25.1	3,003,833
1986	912,578	28.1	788,266	24.3	3,247,381
1991	1,070,627	28.5	893,445	23.8	3,755,554

Sources: Australian Bureau of Statistics Censuses of 1947, 1954, 1966, 1971, 1976, 1981, 1986, 1991.

policy and the national and global economic and political situation has changed. The UK/Eire-born have remained a constant element in the postwar immigration streams, although their share of the total intake has declined significantly from 78.7 percent in 1947 to 18 percent in 1991. The mix of other (mainly non-English speaking) birthplace groups in the incoming stream has undergone significant change with different groups dominating successive waves. Eastern European refugees formed the first of these waves in the late 1940s and early 1950s and were followed by a substantial influx of Dutch and German settlers in the early 1950s who in turn were followed in the mid- and late 1950s by Italians, Greeks, and Yugoslavs. Subsequent flows included Turks, Lebanese, and Egyptians, and very recent flows involved New Zealanders, Vietnamese, Filipinos, Malaysians, and ethnic Chinese.

Each group has added another element of diversity to the national population, but their representation in the two cities has varied. Broadly, the groups dominant in the first half of the period are more strongly represented in Melbourne. In the subsequent postindustrial period, however, Sydney has been growing faster so that the groups peaking during this time are disproportionately represented in Sydney.

Changing Ethnic Composition

The examination of the changing ethnic profiles of Sydney and Melbourne will predominantly utilize birthplace data. While this is an imperfect indicator because of its failure to capture the Australian-born children and other descendants of immigrants (Hugo 1993), it is appropriate to use here because of the recency of the bulk of non-English-speaking migration to the cities and its availability for all postwar censuses. Australia included an ancestry question in the 1986 census and those data for Sydney and Melbourne are analyzed elsewhere (Hugo 1991, 1992). A birthplace of parents question was included in Australian censuses in 1971 so that some analysis of the second generation is possible.

One important component in Australia's ethnic mosaic that is not detected by the birthplace question in the census is the Aboriginal-Torres Strait Islander origin population. The census includes a self-identifying question on Aboriginality, although in the early postwar years its accuracy is questionable. In 1991, 257,333 Australians indicated they were of Aboriginal or Torres Strait Islander origin, 1.5 percent of the national population. Their numbers increased from about 1,400 in 1961 to over 22,000 in 1991 in Sydney; and from about 300 to 8,000 in Melbourne. Today, they are still significantly underrepresented in the two cities, making up 0.6 percent of Sydney's residents and 0.3 percent in Melbourne.

The Aboriginal population in Australia differs from all other ethnic groups in that the majority live outside of the capital cities. As was the case with the non-English-speaking immigrants, the story of Aboriginal urban settlement within Sydney and Melbourne is overwhelmingly one of the post–World War II period. The Aboriginal movement to cities was encouraged by government agencies and by the growing concentration of job opportunities, services, and facilities. Further impetus was given to the movement when Aborigines belatedly were granted full citizenship and other rights as a result of a 1967 referendum. Sydney now has the largest single community of Aborigines and is the focal point of many Aboriginal organizations. There are indications that there has been a slowing down of rural to urban redistribution of the Aboriginal population and that much of the movement tends to be circular (Gray 1989).

Turning now to immigrant populations, figure 3.1 shows the changes in the proportions of the overseas-born population at various postwar censuses in Sydney and Melbourne. The most striking shift is the consistent pattern of decline in the proportion from the UK and Ireland over the period. The pattern for southern Europeans is one of a rapid increase up to 1971 but a subsequent attenuation as the flow of immigrants from Greece and Italy dried up over the last two decades. The greater significance of southern Europeans in Melbourne than Sydney is also evident.

The trajectory of postwar migration of other European nations has tended to follow that of the southern Europeans. Asian-origin immigrants have increased in number dramatically since 1971 and their settlement has favored Sydney over Melbourne. Overall then, the rapid increase in the overseas-born population in Sydney and Melbourne has been accompanied by an equally striking increase in ethnic diversity among them.

It is difficult to depict this diversity adequately here but in 1986 there were seventy-five separate birthplace groups with more than one thousand people in Sydney, and there are many other smaller but viable communities (Moser et al. 1993). Recent changes in the size of major national groups are shown in table 3.3. Most of the groups have a greater proportional representation in Sydney and Melbourne than the Australian-born, the only exceptions being the Dutch in Sydney and New Zealanders and North Americans in Melbourne.

The stronger southern European element in Melbourne is reflected in the fact that of the four largest overseas-born groups, three in Melbourne are southern European (Italian, Greek, Yugoslav) compared with one in Sydney

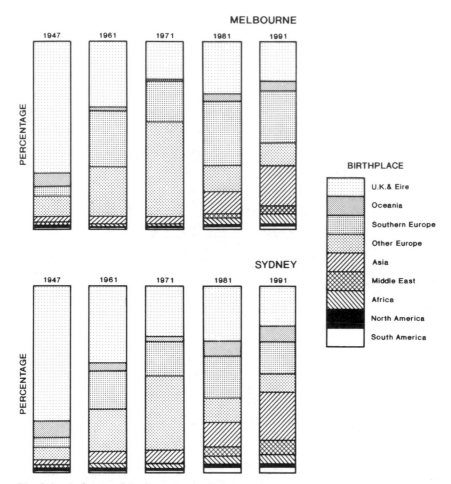

Fig. 3.1   Sydney and Melbourne: Birthplace Composition, 1947–1991. Africa is incorporated with the Middle East in the 1947 figures and the Middle East is incorporated with Asia for the 1961 and 1971 figures. (Australian Bureau of Statistics, Censuses)

(Italian). Lebanese are strongly concentrated in Melbourne. English-speaking-origin groups, UK-Eire, New Zealand, South Africa, United States, and Canada, are more strongly represented in Sydney than in Melbourne. East Asian origin groups favor Sydney with groups from China, the Philippines, and Hong Kong being more than twice as numerous as in Melbourne. On the other hand, the representation of people from India and Malaysia is

Table 3.3 Sydney and Melbourne: Representation and Growth of Major Birthplace Groups, 1981 and 1991

Birthplace	Sydney 1981	1991	% nat'l total	% change	Melbourne 1981	1991	% nat'l total	% change
United Kingdom/Ireland	246,742	225,493	21.6	-8.6	210,001	193,142	16.9	-8.0
New Zealand	53,025	64,779	23.5	-22.2	23,373	35,430	12.8	+51.6
Italy	62,682	57,212	22.4	-8.7	102,326	94,049	36.9	-8.1
Lebanon	36,010	50,056	72.6	+39.0	9,938	13,474	19.5	+35.6
Vietnam	15,385	47,673	39.0	+209.9	12,523	43,991	36.0	+251.3
Yugoslavia	44,351	46,904	29.1	+5.8	51,884	56,389	35.0	+8.7
China	13,162	42,165	53.4	+220.4	4,971	19,518	24.7	+292.6
Greece	43,628	40,654	29.9	-6.8	69,694	64,660	47.5	-7.2
Philippines	7,734	33,555	45.7	+333.9	3,198	14,992	20.4	+368.8
Hong Kong	7,964	30,342	51.5	+281.0	3,260	13,241	22.5	+306.2
Germany	24,097	21,886	19.0	-9.2	27,236	24,469	21.2	-10.2
Malta	21,265	19,418	36.3	-8.7	26,323	23,814	44.5	-9.5
India	10,182	17,917	29.3	+76.0	11,660	18,656	30.5	+60.0
Malaysia	8,076	17,651	24.3	+118.6	9,079	21,505	29.7	+136.9
Poland	14,134	16,262	23.6	+15.1	19,972	21,420	31.1	+7.3
South Africa	9,012	16,228	32.7	+80.1	5,819	10,320	20.8	+77.4
Netherlands	16,780	14,561	15.2	-13.2	20,573	18,714	19.6	-9.0
USA/Canada	13,595	19,686	26.3	+44.8	7,035	11,992	16.0	+70.5
Former USSR	15,525	13,253	30.1	-14.6	14,303	13,634	31.0	-4.7
Australia	2,322,193	2,366,921	18.6	+1.9	1,933,694	2,056,387	16.2	+6.3

Sources: Burnley 1986; Australian Bureau of Statistics Census of 1991.

somewhat greater in Melbourne. The proportion of Vietnamese in the two cities is in both cases twice that of the Australian-born, and the Vietnamese are the fifth largest overseas-born group in each city.

In both cities the increasing Asian presence is in evidence (table 3.3). In Sydney the ten largest overseas-born groups in 1981 did not include a single Asian-origin group, yet by 1991, Vietnam, China, the Philippines, and Hong Kong-born were among the largest ten. In Melbourne in 1981, there were no Asian-born groups in the largest ten birthplace categories, but by 1991, the Vietnamese and Malaysians were the fifth and ninth largest groups respectively. All of the Asian-born groups more than doubled in numbers in the 1980s in both cities while most of the European-origin groups actually declined as death and return migration reduced their numbers. Notable exceptions were groups born in Poland and what was Yugoslavia. Among the English-speaking-origin groups, there was a decline in the UK-Eire-born but significant increases in New Zealanders, South Africans, and North Americans.

Settlement of Ethnic Groups

The spatial distribution of ethnic groups in Sydney and Melbourne is of particular interest because, as Price demonstrates in his classic study of Southern Europeans in Australia (1963,140), patterns of settlement are inextricably bound up with a whole range of social and economic elements that impinge upon the well-being of those groups. There are several factors influencing where individual overseas immigrants settle upon arrival in Australia ultimately shaping the pattern of distribution of each birthplace group within Sydney and Melbourne. These are summarized as follows:

• *Job opportunities*. The concentration of southern European immigrants of the 1950s and 1960s in Sydney and Melbourne was partly a function of job opportunities associated with the rapid expansion of manufacturing. The pattern of settlement of these groups within those cities was partly influenced by proximity to the location of factories offering those jobs.

• *Housing opportunities*. During the 1950s and 1960s the bulk of cheap rental housing was located in the inner suburban areas of the major cities, a factor attracting southern European immigrants to those areas.

• *Timing*. When the peak immigration of the waves of particular groups occurs makes a difference. The spatial distribution of particular job and housing opportunities is constantly changing so that the pattern that existed during the peak immigration of one group will not necessarily apply during the peak period of settlement of another group.

• *Scale*. The size of a particular group arriving in a city matters. Small numbers of immigrants are more likely to be dispersed throughout a city than large numbers. When there is a very large influx, it will tend to be absorbed at the contemporary fringe of the city where the main stock of newly constructed housing is concentrated.

• *Initial place of arrival*. This not only applies at the level of the city, but can also apply to the place in that city that immigrants live upon arrival. Hence, it is characteristic of Melbourne and Sydney's Vietnamese to be clustered in suburbs around the location of now-closed migrant hostels where the bulk of refugee-humanitarian migrants were initially placed. This was also true for the Eastern European refugees arriving in Australia some three decades earlier.

• *Location of family members and fellow countrymen*. As Burnley (1982,92) points out, the nuclei of original "pioneer" settlers often become important anchors for later generations of immigrants. This is partly because later migrants often spend an initial period living with established relatives so that their information about housing opportunities is biased toward that area, and also because of a desire to locate near relatives and friends for the economic and emotional support. Once such a nucleus is established, it will tend to attract ethnic-specific shops, restaurants, and institutions that will be a further inducement for newcomers from that country to settle in that part of the city.

• *Language*. Non-English-speaking (NES) groups have a tendency to concentrate together for mutual support. Moreover, once a community is established, many local shops and services will have at least one employee who can speak the group's language.

• *Marginalization through social control mechanisms*. As Winchester and White (1988,37) point out:

> Social controls given legitimacy by political forces and then operationalised through such mechanisms as allocation systems in the housing market, result in certain subgroups of the population becoming stigmatised as socially unacceptable as well as economically weak. This phenomenon then takes on a spatial dimension, with the residential areas of these inhabitants becoming similarly characterised, consequently reinforcing the image of both area and people in the minds of those exercising power and social control.

Some Australian ethnic groups, at some stages in their settlement in Australia, have been socially, economically, and even legally marginalized. Discrimination in the housing market is one way in which this marginalization occurs with various gatekeepers preventing particular groups from entering particular housing markets.

• *Type of immigration.* Among groups in which sponsored migrants are a substantial proportion, there is often a greater tendency toward spatial concentration than there is for groups who tend to migrate independently.

Spatial Patterns

Ethnic groups in Sydney and Melbourne vary considerably with respect to their contemporary degree of spatial concentration. Here the index of dissimilarity, D, is used to assess the degree of concentration of major overseas-born groups and the Aboriginal-Torres Strait Islander population among local government areas (LGAs) within Sydney and Melbourne in 1986 (table 3.4). The D index can be interpreted as a measure of net displacement, showing the percentage of one population (e.g., Italian-born) that would have to move into other areal units in order to reproduce the

Table 3.4 Sydney and Melbourne: Indices of Dissimilarity for Birthplace Groups and Aboriginals-Torres Strait Islanders, 1986

Origin	Sydney	Melbourne	Origin	Sydney	Melbourne
Aboriginal-Torres Strait Islander	.32	.27	Philippines	.32	.30
UK-Ireland	.11	.16	Spain	.40	.36
Germany	.13	.15	Turkey	.49	.54
Greece	.50	.35	USSR	.35	.35
Italy	.35	.38	Czechoslovakia	.27	.27
Netherlands	.17	.29	Austria	.20	.18
New Zealand	.25	.18	Hungary	.34	.27
Poland	.33	.38	Canada	.29	.19
Scotland	.09	.15	Cyprus	.40	.40
England	.12	.17	Sri Lanka	.29	.33
Yugoslavia	.37	.43	Chile	.41	.46
Vietnam	.67	.56	France	.31	.20
India	.19	.26	Hong Kong	.35	.35
Ireland/Eire	.14	.12	Indonesia	.35	.25
Lebanon	.53	.46	Latvia	.25	.20
Malaysia	.30	.35	Northern Ireland	.13	.17
Malta	.41	.54	Papua New Guinea	.24	.18
South Africa	.26	.27	Portugal	.65	.49
USA	.32	.27	Singapore	.28	.29
China	.37	.36	Wales	.11	.19
Egypt	.32	.27			

Source: Calculated from Australian Bureau of Statistics Census of 1986.

same percentage distribution as the remainder of the population. A D value of 0 means the two populations have the same relative distribution, a D of 1 represents a complete apartheid situation.

The Aboriginal and Torres Strait Islander population is a moderately concentrated group having D values that are lower than many immigrant groups, especially NES groups (table 3.4). Its spatial distribution in Sydney is displayed in figure 3.2. There has been an increase in the degree of residential concentration of Aborigines in Sydney over the last two decades (Hugo 1992,230). They are concentrated in inner suburbs having significant stocks

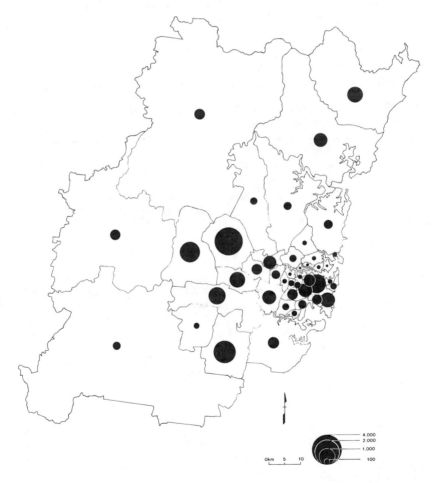

Fig. 3.2   Sydney: Distribution of Aborigines, 1991 (Australian Bureau of Statistics, 1991 Census)

of Housing Commission and Special Aboriginal Housing Schemes, and also in low-income, industrial western and southwestern suburbs. A western suburb, Blacktown, has the largest single Aboriginal community in Sydney, but even there they make up only 1.6 percent of residents.

The evolution of Aboriginal settlement in Sydney has shared many characteristics with that of the postwar, NES-origin immigrants. Aboriginal settlement (especially in its initial stages) has been similar to that of southern Europeans in that kinship linkages played a major role as did the distribution of cheap, rundown rental housing. Accordingly, the initial settlement of both groups was strongly concentrated in the inner suburbs and southern and western industrial areas. Subsequently, with gentrification and adjustment to the city, the inner suburban concentrations of both groups have been somewhat diluted. Aboriginal settlement also has been influenced by the distribution of Housing Commission housing, a characteristic shared with postwar immigrants from the UK and Eire.

In the main, however, the distribution of the Aboriginal population in Sydney reflects strongly its disadvantaged position within the total community. The patterns of Aboriginal settlement in Melbourne, although involving much smaller numbers, are similar to those of Sydney (Hugo 1991,206–11).

The most highly concentrated foreign-born groups tend to be from NES backgrounds (table 3.4). Those having high D values in both cities include Vietnamese, Lebanese, Maltese, Turks, and Portuguese. In contrast, Germans, Irish, Scots, and other United Kingdom natives are much less concentrated. In between these extremes, a great variety of settlement patterns are revealed.

Figures 3.3 and 3.4 show the distribution of the NES-origin populations of Sydney and Melbourne at the beginning of the postwar period and in 1961 after more than a decade of predominantly European NES-origin migrant settlement. In Sydney in 1947, the 33,820 NES-origin residents were strongly concentrated in the inner southern areas of the city (fig. 3.3). Indeed, the LGA of the city of Sydney had one-fifth of the total NES population but only 4.6 percent of the total metropolitan population.

This inner-suburban concentration had two major elements. First were the postwar NES migrants who were predominantly unskilled and with very limited financial means. They had little choice but to locate in areas of cheap rental housing, which at that time was located primarily in the inner-industrial suburbs. However, there also were substantial numbers of NES-origin migrants in high-status, harborside eastern-inner suburbs (Poulsen and Spearritt 1981,118), including many Jewish immigrants.

By 1961, the spatial pattern had changed substantially, quite apart from the sevenfold increase in the NES-origin population. There was still a very strong inner-suburban orientation of the NES-born, although the domination

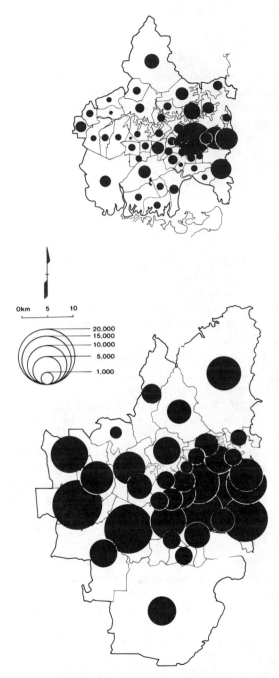

Fig. 3.3   Sydney: Distribution of Non-English-Speaking, Overseas-Born Population, 1947 and 1961 (Australian Bureau of Statistics, 1947 and 1961 Censuses)

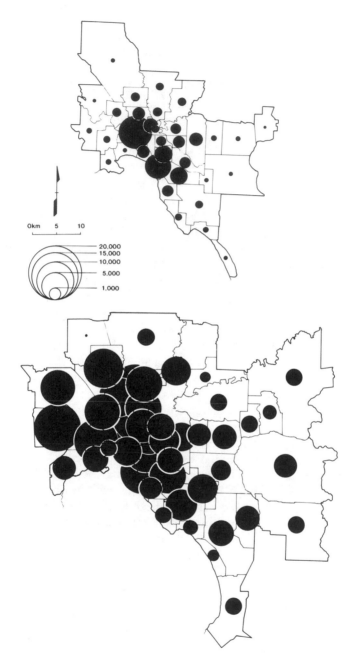

Fig. 3.4   Melbourne: Distribution of Non-English-Speaking, Overseas-Born
Population, 1947 and 1961 (Australian Bureau of Statistics, 1947 and 1961 Censuses)

of the central city of Sydney LGA had been reduced somewhat. The major difference in the 1961 map is the substantial extension of the concentration of the NES-origin group in a corridor to the west of the city of Sydney into nearby industrial suburbs. While there remained significant numbers of NES-origin settlers in the well-off eastern suburbs as was observed for 1947, by 1961, the NES-origin groups were overwhelmingly located in the low socioeconomic status, industrial-western suburbs.

As in Sydney, the 1947 distribution in Melbourne (fig. 3.4) was dominated by the central city area. Melbourne LGA in 1947 had a quarter of the 27,243 NES-origin overseas-born residents in the metropolitan area. An important secondary concentration in the southeastern suburbs predominantly reflected Jewish settlement. Melbourne in 1986 was home to 46 percent of Australia's Jews. The inner city was the major focus of Jewish settlement in the nineteenth century but this moved to the southeast, especially during the 1920s, 1930s, and 1940s. Hence, in Melbourne, as in Sydney, at the beginning of the postwar period, the small NES-origin population was heavily concentrated in the inner-city area but with two distinct foci—one in the industrial, poorer areas and the other in better-off inner-seaside suburbs.

By 1961, there had been a tenfold increase in Melbourne's NES-origin population and a distinct change in the pattern of distribution with a strong western and northwestern orientation replacing the southeastern bias evident in 1947 (fig. 3.4). Major concentrations increased in the inner suburbs and the City of Melbourne's dominance was considerably reduced. Other large concentrations, however, were located in the industrial suburbs of the western part of the city. The long-standing Jewish-based concentration in the southeast is still in evidence.

By 1991, there was a substantial decentralization of the NES-born population in Sydney (fig. 3.5). The city of Sydney's share fell from 16.6 percent (38,257 persons) in 1961 to 0.3 percent (3,094 persons) in 1991. There was a substantial shift in the focus of settlement out to what were the middle and outer western industrial areas during the 1960s and now are best considered "middle" suburbs. In addition to the concentration of mainly Jewish settlers in the inner-eastern suburbs identified earlier, another important element has been the growth of the NES-origin population in some of the higher status suburbs. Many of the Asian-origin people coming to Sydney in the 1980s have arrived with substantial financial assets and skills and settled in high-income areas. This is especially true of the Hong Kong and Malaysian-born groups but not of groups such as the Vietnamese who have entered Australia under the refugee or family migration programs.

Similar trends in Melbourne are in evidence (fig. 3.6). The inner-middle

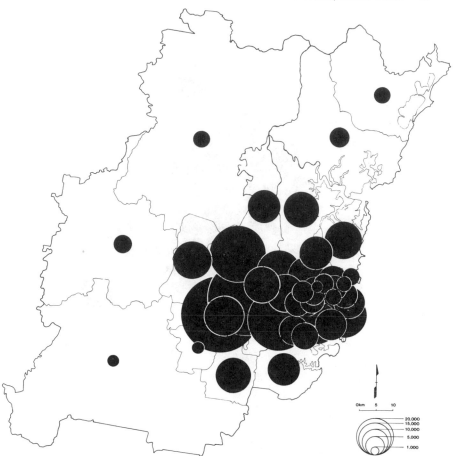

Fig. 3.5   Sydney: Distribution of Non-English-Speaking, Overseas-Born Population, 1991 (Australian Bureau of Statistics, 1991 Census)

western suburb orientation evident in the 1961 map has been reduced somewhat. There are now substantial concentrations in the outer-middle suburban industrial areas along the major arterial routes to the north, southeast and east. On the other hand, the NES-origin population declined in the central city of Melbourne from 21,673 in 1961 to 16,253 in 1991. While the NES population is still concentrated in lower status, industrial suburbs, this is not as marked as it was in 1961, reflecting the shift in the immigration intake. Skilled and business migrants made up a much greater proportion of all immigrants in the 1980s than in previous postwar decades.

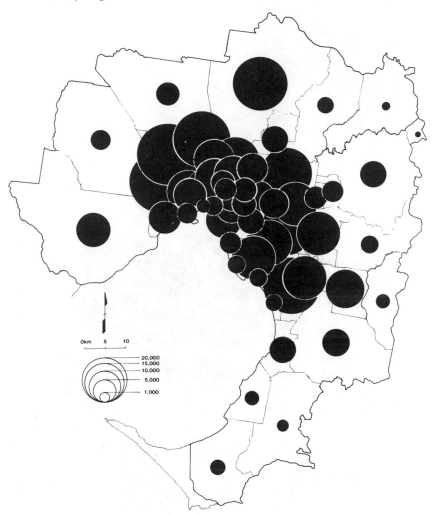

Fig. 3.6   Melbourne: Distribution of Non-English-Speaking, Overseas-Born Population, 1991 (Australian Bureau of Statistics, 1991 Census)

Models of Ethnic Concentrations

There is insufficient space here to examine the changing distribution of individual birthplace groups in any detail (see Hugo 1991, 1992, 1993). However, it is possible to make some generalizations about the changes that have occurred in the distribution of these groups in Sydney and Melbourne over the postwar period. It is clear, first of all, that the degree of concentration of a particular ethnic group at a particular point in time is influenced by the stage in the life cycle of the migration flow of that group. Lieberson and Waters (1987) in analyzing the changing locational patterns of thirty-three ethnic groups in the United States, found that for all groups except Blacks and American Indians, the forces generating distinctive ethnic locational patterns are strongest at the time of initial settlement, so that the longer a group has been present, the less geographically concentrated it will be.

The generalization that over time there will inevitably be a deconcentration of ethnic groups needs some modification. The distinctive settlement patterns of each birthplace group in Sydney and Melbourne partly reflects both the stage that the immigration and settlement of the group has reached and also the distinctive characteristics and specific settlement experience of that group. In the Sydney and Melbourne cases, we can postulate five general models of transition that the spatial distribution of ethnic groups goes through over time.

1. *Model A* includes situations in which the initial pioneer migrants from a particular country immediately upon arrival establish a settlement pattern that is similar to that of the Australian-born population. This pattern of dispersed settlement is maintained by later "vintages" of settler arrivals from that particular country. An example of this type of pattern in Sydney and Melbourne would be the German-born who during the postwar period have shown very little tendency toward concentration.

2. In *Model B* the initial pioneer migrants from a particular origin settle in concentrations in certain ecological niches. Later generations are attracted to those concentrations and they are maintained. However, over time, especially if the numbers of new immigrant arrivals decline, the ethnic concentrations begin to break down and the settlement pattern becomes a more dispersed one. There are several variants of this model depending on the period that elapses before dispersal begins. The Greek-born population appears to fit into this category with significant outward diffusion from initial communities of concentration in the inner suburbs established in the 1950s and 1960s. This diffusion often occurs along a major transport route so that a sectoral pattern of development results and a considerable degree of spatial concentration is maintained.

3. *Model C* is a variant on Model B in which initial spatial concentrations are established, but as newcomers arrive among that birthplace group, they cannot be accommodated in the existing concentrated community. Thus, new concentrations are established farther out from the city center. The group retains a high degree of spatial concentration although the number of concentrations increases. This pattern applies to the Italian populations in Sydney and Melbourne.

4. *Model D* is a situation in which, as in Model B, initial ethnic concentrations are created; however, in this model the pattern of concentration is largely maintained over time and undergoes little change with the aging of the immigrant community. This model tends to fit several of the Eastern European and Polish communities.

5. *Model E*, described by Burnley (1989) in relation to Vietnamese in Sydney, involves a high degree of concentration in the initial stages but over time those who settle outside the major foci of settlement gradually gravitate to those centers leading to an even greater degree of spatial concentration. The cause of this secondary migration is the pull exerted by the growing number of ethnic specific shops and services and community support systems in the major centers.

Some Policy-Related Implications

Spatial segregation of ethnic communities in Australia has not reached the extent that it has in most other migration destination countries (Jupp, McRobbie, and York 1990). This is partly due to the fact that there is such diversity in the populations of the cities and no single group dominates among the non-Anglo/Celtic-origin population. Nevertheless, it is important to consider some of the implications of the changing patterns of concentration of groups in Sydney and Melbourne. Where people live is important in shaping many aspects of their day-to-day lives. With many NES-origin immigrants living in Sydney and Melbourne, especially recent arrivals, the community and the local living situation assume great importance.

The most obvious policy implications relate to the planning and provision of goods and services at the community level. This applies to both the range of ethnic-specific services provided as a major plank in Australia's multiculturalism policy as well as general health, education, welfare, employment, and community services. The NES-origin groups are underusers of many mainstream services in comparison with the population as a whole due to institutional, language, cultural, and other barriers that prevent them from gaining information about the services or feeling comfortable enough to access services. There is a need for such services to be provided in such a way that the minority groups gain equitable access to them.

In Sydney and Melbourne, the bulk of concentrations of Aboriginal and NES-origin immigrant groups is located in areas of low socioeconomic status that tend to be underprovided with goods and services. The Australian government in recent years has developed an access and equity policy and strategy that seeks to overcome barriers of language, birthplace, race, religion, culture, or prejudice. This was encapsulated in the National Agenda for a Multicultural Australia. Most of the discussions about this strategy (see OMA 1990), however, do not include a spatial dimension. However, this is a crucial dimension in achieving the objectives of the access and equity policy since it is the community level at which such policies actually work to influence the day-to-day lives of Australians.

In 1990, the government extended its social justice and access and equity strategies to encompass the issue of locational disadvantage. This relates to "the disadvantages which arise when people live in areas where there are deficiencies in physical and social infrastructure and inadequate access to jobs, training and education opportunities and recreational facilities, thereby reducing the standard of living of those affected and exacerbating other disadvantages they may face" (Hawke and Howe 1990,9).

It is apparent that there is considerable overlap between the distribution of many ethnic groups in Australia and areas of locational disadvantage. As a result, in the process of addressing the problem of locational disadvantage, a multicultural dimension must be incorporated. The concept of multiple disadvantage is important in this context, whereby particular groups and regions are disadvantaged in a number of ways and hence should be the subject of comprehensive strategies designed to overcome those disadvantages.

Another important area of policy relevance relates to the role of concentrations of ethnic groups in the process of adjustment of recently arrived migrants. The conventional view of ethnic enclaves is a generally negative one (Gamage 1992). That is, they tend to foster separatism and delay and impede adjustment to the wider society. However, the research evidence does not support such a view; rather it tends to reflect the role of those enclaves in assisting the adjustment of new arrivals into the Australian economy and society by mediating that adjustment through the filter of day-to-day contact with and assistance from people of the same linguistic and cultural background.

Burnley (1982,105) points out that concentrations are "a natural consequence of the need to adjust to a new and strange environment. There is no evidence that they in themselves inhibit the life chances of individuals or create conflict with the wider society. . . . The general consensus is that spatial concentration indicates less integration although by no means no learning of the new environment."

Desbarats (1985,525) similarly indicates that immigrant clustering "has been found to be beneficial not only to psychological adjustment but also to economic adaptation. Networks organised along ethnic lines have frequently proved decisive in providing newly arrived immigrants with the information and assistance necessary to attain at least basic self sufficiency."

From the limited information available, it appears that this is also a good summary of the situation in Australian cities. For example, the established concentrations of Vietnamese cushion the arrival of new settlers assisting their absorption into the city via a partially familiar subcommunity with which they have language, culture and often kinship links (Viviani 1980,14).

However, in the long term it may be that there are some negative effects of continued patterns of ethnic concentration (Desbarats 1985,525). For example, some people living in an ethnic enclave may be discouraged from learning English and acquiring knowledge about Australian bureaucracies, institutions, and so on, which will hamper long-term adjustment, prosperity, and well-being. Consequently, the small proportion able to speak English among older members (especially women) of long-established, highly concentrated birthplace groups (e.g., southern Europeans) may be a function of the fact that they have lived most of their lives in Australia in such an enclave. It could be that their well-being in their later years may be detrimentally affected as a result (Hugo 1993).

The negative perception of ethnic concentration has led some to call for dispersal policies designed to reduce ethnic concentrations (Castles 1993,16). Such policies have been initiated in Australia in the case of Aborigines where at times housing programs have consciously attempted to disperse the Aboriginal-Tores Strait Islander population and prevent its "ghettoization" (Gale 1980,16). However, there have been no substantial attempts to develop programs to disperse other groups who are concentrated in ethnic enclaves. As Castles (1993,16) points out, "in the absence of economic opportunities and political structures needed to overcome the powerful forces of marginalization, dispersal policies are difficult to implement."

Given the positive functions that these enclaves perform, it would seem misguided to attempt to disperse them. This is particularly the case since in Australia there is little, if any, conflict between low-income groups in ethnic enclaves, which has occurred in other high-immigration countries (Cope, Castles, and Kalantzis 1991).

The only realistic way a dispersal policy could be initiated is through housing programs. In France, for example, in the late 1960s, public housing was made available to immigrants and the concept of *seuil de tolerance* (threshold of tolerance) was introduced (Verbunt 1985). This limited the immigrant presence to a maximum of 10–15 percent of residents in a housing estate or 25 percent of students in a school class. In Australia, access to public housing has been an important factor in the concentrations of some immigrant groups and Aborigines, but in Sydney and Melbourne, the incidence of overseas-born persons living in public housing is lower than for the Australian-born, especially among those from NES origins.

In contrast, the incidence is high among particular groups such as the Turks (15.3 percent) and Vietnamese (21.2 percent). For such groups, housing authorities need to be sensitive to the importance of striking a balance between creating concentrations that are sufficiently large to provide mutual support systems for the groups, but not so large as to create too great a majority of the population in an area and thereby marginalize other residents. This is obviously a very sensitive and complex issue and needs to be carefully analyzed and monitored in each individual situation.

A further policy issue concerning patterns of immigrant settlement is that of whether there should be government intervention to influence where immigrants should settle upon arrival in Australia. It has been suggested that the disproportionate concentration of overseas migrants in Sydney and Melbourne is causing a range of negative environmental and economic consequences (NPC 1992) and that some immigrants should be diverted away from those cities upon arrival in Australia. There have been some previous attempts to influence where immigrants settle in Australia during the postwar period (Hugo 1993). However, such policies would be difficult to justify in the contemporary context since they would create two classes of citizens with different rights. The real answer to any perceived imbalance in the distribution of population will not be solved by micromanipulation of immigrant settlement patterns. It will only be tackled if fundamental biases and blockages in the economic system that favor the growth of the largest cities are addressed.

Postwar Transformation

Sydney and Melbourne have been transformed during the postwar period. Their populations have more than doubled, they have experienced rapid industrial growth followed by structural change that has seen a decline in manufacturing employment and a growth of tertiary and quaternary sector jobs. The cities have been transformed from ethnic homogeneity to significant diversity. No process has been more important in the parametric changes to the cities than immigration.

Official projections for the growth of Sydney and Melbourne see them having populations of around five million and four million, respectively, by 2031. There seems little reason to believe that the existing pattern of locational preferences for the overseas-born population settling in the two cities will change. Sydney and Melbourne remain the major centers of settlement for most birthplace groups and this inevitably will mean that the networks and migration chains that are so important in shaping immigrant settlement patterns in Australia will channel new arrivals to the two cities.

Anticipating the actual scale of that movement, however, is difficult. At the time of writing, Australia's net immigration intake has fallen to its lowest level for two decades in the face of high unemployment levels, balance of payment problems, and so on. Nevertheless, Australia's immigration history has been one of substantial year-to-year fluctuations in intake levels. The composition of the intake undoubtedly will change as the global political and economic situation changes, although it is likely that a strengthening of the Asian-origin immigration will occur.

There are national concerns about negative environmental and equity consequences arising from the continued expansion of Sydney, and to a lesser degree, Melbourne (NPC 1992). In her review of these, Fincher (1991) concludes that at present, at least, there is insufficient evidence to infer that additional growth of Sydney and Melbourne will necessarily involve substantial additional costs to the community. While there are some uncertainties, especially relating to the management of cities, O'Connor (1991) has concluded that in the evolving international economic context, it is Australia's largest cities that are best placed to compete.

Hence, there is little reason to project significant reduction in contemporary rates of growth of Sydney and Melbourne or the significance of immigration in that growth. The two cities are likely to become even more ethnically diverse and residential segregation of immigrant groups will be maintained and take on new forms. There is a need in Australia to get away from the negative stereotyping of such patterns. There is insufficient recognition of the positive roles played by such concentrations in (1) assisting the adjustment process of newly arrived migrants and in (2) being incubators of new economic enterprises. However, a more balanced assessment of ethnic concentrations in Sydney and Melbourne is unlikely to emerge until we have a better understanding of the roles and functions of such concentrations.

References

Australian Bureau of Statistics (ABS). 1990. *Population Growth and Distribution in Australia*. Catalogue No. 2504.0. Canberra: ABS.

Burnley, Ian H. 1982. *Population, Society and Environment in Australia: A Spatial and Temporal View*. Melbourne: Shillington House.

———. 1986. "Immigration: The Post-War Transformation of Sydney and

Melbourne." *The Sydney-Melbourne Book,* ed. J. Davidson. Sydney: Allen and Unwin.

———. 1989. "Settlement Dimensions of the Vietnam-Born Population in Metropolitan Sydney." *Australian Geographical Studies* 27 (October):129–54.

Castles, Stephen. 1993. "The Process of Integration of Migrant Communities." Paper presented at Expert Group Meeting on Population Distribution and Migration, January 18–22, Santa Cruz, Bolivia.

Cope, Bill, Stephen Castles, and Mary Kalantzis. 1991. *Immigration, Ethnic Conflicts and Social Cohesion.* Wollongong: Centre for Multicultural Studies.

Davidson, J., ed. 1986. *The Sydney-Melbourne Book.* Sydney: Allen and Unwin.

Desbarats, Jacqueline. 1985. "Indochinese Resettlement in the United States." *Annals of the Association of American Geographers* 75(4):522–38.

Fincher, Ruth. 1991. *Immigration, Urban Infrastructure and the Environment.* Canberra: AGPS.

Gale, Gwendoline F. 1980. "Aborigines: Adjustment of Migrants in Cities, with Particular Reference to Adelaide." Paper presented to the 1980 Development Studies Centre Conference, October.

Gamage, S. 1992. "Community Relations in a Multicultural Society: The 'Ethnic Concentrations' Debate and Sri Lankan Immigrants in Melbourne." *Migration Monitor* 25–26:12–17.

Gray, Alan. 1989. "Aboriginal Migration to the Cities." *Journal of the Australian Population Association* 6(2):122–44.

Hawke, Robert J. L., and Brian Howe. 1990. *Towards a Fairer Australia: Social Justice Strategy Statement, 1990–1991.* Canberra: AGPS.

Hugo, Graeme J. 1989. "Australia: The Spatial Concentration of the Turnaround." *Counterurbanization: The Changing Pace and Nature of Population Deconcentration,* ed. Anthony G. Champion. London: Edward Arnold.

———. 1991. *Atlas of the Australian People: Victoria.* Canberra: AGPS.

———. 1992. *Atlas of the Australian People: New South Wales.* Canberra: AGPS.

———. 1993. "The Changing Spatial Distribution of Major Ethnic Groups in Australia, 1961–1986." Revised version of a report prepared for the Office of Multicultural Affairs, April.

Jupp, James, Andrea McRobbie, and Barry York. 1990. *Metropolitan Ghettos and Ethnic Concentrations I and II*. Wollongong: Centre for Multicultural Studies.

Lieberson, Stanley, and Mary C. Waters. 1987. "The Location of Ethnic and Racial Groups in the United States." *Sociological Forum* 2(4): 780–810.

Maher, Christopher, and John McKay. 1986. *1981 Internal Migration Study Final Report: Internal Migration in Australia*. Canberra: Department of Immigration and Ethnic Affairs.

Moser, Susan, Nicola Maher, Andre Kalan, and John Connell. 1993. *Migration and Identity in Sydney: Icelanders, Minangkabau and White Russians*. Research Monograph 6, Department of Geography, University of Sydney.

National Population Council (NPC). 1992. *Population Issues and Australia's Future: Environment, Economy and Society. Final Report of the Population Issues Committee*. Canberra: AGPS.

O'Connor, Kevin. 1991. "Economic Activity in Australian Cities: National and Local Trends in Policy." Paper prepared for Joint CSIRO Department of Health, Housing and Community Services Seminar on Productive Cities of the Twenty-First Century, September 3, Sydney.

Office of Multicultural Affairs (OMA). 1990. *Making It Happen—Access and Equity at Work around Australia*. Canberra: AGPS.

Poulsen, Michael, and Peter Spearritt. 1981. *Sydney: A Social and Political Atlas*. Sydney: Allen and Unwin.

Price, Charles A. 1963. *Southern Europeans in Australia*. Melbourne: Oxford University Press.

Verbunt, G. 1985. "France." *European Immigration Policy: A Comparative Study*, ed. Thomas Hammar. Cambridge: Cambridge University Press.

Viviani, Nancy. 1980. *The Vietnamese in Australia: New Problems in Old Forms*. Centre for the Study of Australian-Asian Relations, Griffith University, Research Paper 11.

Winchester, Hilary P. M., and Paul E. White. 1988. "The Location of Marginalised Groups in the Inner City." *Environment and Planning D: Society and Space* 6:36–54.

Chapter 4

Foreigners in the Paris Agglomeration*

Michelle Guillon and Daniel Noin

Paris has attracted foreigners for over two hundred years. Not only artists, intellectuals, refugees, and dissidents have been drawn to Paris since the French Revolution, but also many others have come in quest of resources since the middle of the nineteenth century. Paris has thus become a city with a major concentration of foreigners and a place where numerous nationalities live side by side.

The importance of the foreign presence has become a point of controversy over the last few years, when impressions have sometimes tended to replace precise information. What is the exact number of foreigners? How is this number changing? Which nationalities are represented? What are the demographic and social characteristics of the foreign population? How are foreigners distributed spatially within the urban area? To what extent have they mixed into the French population? Why does ethnic segregation appear weak when compared to that of New York, Chicago, or Los Angeles, and why is there no real ethnic district? These questions form the foundation for this study of the evolution, structure, and spatial characteristics of the foreign population of Paris.

The Number of Foreigners

Uncertainties in Enumeration

The French census does not collect information on ethnic groups or foreign-born immigrants, in contrast to the censuses of many other countries.

*The authors gratefully acknowledge the assistance of Yvan Chauviré of the Université de Paris in the preparation of this chapter.

77

It does provide data on nationality by enumerating the number of foreigners. This number is slightly underestimated in the census for two reasons: (1) the declaration of the nationality of children born to foreign parents is not always correct, and (2) omissions are more numerous for foreigners than for French nationals because of the mobility of part of the foreign population and because of irregular conditions of their accommodation.

The underestimate of the foreign population was approximately 10 percent in 1975 and about 5 percent in 1982. In spite of attempts to reduce the underestimate, it was probably the same in 1990. Because other sources of information (files of the Ministry of the Interior and the Immigration Service, plus the annual surveys on employment) do not reveal the size of the foreign population more accurately, we use census data in this study. This study is based primarily on demographic, socioeconomic, and geographical information on the foreign population from the 1982 and 1990 censuses.

For 1990, the census indicates 1.28 million foreigners in the urban agglomeration of Paris, and 1.37 million in the Ile-de-France region, which is slightly larger and roughly represents the broader urban region (Recensement Général de la Population de 1990, Nationalités, 1992). The largest concentration of foreigners in France, it is ten times bigger than in Lyon, and sixteen times bigger than in Marseille. It may also be the largest concentration in Europe although direct comparisons are difficult because of varying definitions of ethnic groups. London may have a similar number with more than one million immigrants.

Evolution of the Foreign Population

The concentration of foreigners in Paris was primarily formed over the last four decades. Before that, two cycles were each marked by a growth period followed by a decline. Only the third cycle, which started after the Second World War, will be analyzed here. This third cycle shows a particularly fast pace of growth, since the foreign population has increased more than four times between 1946 and 1990 in the Ile-de-France region (fig. 4.1). This rate of growth is remarkable, on average 3.4 percent per year, compared to about 1 percent for French nationals.

We can divide this period of growth into three distinct phases: (1) a phase of moderate growth between 1946 and 1954 during the postwar restoration of the French economy (2.2 percent per year, slightly greater than for the French); (2) a phase of very fast growth from 1954 to 1974 that corresponds to a period of strong economic expansion (4.7 percent per year compared to 0.8 percent for the French); and (3) a phase of slow growth from 1982 to

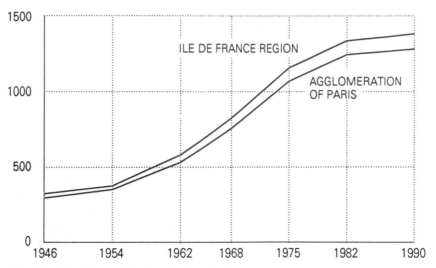

Fig. 4.1 Evolution of the Foreign Population

1990, corresponding to a period of economic difficulties and sometimes crisis (0.3 percent per year—less than for the French population, which remained 0.8 percent). Underlying these patterns were important changes in migratory flows. A turning point came in 1974 when various measures were taken to limit immigration (Weil 1991). In reality, these measures did not put a halt to immigration, but merely slowed it down.

The change in the number of foreigners varies according to a mix of six different elements: entries, exits, births, deaths, naturalizations, and "regularizations" for those who are in France without permit. In 1981–82, after the Socialists came to power, the situation of many illegal aliens was legalized (about 150,000 in France and 70,000 in the Ile-de-France region). From 1982 to 1990, the number of entries dropped as migratory flows were more controlled, but a large number of foreigners were naturalized.

In this most recent period, the increase in the number of foreigners has been small, and their proportion in the total population has even diminished slightly, from 13.3 percent to 12.9 percent in the region between 1982 and 1990. This reduction does not always correspond to the French population's perception of the foreign presence mainly because of the change in national origins of the foreign population, particularly the increase in the number of Africans and Asians whose arrival is more visible to the French.

Foreigners in Paris

Predominance of Mediterranean Peoples

The foreign population of Paris and its suburbs is indeed heterogeneous from many different points of view. The profile of new immigrants is generally comparable in many ways to the population that has been in Paris for several decades: old to young, manual workers with no professional skills to highly qualified executives, migrants from the less-developed countries to those from the more-developed.

The nationalities or groups of nationalities most strongly represented in the foreign population are from the Mediterranean countries, totaling about 70 percent (table 4.1). Those from southern Europe are now slightly less numerous than those from African and Asian countries around the Mediterranean (32 percent compared to 38 percent). The origins of the other peoples are very diverse. Those from the northern countries of the European Union constitute less than 4 percent of the total number of foreigners; they are mainly from Britain, Belgium, and Germany.

Three different groups can be distinguished from the evolution of the diverse nationalities (Guillon 1992) (fig. 4.2):

1. Immigrants who arrived a long time ago and whose numbers have started to diminish quite perceptibly. The number of Italians and Spaniards reached a peak in the early sixties and late sixties respectively.

2. The Algerians, Portuguese, and Yugoslavs who generally did not arrive until later, but whose numbers started to drop slightly during the 1980s.

Table 4.1   Ile-de-France Region: Main Foreign Groups, 1990

Group	Number (000s)	Group	Number (000s)
Portuguese	295	Italians	53
Algerians	246	Turks	40
Moroccans	157	Yugoslavs[a]	32
Tunisians	76	Black Africans[b]	154
Spaniards	57	S. and E. Asians[c]	55

Source: Recensement Général de la Population de 1990, Nationalités, 1992.
[a]Peoples from former Yugoslavia, especially Serbs.
[b]Especially Malians and Senegalese but there are many other nationalities.
[c]Especially Cambodians, Vietnamese, Laotians, and Chinese.

Numbers (in thousands)

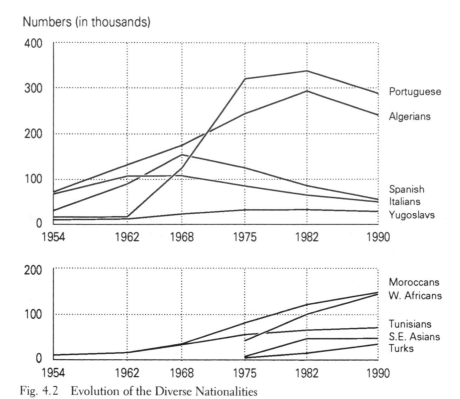

Fig. 4.2   Evolution of the Diverse Nationalities

3. Nationalities who arrived still later, representing the last wave of immigration, and whose numbers are still increasing. These include Moroccans, Tunisians, Turks, Black Africans, and peoples originating in former Indochina. Also included are people from southern Asia, mostly from Sri Lanka and Pakistan, whose numbers remain small although they are easily visible in the population.

The evolution of foreign population as a whole is the sum of varying changes in individual group populations. The slight overall growth of the foreign population over the last period, 1982–90, masks changes of varying direction, and a changing composition of national origins with a growing proportion of Africans and Asians.

Diverse Demographic Characteristics

The diversity of the foreign population is equally marked in its demographic characteristics. The foreign population shows an appreciable imbalance of the sexes, is relatively young, and has varying household characteristics, although these characteristics are gradually changing.

The sex ratio is decreasing because immigration has become more family-oriented since the 1970s and because of the number of births on French territory. The number of men per 100 women dropped from 152 in 1975 to 123 in 1990. Variations are marked from one nationality to another: the ratio is 152:100 for the Algerians in 1990, 135:100 for the Moroccans and Tunisians, 103:100 for the Spaniards, and only 88:100 for foreigners originating from the northern countries of the European Union.

The median age was 30.6 years in 1982 for foreigners as a whole, but shows marked variations between nationalities. Recent migrants are generally young. The median age in the same year was only 26 for the former Indochina populations and 25.5 for Black Africans. Those people who arrived earlier are relatively old: the median age was 40.2 for the Spanish and 45.7 for the Italians. More than half of the Poles were over 65.

The size and structure of households also vary according to nationality, although Italian and Spanish households are similar to French ones. North African, Turk, and Black African households are larger than those of the French, especially because of the high fertility rate of family households. The large size of Portuguese households is linked to the arrival of relatives.

The size and composition of foreign households has changed profoundly with the decrease in migration flows and with the settlement of families in France. The proportion of family households is now two-thirds of the total, most of them with children. This proportion is even a little higher than that of the French due to the relative youth of the foreign population. This is also true of other demographic characteristics—fertility, nuptiality, or composition of households. Variations are great for whatever the chosen indicator.

Socioeconomic Characteristics

When considering socioeconomic factors, we must beware of stereotypes of the foreign population. Many Parisians consider foreigners to be poorly qualified manual workers. This evaluation was in fact applicable in the past. During the decades of economic expansion following the Second World War, foreigners worked at factories and building sites in low-skill positions. Even today the proportion of manual workers is large (being three times that of the French) and the rate of unemployment is high (twice as much as the French). This is not at all surprising, as the majority of migrants come from rural and rather poor regions, with low levels of education and training, and with a rudimentary knowledge of French. Because of this, they are often engaged in hard, repetitive, and poorly paid jobs abandoned by French nationals.

This situation, however, has changed little by little because the job market has been modified. Many foreign workers are now qualified to a higher level and work in more diverse positions. The proportion of blue-collar workers is decreasing, from 68 percent in 1954 to 51 percent in 1990. The proportion of white-collar jobs, craftsmen, and tradespeople is increasing. The most visible aspect of this change is the proliferation of shops and stores run by foreigners, especially restaurants, grocers, greengrocers, and inexpensive clothing shops (Ma Mung 1992; Marie 1992). Even more significant is the growing proportion of workers in management and the liberal professions (almost 8 percent in 1990 compared to 4 percent in 1982). The number of female workers is also changing rapidly, now representing 31 percent of all the jobs occupied by foreign workers. Finally, the foreign population is experiencing a marked shift toward the tertiary sector in which 61 percent of their jobs are now found.

The current image of the economic and social situation of foreigners may also be inaccurate because of the great diversity of the different groups. The Algerians, Moroccans, and Turks are very rarely found among the executive and liberal professions, whereas the rate is 14 percent for the Italians and 40 percent for migrants from the northern countries of the European Union. There are many shopkeepers among Tunisians and Asians. The majority of Turks and Moroccans work as laborers at building sites or factories (75 and 63 percent, respectively), whereas very few northwest Europeans are found in these jobs. North Africans and Turks are severely unemployed (20 percent and 30 percent, respectively), whereas for northwest Europeans the figure is less than 7 percent.

Most of the nationalities that recently arrived in the Ile-de-France region can be found at the lowest level of the socioeconomic pyramid. This is particularly true for Moroccans, Turks, and Black Africans. The Portuguese and Yugoslavs are placed a little higher. On the other hand, the Americans, Canadians, British, and Germans are generally situated at the upper-middle or upper level. This social diversity of foreigners also clearly appears in their spatial distribution.

Housing Conditions: Persistent Inequalities

Housing conditions are also changing for the better, although inequalities in comparison with the French have not disappeared. Foreign households generally occupy smaller flats and houses than the French even though the number of persons per household is greater on average. A large proportion of foreign accommodations are therefore overpopulated. On average, there are 1.14 persons per room instead of 0.77 for the total population; and the large majority of these foreigners are tenants.

In Paris and the inner suburbs, foreigners tend to live in old, dilapidated blocks of flats offering little comfort. They also live in furnished rooms and cheap hostels in working-class districts. In the outer suburbs, foreigners tend to live in newer high-rise blocks of flats with poor public transportation services. Some have acquired old individual houses that they do their best to renovate.

The picture also varies according to nationality. Black Africans are numerous in workers' hostels. Many Portuguese have become owners of individual houses on the periphery. Among Algerians and Moroccans, single men tend to live in dilapidated blocks of flats in the inner suburbs while families tend to occupy flats in social housing of the outer suburbs.

Spatial Distribution of the Foreign Population

Widespread Pattern

The spatial distribution of foreigners shows only slight changes between 1982 and 1990. At first glance, it reveals a concentration in the central part of the urban area. However, the most significant factor of foreign distribution is its wide distribution and its mixing with the French population. Not one commune, district, or neighborhood exists without some degree of mixing between French and foreigners. Only at the scale of a block of flats can we find real concentration, and even in this case, it is exceptional. In the Paris agglomeration there are no ethnic districts, even if some areas are characterized by a marked commercial foreign presence. Examples of the latter include the North Africans in the Goutte d'Or district in the north of Paris (Vuddamalay, White, and Sporton 1991) and the Chinese in the Porte de Choisy district in the south of the city (White, Winchester, and Guillon 1987).

The map representing the proportion of foreigners in the total population holds greater significance (fig. 4.3). It shows a pattern that is both concentric and sectoral though much more sectoral than concentric. Foreign presence is slightly greater in the central part of the agglomeration than on the periphery. It is especially high in working-class areas: in districts of the northeast quarter of Paris, in the suburbs situated in the north, northwest or northeast of the capital, and also in some industrial districts in the periphery

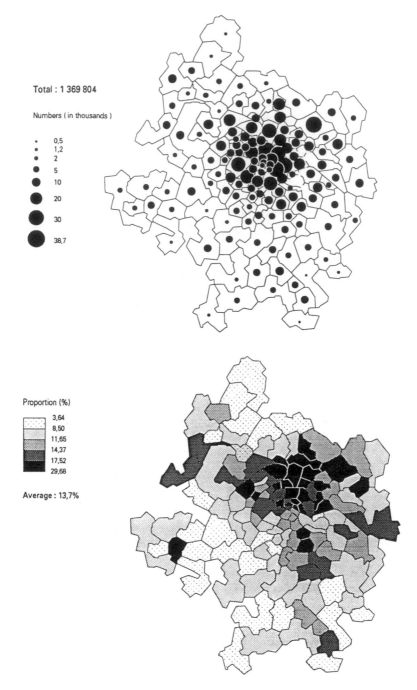

Total : 1 369 804

Numbers (in thousands)

- · 0,5
- · 1,2
- · 2
- 5
- 10
- 20
- 30
- 38,7

Proportion (%)

- 3,64
- 8,50
- 11,65
- 14,37
- 17,52
- 29,68

Average : 13,7%

Fig. 4.3   Foreign Populations in 1990, Distribution and Percentage (INSEE, recensements)

such as Corbeil or Poissy. In these areas, the proportion of foreigners reaches 20 or 25 percent of the total population but no more.

The distribution is nevertheless complex as each nationality has implanted itself differently according to both its migratory history and its position on the social pyramid. Because it is not possible to analyze the detailed distribution of all the various nationalities in the Paris urban space, four examples will be examined to illustrate the variety of patterns.

Algerians provide a good example of the residential distribution of the laboring nationalities (fig. 4.4). In spite of their relatively early immigration, they have conserved their working-class characteristics, are often victim to racial prejudice, and have remained loyal to their initial settlement near industrial areas or former industrial areas. They are found essentially in the working-class districts of Paris and especially in the working-class suburbs of

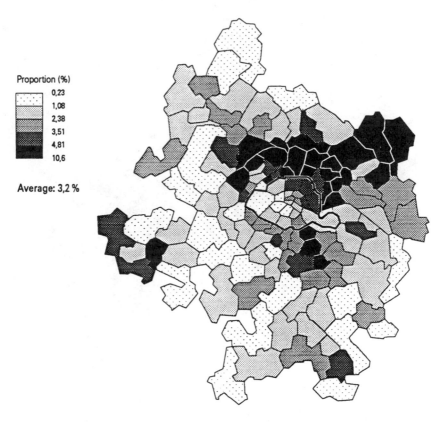

Proportion (%)

0,23
1,08
2,38
3,51
4,81
10,6

Average: 3,2 %

Fig. 4.4   Algerians (INSEE, recensements, 1990, special processing)

the northern zone. In some areas, they constitute more than a tenth of the total population.

The Portuguese arrived later than the Algerians although they have a slightly higher position on the social pyramid. They occupy a diverse range of housing: they can be found in very different areas according to the social level, including the wealthy districts, as they are well accepted by the French population (many Portuguese women work as cleaning ladies or caretakers in blocks of flats). They are especially found in peripheral districts (fig. 4.5), particularly in the south and southeast, near the construction sites of the 1970s, as the men often work in the building industry. Many Portuguese families have acquired inexpensive houses on the periphery.

The Asians have a contrasting distribution (fig. 4.6). Asian immigrants in Paris include Cambodians, Laotians, Vietnamese, and especially people of

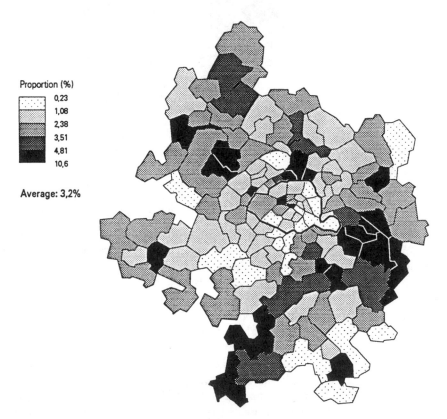

Fig. 4.5   Portuguese (INSEE, recensements, 1990, special processing)

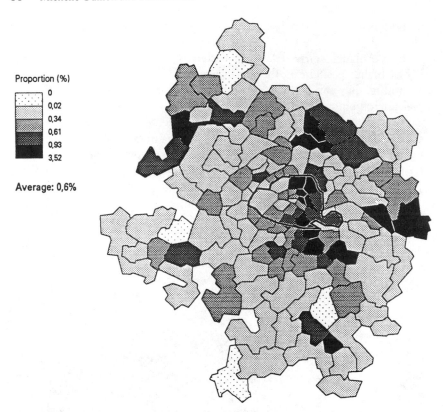

Proportion (%)

	0
	0,02
	0,34
	0,61
	0,93
	3,52

Average: 0,6%

Fig. 4.6   Asians: Cambodians, Chinese, Laotians, and Vietnamese (INSEE, recensements, 1990, special processing)

Chinese descent who came directly from China in the interwar period, or from former Indochina in the 1970s. Their residential locations are varied though there are a few concentrations, the most characteristic being China-town in the thirteenth arrondissement of Paris, and the Asiatic enclave in the new town of Marne-la-Vallée in the eastern suburbs.

The group under the heading of "other nationalities" is the most heteroge-neous of all as it is composed of all foreign nationals except North Africans, Black Africans, Portuguese, Spaniards, Italians, Yugoslavs, Turks, and Asians from China or former Indochina. In fact, it is mainly composed of executives and intellectuals coming from various countries of Europe and America. In this case, it is not surprising to note a different settlement pattern as they have a majority of workers in management and the professions, who have chosen to live in the West End of Paris or the wealthy western suburbs (fig. 4.7).

In order to synthesize the spatial patterns of settlement, a final map was derived from a hierarchical classification based on 1982 data. It shows the overall distribution of types of concentrations of foreign groups (fig. 4.8). Types 1, 2, and 3 are characterized both by a moderate and a barely visible foreign presence, essentially European, marked by the Portuguese or northwest Europeans. Types 5, 7, and 8, on the other hand, are characterized by a strong and visible foreign presence, essentially North African, corresponding to the working-class areas. Type 6 covers a large part of the suburbs: this is the category closest to the average noted in the agglomeration. Type 4 is exceptional in that it is strongly marked by Asians.

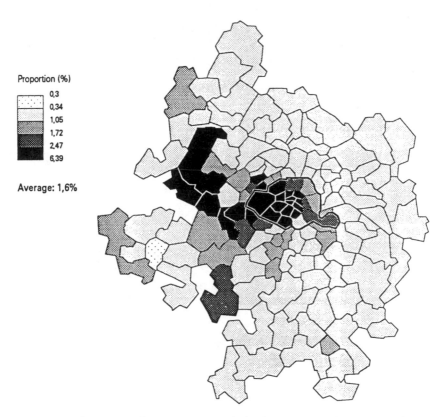

Proportion (%)

0,3
0,34
1,05
1,72
2,47
6,39

Average: 1,6%

Fig. 4.7   Other National Groups. This includes foreign nationals except North Africans, Black Africans, Portuguese, Spanish, Italians, Yugoslavs, Turks, and Southeast Asians. (INSEE, recensements, 1990, special processing)

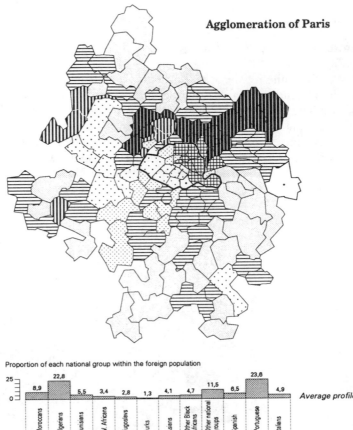

Agglomeration of Paris

Proportion of each national group within the foreign population

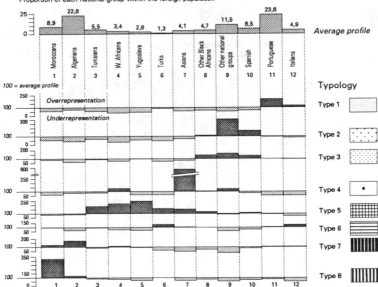

Fig. 4.8   Typology of the Foreign Population (INSEE, recensements, 1982, special processing)

Indistinct Concentration of Foreigners

Globally speaking, the geographical approach leaves the impression of an indistinct spatial concentration of foreigners within the Paris agglomeration. This impression is confirmed by the statistical analysis using the index of dissimilarity (D) for the 136 statistical divisions of the agglomeration. For the foreign population as a whole, the index is low, being only .17 in 1990. This can be interpreted to mean that 17 percent of foreigners would have to change their place of residence in order to achieve an identical distribution to that of the overall population. This index has increased slightly, from approximately .15 in 1975 and .16 in 1982. This slight rise seems to be linked to the reinforcement of neoimmigrant concentrations, such as the Turks, and to the reduction in number of well-integrated and highly dispersed groups, such as the Italians and the Spanish.

The index obviously varies according to nationality. In 1982, it was .41 for the Turks and .40 for the Yugoslavs. The index is equally high for the Asians and West Europeans. It is moderate for the Moroccans at .31, Tunisians at .30, Algerians at .28, and Black Africans at .25. It is low for the Italians and Portuguese (.16). This index would be a little higher if smaller regional units had been chosen (at a commune or block level for instance), although even in this case, it probably would remain low to moderate.

The intensity of the ethnic segregation, just as with social segregation, also varies in the different parts of the Paris agglomeration. In Paris itself, it is more clearly apparent in the peripheral areas than in the central ones. There are some concentrations of poorer foreigners such as in the Goutte d'Or district. In the suburbs, segregation is particularly marked in the periphery and in the newer districts where some concentrations can also be found.

These concentrations are exceptional, however. The foreign population as a general rule is largely dispersed, with a relatively high mix of diverse nationalities and of foreigners within the French population. The process of segregation here is in no way similar to that observed in many industrial nations, and particularly in North America. The urban area of Paris is heterogeneous as all big cities are, but this heterogeneity is essentially social. The ethnic composition is only a secondary element of variation.

Some Explanations

The contradictory elements of this situation make interpretation quite difficult. It is not surprising that opposing judgments emerge. It is undeniable that segregation is weak compared to that observed in other European countries such as England or Germany, and especially to non-European countries such as the United States and Australia. The Paris agglomeration does not have ethnic districts like those seen in New York, Los Angeles, or Sydney. The only areas that could in any way fall within this category are the North African district of the Goutte d'Or and the Chinese district of the Porte de Choisy. However, here, the latter concentration is not nearly as strong as in the North American Chinatowns (Guillon and Taboada-Leonetti 1988). Moreover, even if segregation could be said to exist, it would be characterized as voluntary segregation, arising from a desire of foreigners to live their way of life among their own people.

Within the agglomeration, communes with over 25 percent of foreigners in the total population in 1990 are rare. No more than a dozen out of four hundred could be noted at this time (Atlas des Franciliens 1991). Only one commune showed more than 30 percent foreigners (Clichy-sous-Bois, in the working-class suburb north of Paris), which signifies a French population of 70 percent in this extreme case.

The roots of this situation for the foreign population go back to the eighteenth century, to the age of Enlightenment, and the French Revolution. A universalist and egalitarian ideal has existed since then. The ideal vision of the nation is of a homogeneous country where juridical and territorial particularities are excluded, and where minorities do not exist.

The formation of ethnic or foreign communities is strongly contrary to the ideals prevalent in French politics which have long been central to people's way of thinking. Since the eighteenth century, there has been tolerance toward foreigners in France, whether they be intellectuals, artists, political refugees, or simple workers. This tolerance is certainly more notable in Paris than elsewhere as this big city has long been home to a large number of humanist intellectuals. Paris has thus played the role of the "melting pot" for France as a whole (Noiriel 1988).

Moreover, the egalitarian ideal has had a strong influence on French politics since the eighteenth century and has helped in leveling social inequalities, or at least in reducing them as far as possible within the spheres of education, health, and housing. This occurred violently for the first time during the French Revolution in 1789–93, but has occurred at various times since then: in 1848, at the turn of the twentieth century, in 1936, in 1968, and at the beginning of the 1980s. This marked reduction of inequalities in urban policy gave rise to a strong social mix in most of the communes in the agglomeration. It is hard to find socially homogeneous districts like those in the cities of North America. Of course, there are favored and disadvantaged communes but nearly all of them contain a large social mix. This mix of social groups also played in favor of the mix of foreigners into the French population.

Even if there is no ethnic segregation as such, this does not mean that there is no process of segregation tending to isolate certain foreign groups. This process can only be found for foreign groups that are markedly different from the French in physical aspect and especially in their education and level of qualification. Xenophobic attitudes are exceptional, but when they do arise, they are particularly directed toward Algerians, Moroccans, Turks, and Black Africans. Having generally low levels of skill and education, these groups are in a weak position on the job market and their unemployment rate is relatively high. They are also in a weak position in the housing market and thus tend to occupy old dilapidated flats or new mediocre quality housing in the northeast quarter of Paris and the most disadvantaged working-class suburbs.

It is probable, moreover, that the economic difficulties, persistent over the last twenty years, have worsened the situation of the more disadvantaged groups of the population. Once again, it must be emphasized that these groups do not contain a majority of foreigners. The segregation process is essentially of social and not of ethnic character. Assimilation will depend on the economy.

Foreign Population in Perspective: Cautious Hypotheses

To conclude this analysis of the evolution, structure, and spatial distribution of the foreign population in Paris, we shall tentatively consider the situation in the years to come, taking into account the trends observed. All international migratory flows are subject to unpredictable fluctuations, which makes this task highly uncertain. We shall therefore focus on the present foreign population rather than the flows, and we shall only consider the near future.

The third large migratory wave that France experienced in her recent past seems to have ended. The size of the foreign population is more or less stable. In all probability, the number of foreigners in the Paris agglomeration will remain approximately the same in the years to come. There will always be small migratory flows from various origins due to the strong attraction of Paris, but these will be balanced by the number of foreigners returning home or being naturalized.

Over recent years, new arrivals tended to come from countries farther and farther away. This trend should continue or even become more pronounced. The number of foreigners originating from southern Europe will probably continue to decline gradually into the future while the number of Asians and

Africans, especially from southern Asia and Black Africa, will increase, resulting in more and more visible foreign immigrants in Paris.

The immigrants of recent years are no longer the illiterate peasants of the prosperous years. The job market has changed profoundly. New arrivals increasingly come from urban areas and this trend should become even more marked with the rapid urbanization of the less-developed countries. These migrants are more educated, some with professional qualifications, which is a characteristic that should become more pronounced in the years to come and would normally facilitate assimilation.

In considering assimilation, it is difficult even to sketch a picture of the future. The rhythm of integration is dependent on numerous factors, and particularly on the economic situation. If the economic crisis continues into the coming years, which is not improbable, the process of integration will undoubtedly be difficult for a large part of the foreign population, whether it has recently arrived, has been installed for a long time, or is made up of children of immigrants. If the economic situation gets better, which is also possible, the process of assimilation should continue. This was the case at different times in the past and there is no reason to think that it could not happen again, even for those African and Asian populations that are culturally very different from the French population. In this case, we can put forward the hypothesis that the spatial diffusion of foreigners in the urban agglomeration, which is already very high, will continue in the years to come. In this domain as in many others, the evolution will depend to a large extent on the job situation.

References

Atlas des Franciliens. 1991. Paris: IAURIF, INSEE, Dir. Rég. d'Ile-de-France. 2 vol.

Guillon, Michelle. 1992. *Etrangers et immigrés en Ile-de-France, synthèse des travaux.* Thèse, Université de Paris I, Travaux et Documents de l'INED. Paris: PUF.

Guillon, Michelle, and Isabelle Taboada-Leonetti. 1988. *Le triangle de Choisy.* Paris: CIEM-L'Harmattan.

Ma Mung, Emmanuel. 1992. "L'expansion du commerce ethnique. Asiatiques et Maghrébins dans la Région Parisienne." *Revue Européenne des Migrations Internationales* 8(1):39–59.

Marie, Claude-Valentin. 1992. "Les étrangers non salariés en France, symbole de la mutation économique des années 80." *Revue Européenne des Migrations Internationales* 8(1):27–38.

Noiriel, Gérard. 1988. *Le creuset français*. Paris: Seuil.

Recensement Général de la Population de 1990. Nationalités. 1992. *INSEE Résultats*, n° 217.

Vuddamalay, Vasood, Paul White, and Deborah Sporton. 1991. "The Evolution of the Goutte d'Or as an Ethnic Minority District of Paris." *New Community* 17(2):245–58.

Weil, Pierre. 1991. *La France et ses étrangers*. Paris: Calmann-Lévy.

White, Paul, Hilary Winchester, and Michelle Guillon. 1987. "South-East Asian Refugees in Paris." *Ethnic and Racial Studies* 10(1):48–61.

Chapter 5

Greater London in Britain's First Ethnic Census

David McEvoy

The social, economic, and political status of minority populations has been a major interest for social scientists since the days of the Chicago School of Human Ecology. For British geographers this interest has often focused on the spatial distribution and segregation of ethnic minorities (Cater and Jones 1989, 139–52). Higher degrees of separation from the White majority are usually seen as strongly indicative of varied types of socioeconomic deprivation. While it is also possible to contribute to geographical understanding through an emphasis on the cultural values of specific ethnic groups, and by the dissection of the significance and meaning attached by them to particular places, it remains useful to continue the disciplinary tradition of spatial inquiry. Through an analysis of the size and distribution of ethnic minorities, it becomes possible to understand some of the ways in which they differ from one another and from the majority.

This paper takes advantage of newly available ethnic data to continue this tradition in relation to Greater London, which is not only by far the largest of Britain's cities, but also the main center of immigration and continuing ethnic minority residence. Censuses from 1841 have asked about country of birth; the 1971 census asked about parental birthplace; and in 1981 the population was classified by the birthplace of the so-called head of household. Only in 1991, however, were census respondents asked to categorize themselves, and the other members of their households, according to ethnic group.

The information thus derived has plugged a significant gap in British population geography, since birthplace-based data have become an increasingly weak device for use in the study of minority populations, which include not only immigrants but also their descendants in the second, third, and subsequent generations. In 1991, the direct question on ethnicity suggested a non-White population of 3.02 million in Great Britain, but use of the 1981 measure, the number of people living in a household headed by a person born in the New Commonwealth or Pakistan, gives a count of only 2.64 million (Owen 1993a).

The use of the term *non-White* in the previous paragraph is an important indicator of the way ethnic minorities are viewed in Britain. The label *ethnic minority* is understood to refer to the non-White populations derived overwhelmingly from post-1945 immigration: non-White, visually identifiable, problematic. This arguably racist understanding clearly manifests itself in the way census data are collected and published.

Before the new data are examined, a brief review of London's ethnic history is presented, with emphasis on the way in which changes in immigration law have partially restricted the growth of minority populations. Next comes an account of the ethnic categories used in the 1991 census, together with an indication of size of the groups thus defined. The spatial concentration or dispersal of the individual groups is then described. Finally, these patterns are analyzed through statistical measures of segregation and interaction. At appropriate points the processes underlying the numbers, distributions, and index values that make up this account of London's contemporary ethnic geography are discussed.

Historical Background

As the dominant city in Britain and as a long-standing member of the upper reaches of the global urban hierarchy, London has an extended history of immigration and of ethnic minority residence. More recently, a major change in Britain's, and London's, population pattern has been the emergence of substantial non-White minorities that derive from a very limited period of primary immigration lasting from 1948 to 1962. The British Nationality Act of 1948 made it clear that residents of Britain's considerable surviving colonial empire, and also citizens of independent Commonwealth states, such as India, retained the right of unrestricted entry to Britain (Coleman and Salt 1992, 439). Economic growth in the 1950s and decreasing relative costs of international transport provided the incentive and means for increasing numbers of Commonwealth and colonial citizens to migrate to Britain. Particularly in the major cities, employment vacancies developed, especially in unpleasant or poorly paid jobs, in both manufacturing and services. Employers such as London Transport actively recruited labor in countries of origin.

The majority of immigrants to London and the rest of Britain came, however, to seek work rather than to prearranged positions. At first the main flow was from the Caribbean, but as the 1950s progressed, increasing numbers came from India and Pakistan. The numbers involved were not large, even at the national level; Coleman and Salt (1992, 449) suggest that in the year and a half from January 1961, 98,000 people arrived from the West Indies, 42,000 from India, and 50,000 from Pakistan. Nevertheless, both the main political parties expressed concern that increasing immigrant numbers were becoming a "threat" to race relations (Smith 1989, 122–24). In consequence, the first of a series of restrictions on immigration, the Commonwealth Immigrants Act, was approved by Parliament in 1962. Entry of Commonwealth citizens was now restricted to holders of work vouchers, their dependants, and the dependants of existing residents.

Legislation in 1968, 1971, 1981, and 1988 has further limited the immigration of Commonwealth citizens, although a careful loophole has been left for "patrials," the predominantly White overseas descendants of British citizens (Coleman and Salt 1992, 438–42). Movement from India and Pakistan followed that from the Caribbean into decline, although the reunification of Bangladeshi families has proved a continuing source of immigration in the 1980s. So successful have immigration restrictions become that by the mid-1980s only a third of the growth of the ethnic minority population derived from continued net immigration; the balance came from natural growth (Shaw 1988).

Overall Composition

The 1991 census form required respondents to indicate the ethnicity of each member of their household as one of White, Black Caribbean, Black African, Black Other, Indian, Pakistani, Bangladeshi, Chinese, or (any) Other. Further details were requested for the Black Other and (any) Other answer given. In reporting the census results, the (any) Other category has been subdivided into Other Asian and Other Other. There are thus ten ethnic categories used for most census output, which can be further reduced to four broad groupings: White, Black, South Asian, and Chinese and Others (table 5.1) (Teague 1993; Johnson 1993).

It can be seen that the census has made the assumption that being White involves membership of a group that requires no subdivision. In a city like London this suppresses the identification of White subgroups with their own

Table 5.1   Greater London and Great Britain: Resident Population of Ethnic Groups

	Greater London		Great Britain		% of Great Britain in Greater London
	Number (000s)	%	Number (000s)	%	
White	5332.9	79.8	51843.9	94.5	10.3
All ethnic minorities	1345.0	20.1	3006.5	5.5	44.7
Black	534.3	8.0	885.4	1.6	60.3
Caribbean	290.5	4.4	499.1	0.9	58.2
African	164.5	2.4	207.5	0.4	79.3
Other	79.3	1.2	178.8	0.3	44.4
South Asians	521.8	7.8	1476.9	2.7	35.3
Indian	346.5	5.2	840.8	1.5	41.2
Pakistani	88.5	1.3	475.8	0.9	18.6
Bangladeshi	86.8	1.3	160.3	0.3	54.1
Chinese and Others	288.9	4.3	644.3	1.2	44.8
Chinese	56.8	0.8	157.5	0.3	36.1
Other Asian	111.9	1.7	196.7	0.4	56.9
Other Other	120.2	1.8	290.1	0.5	41.4
Total	6677.9	99.9	54850.4	100.0	12.2

Source: Owen 1992.

distinctive geography, such as the large Irish population (Chance 1987), the Jews of Barnet (Waterman and Kosmin 1987), and the Greek Cypriots of Haringey (Constantinides 1977). Birthplace data allow the census to illuminate some such groups, but only for the immigrant generation. Data limitations therefore explain why the remainder of this paper conforms to an understanding of ethnicity of which it has been critical.

It is a commonplace that New York is not America. Equally, London is not England, and certainly not Great Britain or the United Kingdom. This is clearly true for ethnic composition (table 5.1). While Greater London has a population that is over 20 percent ethnic minority, the national proportion is only 5.5 percent.

Within London, as previous studies have noted (Jackson 1986; Jones 1991), Black and South Asian populations are the dominant broad groups and together account for almost four-fifths of the ethnic minority residents. On a more detailed level, Indians are clearly the most numerous group, followed by Black Caribbeans. We may note that intercensal change has caused the Indians to replace the Black Caribbeans as the most numerous group. While we can attribute this change partly to higher natural increase among Indians, and partly to their higher net immigration during the 1980s (Shaw 1988), it is also possible that the changed ethnic classification has been a factor. Both nationally and in London the number of Black Caribbeans recorded by the census in 1991 is lower than the number of persons counted by the 1981 census as being resident in households headed by someone born in the Caribbean. For London the figures are 306.8 thousand in 1981 and 290.5 thousand in 1991. The difference is unlikely to be accounted for by movement out of London since Robinson (1991) has shown that Indians are much more mobile in this respect than Caribbeans. The "missing" Caribbeans may be found in other 1991 census categories, particularly Black Other, a classification used by many British-born Black census respondents.

Changes in census classification also account for the emergence of Black Africans as London's third ethnic minority category in 1991. In 1981 this group was dispersed in the statistics between headings such as East African New Commonwealth, Remainder of New Commonwealth, and the Rest of the World. As such diverse labels indicate, this particular census variable in no sense represents a community. It is a portmanteau into which numerous small minorities have been loaded, similar features of heterogeneity relate to three of the remaining categories in table 5.1, Black Other, Other Asian, and Other Other.

The largest of the remaining ethnic minorities in 1991 was that from Pakistan, which just outnumbered that from Bangladesh. The relative position of these two groups has probably changed in the short period since the census, for although both groups are growing rapidly, the Bangladeshi population of Britain has the younger age structure and an estimated growth rate, deriving both from natural change and immigration, approximately twice that of the Pakistani population (Owen 1993a). Finally, London has a Chinese minority numbering almost 57,000.

It can be seen from the final column of table 5.1 that London houses a much greater share of all ethnic minority populations than it does of the White population. Almost 45 percent of the ethnic minorities live in London, but only just over 10 percent of the White population. For Blacks the capital is more significant (60.3 percent) than for either South Asians (35.3 percent) or Chinese and Others (44.8 percent). All three of these broad categories are substantially differentiated internally especially the South Asians.

Over half of the nation's Bangladeshis are in London, but only 18.6 percent of Pakistanis. Both groups followed a similar path on immigration, finding employment in a restricted range of industries in a few regions. The Pakistanis came originally to fill ill-paid unskilled jobs in the engineering industries of the West Midlands and the textile industries of Lancashire and Yorkshire (Dahya 1974). For Bangladeshis, the principal focus was in London in the clothing, leather, and footwear industries in the Brick Lane area of the East End (Rhodes and Nabi 1992).

Spatial Distributions

This reference to the site of Bangladeshi incorporation in the economy of London serves as an introduction to the more general issue of spatial pattern of the city's minorities. Through an account of this pattern, an appreciation of the socioeconomic position of ethnic groups will be derived, thus helping to underpin the analysis of segregation and interaction that follows.

Spatial patterns can be examined in many ways. Because this chapter uses census data, it is convenient to examine patterns through a selection of the spatial scales at which census information is released. We begin on the broad scale of local administration. For purposes of local government, Greater London consists of thirty-two London boroughs and the city of London. This borough scale is a useful one for the analysis of the geographical distribution of ethnic minorities. It is the scale at which many important governmental services and obligations, such as education, social work, public housing, and local taxation, are administered.

The Black and South Asian populations of London have significantly different spatial distributions (table 5.2, fig. 5.1, and fig. 5.2). The Black population is the more centralized of the two, with the principal boroughs of residence forming a discontinuous ring surrounding the most central boroughs and the city of London. South Asians, in contrast, are relatively decentralized. Their major boroughs of residence form a continuous belt in the west of the metropolitan area. There is a secondary focus stretching from the inner East End into the northeastern suburbs. The heterogeneous Chinese and Other group peaks in the inner West End and gradually declines toward the periphery of Greater London, especially in the east and southeast (fig. 5.3). More specific Black and South Asian minorities generally follow the distribution of their wider group, except that Bangladeshis are concentrated into the single borough of Tower Hamlets and are relatively few in west London. The Chinese, by contrast, appear to be the most evenly distributed of London's minorities.

This borough-level analysis does not complete the picture of London's ethnic minority geography. Within each borough there is considerable variation in the distribution of minorities on more local scales. As an indication of these variations, Figure 5.4 illustrates the distribution of ethnic minorities in total at the level of the ward.

The explanation of London's ethnic spatial patterns is, like that in many other cities, complex. The presence of an individual minority in a specific locality may be the result of highly particular causes. For example, chain migration to Southall, originating in recruitment in Punjab to the Wolf rubber factory, has given the Northcote ward of the borough of Ealing a

Table 5.2 Greater London: Ethnic Composition, 1991 (Borough Level)

Percent of Resident Population

	All ethnic minorities	Indians	Black Caribbeans	Black Africans	Other Other	Other Asians	Pakistanis	Bangla-deshis	Black Other	Chinese
Brent	44.8	17.2	10.2	4.1	3.2	3.6	3.0	0.3	2.2	1.1
Newham	42.3	13.0	7.2	5.6	1.4	3.0	5.9	3.8	1.6	0.8
Tower Hamlets	35.6	3.5	3.6	2.4	1.5	1.1	0.7	22.9	1.1	1.1
Hackney	33.6	3.5	11.2	6.8	2.9	1.4	1.0	1.8	4.0	1.1
Ealing	32.3	16.1	4.4	1.6	2.6	2.7	2.7	0.3	1.1	0.9
Lambeth	30.3	2.1	12.6	6.5	2.3	1.2	0.8	0.7	2.7	1.3
Haringey	29.0	3.6	9.3	5.5	2.7	2.3	0.7	1.5	2.3	1.1
Harrow	26.2	16.1	2.2	0.8	1.8	2.3	1.2	0.3	0.7	0.9
Waltham Forest	25.6	3.3	6.8	2.8	1.6	1.6	6.3	0.3	1.7	0.6
Southwark	24.4	1.2	8.3	7.2	1.7	1.6	0.4	1.0	2.2	1.3
Hounslow	24.4	14.3	1.1	1.1	2.0	1.9	2.6	0.3	0.5	0.6
Lewisham	22.0	1.2	10.1	3.7	1.6	1.3	0.3	0.3	2.5	1.0
Redbridge	21.4	10.2	2.5	1.1	1.3	1.3	2.8	0.8	0.7	0.7
Westminster	21.4	2.0	3.7	2.8	4.3	2.9	0.7	2.3	1.1	1.6
Wandsworth	20.0	3.1	6.1	2.9	1.7	1.8	1.7	0.4	1.7	0.8
Islington	18.9	1.5	5.1	3.6	2.1	1.4	0.4	1.6	1.9	1.3
Barnet	18.4	7.3	1.0	2.1	2.0	2.9	0.8	0.4	0.5	1.3
Camden	17.8	1.7	1.8	2.7	2.8	2.3	0.4	3.5	1.0	1.5
Croydon	17.6	4.7	4.9	1.6	1.9	1.5	1.1	0.3	1.1	0.5
Hammersmith and Fulham	17.5	1.6	5.9	2.5	2.5	1.3	0.8	0.5	1.8	0.7
Merton	16.3	3.4	2.9	2.0	1.8	2.7	1.3	0.5	0.9	0.7
Kensington and Chelsea	15.6	1.2	2.5	2.2	3.6	2.8	0.6	0.5	1.1	1.1
Enfield	14.1	3.5	3.7	1.6	1.4	1.4	0.4	0.8	0.8	0.4
Greenwich	12.7	3.4	2.5	1.9	1.2	1.1	0.6	0.2	1.0	0.8
Hillingdon	12.3	6.7	0.9	0.4	1.1	1.1	0.9	0.4	0.4	0.5
Kingston	8.6	2.3	0.4	0.4	1.3	2.5	0.6	0.1	0.2	0.8
City of London	7.3	1.7	0.3	0.3	1.1	1.5	0.5	0.2	0.3	1.4
Barking and Dagenham	6.8	2.0	1.2	0.6	0.5	0.4	1.2	0.1	0.4	0.4
Surbiton	5.9	1.6	0.7	0.4	0.9	1.0	0.3	0.2	0.3	0.5
Bexley	5.8	2.4	0.7	0.4	0.6	0.5	0.1	0.1	0.3	0.6
Richmond	5.5	1.6	0.3	0.2	1.2	1.0	0.2	0.2	0.2	0.5
Bromley	4.7	1.1	0.9	0.3	0.8	0.6	0.1	0.2	0.3	0.4
Havering	3.2	1.1	0.6	0.2	0.4	0.2	0.2	0.1	0.2	0.4

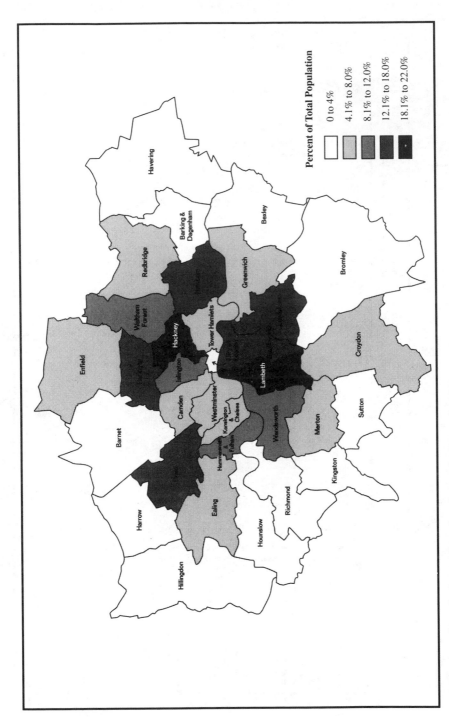

Percent of Total Population

- 0 to 4%
- 4.1% to 8.0%
- 8.1% to 12.0%
- 12.1% to 18.0%
- 18.1% to 22.0%

Havering

Barking &
Dagenham

Bexley

Redbridge

Greenwich

Bromley

Waltham
Forest

Newham

Hackney

Tower Hamlets

Enfield

Islington

Croydon

Lambeth

Camden

Westminster

Wandsworth

Barnet

Kensington
&
Chelsea

Hammersmith
&
Fulham

Merton

Sutton

Brent

Ealing

Hounslow

Richmond

Kingston

Harrow

Hillingdon

Fig. 5.1   London: Black Caribbean Population, by Borough, 1991

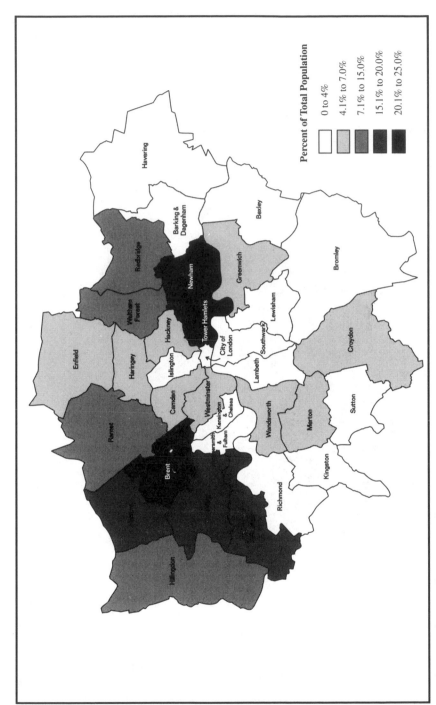

Fig. 5.2 London: South Asian Population, by Borough, 1991

Percent of Total Population

0 to 4%

4.1% to 7.0%

7.1% to 15.0%

15.1% to 20.0%

20.1% to 25.0%

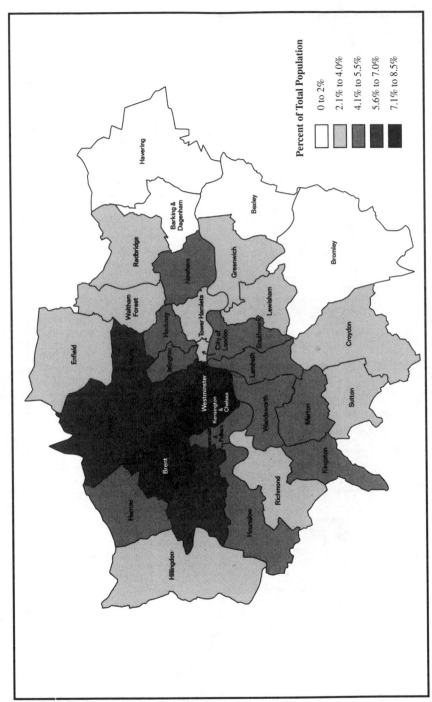

Percent of Total Population

- 0 to 2%
- 2.1% to 4.0%
- 4.1% to 5.5%
- 5.6% to 7.0%
- 7.1% to 8.5%

Fig. 5.3   London: Chinese and Other Minority Population, by Borough, 1991

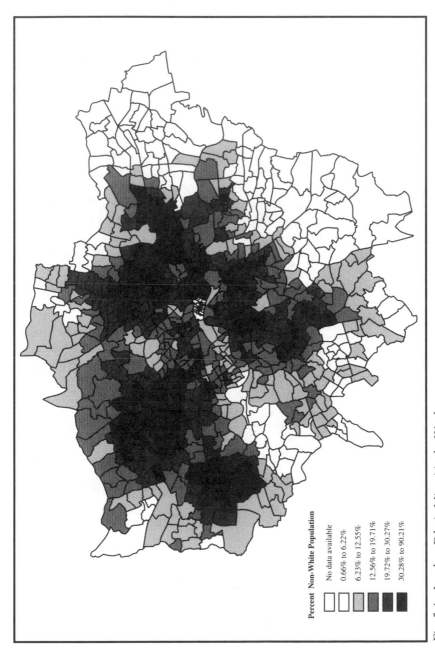

Percent Non-White Population

No data available
0.66% to 6.22%
6.23% to 12.55%
12.56% to 19.71%
19.72% to 30.27%
30.28% to 90.21%

Fig. 5.4   London: Ethnic Minorities by Ward

population that is 67 percent Indian, 11 percent Pakistani, and 90 percent ethnic minority. It has a higher population of ethnic minorities than any other ward in Greater London, or in Britain. London's Caribbean geography, with a Jamaican stronghold in South London, and "an archipelago of Windward and Leeward Islanders" north of the Thames, also derives significantly from chain migration (Peach 1984, 224). Carey and Shukur (1986) describe a complex sequence for Bangladeshis, starting with dockland cafés, established by former cooks in the British merchant navy, and progressing eventually into the ill-paid garment manufacturing sector as the industry was abandoned by the upwardly mobile Jewish community.

Jones (1991) explains Caribbean and South Asian distributions in relation to the housing market. Caribbeans found widespread opportunities for "colonization" in the older housing of the inner city as it was vacated by White residents encouraged to the new towns by the housing overspill policies of the 1950s and 1960s. South Asians, arriving in London later than the Caribbean minority, became focused in different areas. In the Indian case, there is a strong association with the international airport at Heathrow, in the western borough of Hounslow. Jones (1991, 185) attributes this to the unusual availability of reduced-cost housing, arising from the departure of Whites who could no longer tolerate airport noise.

What all ethnic minorities have shared recently in London is concentration at the bottom of the labor market. Initial recruitment as replacement labor, in times of economic growth, has now given way in time of recession to disproportionate experience of unemployment. In 1991 London's Whites had a historically high unemployment rate of 10 percent. For the three Black groups combined, however, the figure was 22.5 percent, and for South Asians 15.8 percent (for Chinese and Others the figure was 16 percent) (Owen 1993b).

For those who remain in employment, the level of unemployment is nevertheless important. It signifies that the general level of eonomic activity is far from buoyant. The prospect of switching jobs to a more lucrative position is reduced; and for many, high unemployment means that a member of the household or the family is not generating the income that might be expected. The chances of being able to afford residential relocation are therefore reduced. In the first half of the 1990s, this has meant a widespread reduction in house prices from the levels of the 1980s.

This contributes to a consolidation of the ethnic map. If residential mobility is reduced, then the location and distribution of minority groups persists. There is a reinforcement of the existing tendency of any ethnic group to remain more characteristic of certain parts of the city than others. In London the rich infrastructure of cultural and economic institutions that has built up over the decades contributes to this tendency (McAuley 1987). The particular factors that led to the original location of a community may disappear, but their consequences survive.

Segregation and Interaction

The preceding descriptions have made it clear that there is an element of segregation between groups delineated by London's ethnic census categories. A degree of precision can be given to our understanding of this phenomenon by the use of the segregation index and the exposure or interaction index. The segregation index has been widely used in the analysis of the ethnic geography of cities in North America (Taeuber and Taeuber 1965; Massey and Denton 1993; Mercer 1989) and in Europe (Peach 1987). It is commonly understood to measure the percentage of an ethnic group that would have to move to other spatial units within the city in order to reproduce the same geographical distribution as some other group.

In any particular city the value of the segregation index for any two ethnic groups is influenced by the size of the spatial units used in its calculation (Jones and McEvoy 1978). In London use has been made of the borough scale (Peach 1987, 43–45), ward scale (Jones 1991,183), and multiple scales (Lee 1977). The effect of moving from the borough level to the ward level, or from the ward level to that of the enumeration district, is to introduce large numbers of additional spatial units into the calculation of the index. Thus, the value of the index increases because there are more units between which the hypothetical movement of an ethnic group could occur.

In this study, two scales have been used—the London borough and the ward (table 5.3). Ideally, the census enumeration district data would also have been examined. However, because the number of persons in many ethnic groups is very small at this scale of analysis, the census has chosen to report only at the four-category level for enumeration districts. If we want spatial precision we lose ethnic precision; hence the limitation on our choice of scales. Broadly speaking, the picture of segregation is similar at the two scales examined, although the ward scale has higher values and the differential fluctuates.

Segregation from Whites is highest among the three South Asian groups, with the Bangladeshis exhibiting values markedly higher than either Indians or Pakistanis. The three Black groups are somewhat less segregated from Whites than South Asians, while the Chinese and Other categories display lower values still. Some of the more extreme values are perhaps most easily explained. The high Bangladeshi value reflects the concentration of this

Table 5.3 Greater London: Segregation Indexes, 1991

	(1)	(2)	(3)	(4)	(5)	(6)	(7)	(8)	(9)	(10)
(1) White	—	.48	.46	.41	.51	.53	.65	.29	.34	.28
(2) Black-Caribbean	.39	—	.21	.15	.56	.51	.62	.42	.43	.35
(3) Black-African	.37	.15	—	.19	.56	.52	.58	.34	.40	.33
(4) Black-Other	.33	.10	.13	—	.55	.51	.60	.35	.39	.29
(5) Indian	.42	.47	.48	.48	—	.33	.67	.49	.38	.45
(6) Pakistani	.43	.42	.44	.43	.28	—	.65	.51	.41	.46
(7) Bangladeshi	.58	.56	.51	.54	.63	.61	—	.59	.61	.60
(8) Chinese	.21	.31	.26	.24	.41	.43	.51	—	.27	.23
(9) Other Asian	.24	.32	.32	.30	.31	.33	.53	.18	—	.22
(10) Other Other	.21	.28	.28	.24	.38	.39	.52	.14	.14	—

Note: Above diagonal: ward level; below diagonal: borough level

relatively small group within the borough of Tower Hamlets. The low Chinese value, in contrast, derives from a pattern of dispersal that is clearly connected to the concentration of Chinese workers in the catering trade. If an ethnic group serves the rest of the population through its restaurants, it may develop a pattern of residence that broadly reflects that of the target market. This is the classic pattern of a "middleman minority" community (Waldinger, McEvoy, and Aldrich 1990).

Segregation between ethnic minorities is more polarized than that between Whites and ethnic minorities. The three Black groups are little segregated from one another at either scale, and the three subdivisions of Chinese and others also have low levels of segregation. The three Black groups are more strongly segregated from South Asians than they are from Whites, and like Whites, their most extreme difference is with Bangladeshis. Within the South Asian groups, unlike the Black groups, there is considerable spatial separation. While Indians and Pakistanis have their lowest segregation with each other, both have their highest segregation from the Bangladeshi group. The segregation between Indians and Bangladeshis is the highest between any groups at both scales. Moreover, all other groups have their highest segregation from the Bangladeshis.

The existence of higher segregation levels between certain ethnic minority groups than between ethnic minorities and Whites has led some authors to surmise that segregation is a matter of choice, based on the cultural preferences of the ethnic minorities. Others have favored explanations of segregation based on White racism and discrimination (Jones and McEvoy 1978). No attempt is made here to definitively resolve this issue, but it should be recognized that if choice is at work, then it often acts to provide minorities with the least desirable housing in the parts of the metropolitan area that they occupy.

Reliance on the single measure of the segregation index was strongly criticized by Lieberson (1980, 1981) who pointed out that a given level of the segregation index means very different things to majority and minority groups. We have noted above the relatively low segregation of Chinese and Whites in London. For most Whites this means that they live in areas in which Chinese are a small minority, but for most Chinese it means living in areas where the vast preponderance of the population is White. In order to assess such asymmetrical experiences, Lieberson proposed the more widespread use of so-called p* indexes. In their subsequent use (e.g., Robinson 1980; Jones 1983), these have come to be known as exposure, isolation, or interaction indexes. They measure the chances that members of an ethnic group have of encountering, in their neighborhood, a member of another ethnic group.

Like segregation indexes, the value of p* indexes is influenced by the scale of the neighborhoods used in their calculation. The effects of scale are not however as straightforward as those of segregation indexes. Because p* indexes measure the chances (or probability) members of a particular group have of coming into contact with members of other groups, they must, when added to the chances of a group's members encountering each other, add up to unity. Thus, if a scale change results in a group's chances of self-interaction *increasing*, then it follows that its chances of interactions with other groups must, in aggregate, be *decreasing*.

When we consider interaction probabilities at borough level (table 5.4), we can immediately see that the highest figure for any group is that indicating the chances of encountering White people. The highest figure of all is for White self-interaction. The value of .81 indicates that the average White person in London in 1991 would find that 81 percent of the other residents in his or her borough were also White. Members of other ethnic groups had at least a 70 percent chance of finding that their borough coresidents are White. The lowest figure is for Bangladeshis, who, we have already seen, have the greatest segregation index when compared with Whites (table 5.3). The highest figure is for the Chinese, previously identified as the group least segregated from Whites at borough level. The high probability of minority interaction with Whites is in contrast with the low probability of White interaction with members of minorities. Only for Indians and Black Caribbeans do White chances of encountering members of an ethnic minority rise above 2 percent. Lieberson's asymmetry is thus starkly revealed.

Turning to the possibilities of interaction between members of minorities at borough level, we can see that the three Black groups have their highest probability of interaction with Black Caribbeans. Thus, Black Africans and Black Others are more likely to find their borough coresidents are Caribbeans rather than members of their own group. This reflects both the low segregation index values between Caribbeans and the other two groups, and the larger size of the Black Caribbean population.

Indians have an approximately 10 percent chance of finding that their borough neighbors are also Indians. Pakistanis also find that their highest chance of interaction is with Indians, an 8 percent chance compared with only a 3 percent chance of encountering fellow Pakistanis. This can be understood by reference to the four times greater size of the Indian population and to the relatively low segregation index of 28.2 for the two groups.

Although Bangladeshis are no more numerous than Pakistanis in London, their chances of encountering Indian coresidents are much lower. This is clearly related to the high segregation index already noted between Indians and Bangladeshis. Indeed, the segregation of Bangladeshis from other groups

Table 5.4 Greater London: Interaction Indexes (p*), 1991 (Borough Level)

		(1)	(2)	(3)	(4)	(5)	(6)	(7)	(8)	(9)	(10)
(1)	White	0.8129	0.7354	0.7371	0.7473	0.7357	0.7267	0.7012	0.7762	0.7639	0.7693
(2)	Black - Caribbean	0.0403	0.0732	0.0702	0.0683	0.0455	0.0541	0.0470	0.0502	0.0479	0.0514
(3)	Black - African	0.0222	0.0385	0.0406	0.0370	0.0235	0.0286	0.0305	0.0289	0.0267	0.0282
(4)	Black - Other	0.0113	0.0189	0.0187	0.0184	0.0117	0.0137	0.0138	0.0139	0.0129	0.0142
(5)	Indian	0.0483	0.0546	0.0514	0.0507	0.1030	0.0848	0.0355	0.0532	0.0681	0.0583
(6)	Pakistani	0.0121	0.0164	0.0158	0.0149	0.0214	0.0302	0.0142	0.0128	0.0165	0.0140
(7)	Bangladeshi	0.0113	0.0138	0.0163	0.0146	0.0087	0.0138	0.1123	0.0160	0.0124	0.0135
(8)	Chinese	0.0081	0.0096	0.0101	0.0096	0.0085	0.0081	0.0104	0.0096	0.0093	0.0095
(9)	Other Asian	0.0161	0.0184	0.0187	0.0180	0.0219	0.0210	0.0163	0.0187	0.0212	0.0197
(10)	Other Other	0.0174	0.0212	0.0212	0.0211	0.0201	0.0190	0.0189	0.0205	0.0211	0.0221

Note: Index measures chances a member of an ethnic group (columns) has of encountering, in his or her borough, a member of another or the same ethnic group (rows).

ensures that, after Whites, Bangladeshis are far more likely to encounter fellow Bangladeshis than they are members of another individual minority. Even for Bangladeshis, however, the *combined* chances of interaction with other ethnic minorities are larger than those of self-interaction.

The Chinese and Other groups find that their principal chances of minority interaction, at borough level, are with the two largest groups, the Indians and the Black Caribbeans. None of these groups displays high levels of self-interaction. In the Chinese case, this reflects relatively small numbers and relatively even distribution across the city. For Other Others, the heterogeneous nature of the category would have made high levels of self-interaction highly surprising. For Other Asians, too, diversity is the key to understanding the low probability of self-interaction; while most members of the group are of South Asian extraction, they are divided in their origins, principally between India and Pakistan.

When we examine the p^* indexes at ward level (table 5.5), the same general picture appears as at borough level, but the values are somewhat more divergent. Thus, the White self-interaction value is higher at ward level than at borough level and the aggregate chances of White interaction with minorities is therefore lower. White chances of encountering members of individual minorities remain low. Minority chances of encountering Whites remain high at ward level, but are somewhat reduced from the borough-level figures. Self-interaction among minorities is markedly higher for some groups at ward level when compared with borough level: Indians have a 17 percent chance of encountering coethnics, Bangladeshis a 16 percent chance, and Black Caribbeans a 10 percent chance.

We can perhaps summarize the information contained in the p^* indexes by indicating that for all ethnic minorities, at either scale level, the experience of the average group member is residence in an area in which Whites are the majority. This majority is lower at the ward level, and for certain groups at this scale, self-interaction is becoming a strong subsidiary theme. For Whites, in contrast, the average experience is one in which over 80 percent of coresidents are coethnics.

The Broad Picture

Much work remains to be done on Britain's and London's ethnic minorities. It seems unlikely, however, that the broad picture implicit in the spatial distribution and segregation calculations will be challenged. Ethnic minorities are concentrated, though in a differential manner, in those

Table 5.5 Greater London: Interaction Indexes (p^*), 1991 (Ward Level)

		(1)	(2)	(3)	(4)	(5)	(6)	(7)	(8)	(9)	(10)
(1)	White	0.8265	0.6928	0.6978	0.7184	0.6431	0.6418	0.6313	0.7663	0.7337	0.7547
(2)	Black - Caribbean	0.0379	0.0963	0.0853	0.0835	0.0474	0.0598	0.0476	0.0517	0.0497	0.0555
(3)	Black - African	0.0210	0.0468	0.0533	0.0437	0.0242	0.0309	0.0315	0.0339	0.0285	0.0306
(4)	Black - Other	0.0109	0.0231	0.0220	0.0221	0.0117	0.0147	0.0139	0.0146	0.0133	0.0151
(5)	Indian	0.0422	0.0568	0.0529	0.0505	0.1746	0.1307	0.0455	0.0505	0.0816	0.0596
(6)	Pakistani	0.0106	0.0181	0.0170	0.0160	0.0330	0.0485	0.0194	0.0129	0.0204	0.0151
(7)	Bangladeshi	0.0102	0.0140	0.0168	0.0148	0.0111	0.0188	0.1645	0.0153	0.0130	0.0138
(8)	Chinese	0.0080	0.0099	0.0118	0.0101	0.0081	0.0082	0.0099	0.0126	0.0103	0.0099
(9)	Other Asian	0.0155	0.0192	0.0200	0.0185	0.0263	0.0259	0.0170	0.0208	0.0271	0.0209
(10)	Other Other	0.0171	0.0229	0.0230	0.0226	0.0206	0.0206	0.0194	0.0215	0.0224	0.0248

Note: Index measures chances a member of an ethnic group (columns) has of encountering, in his or her ward, a member of another or the same ethnic group (rows).

parts of London's society and space that are no longer desirable to the White majority.

Black Caribbeans, for example, remain most strongly represented in the inner boroughs. Where they have escaped the lower standard housing of the private rented sector, in which they were originally accommodated, many became resident in public-sector housing. National government policies have encouraged the purchase of such properties by residents. Because of the downturn in property values, many residents are now trapped in a position of "negative equity," owing more to the providers of their home loans than they could realize by sale of the property. Those who remain in the residual public-sector housing, typically the least-desirable property, are also trapped since the more desirable housing, to which they might have once sought transfer, is now in private hands (Dorling 1994).

The experience of South Asian groups parallels that of Black Caribbeans. For example, the Indian community in the western borough of Ealing is most heavily concentrated in low-status owner occupation in terraced housing areas of the Southall district, and where it owns semidetached housing, it often suffers from airport externalities. In both instances, slow housing markets and negative equity combine with general economic uncertainty to restrict movement into other, better, areas.

The Bangladeshis meanwhile are quite clearly occupying the least-desirable council houses in Tower Hamlets (Hyndman 1990). Their residence in this borough has also exposed them to Britain's most violently expressed examples of White racism. The sense of insecurity that this violence engenders, coupled with the rapid demographic growth of the group, goes some way to explaining why Bangladeshis endure the greatest levels of segregation that this chapter has identified.

Because this chapter has used a new data set, it has necessarily concentrated on the position in 1991. The most valuable statistical accounts of ethnic minority residence, such as that of Massey and Denton (1993), incorporate temporal analyses. It is to be hoped, therefore, that the 2001 census will allow the continuance or change of current patterns to be analyzed by the continued use of the same ethnic question as the 1991 census. It may be that alternative ways of aggregating the detailed answers into broad ethnic categories will be found. If this is the case, however, we will also need a continuation of reporting on current categorizations if comparability is to be established.

A major feature of the intercensal decade is likely to be the continued growth of many minorities, most notably perhaps the extremely youthful Bangladeshis. Will this growth be accommodated by the spread of more minority members into the peripheral areas of London that remain predominantly White? Or will we have the development of more and more localities like the Northcote ward? Some time ago Jones and McEvoy (1978) argued that "ghetto" was as appropriate a label for minority quarters in Britain as it was in America. Such a judgment may have been premature, but for how long?

References

Carey, Sean, and Abdus Shukur. 1986. "A Profile of the Bangla Deshi Community in East London." *New Community* 12:405–17.

Cater, John C., and Trevor P. Jones. 1989. *Social Geography: An Introduction to Contemporary Issues.* London: Edward Arnold.

Chance, Judy. 1987. "The Irish in London: An Exploration of Ethnic Boundary Maintenance." In *Race and Racism*, ed. Peter Jackson. London: Allen and Unwin.

Coleman, David, and John Salt. 1992. *The British Population: Patterns, Trends and Processes.* Oxford: Oxford University Press.

Constantinides, Pamela. 1977. "The Greek Cypriots: Factors in the Maintenance of Ethnic Identity." In *Between Two Cultures*, ed. James L. Watson. Oxford: Basil Blackwell.

Dahya, Badr. 1974. "The Nature of Pakistani Ethnicity in Industrial Cities in Britain." In *Urban Ethnicity*, ed. Abner Cohen. London: Tavistock.

Dorling, Daniel. 1994. "The Negative Equity Map of Britain." *Area* 26:327–42.

Hyndman, Sophie. 1990. *Housing and Health among British Bengalis in Tower Hamlets.* Research Paper No. 3. London: Department of Geography, Queen Mary and Westfield College.

Jackson, Peter. 1986. "Ethnic and Social Conflict." In *London: Problems of Change*, ed. Hugh Clout and Peter Wood. London: Longman.

Johnson, Mark R. D. 1993. "A Question of Ethnic Origin in the 1991 Census." *New Community* 19:281–89.

Jones, Emrys. 1991. "Race and Ethnicity in London." In *London: A New Metropolitan Geography*, ed. Keith Hoggart and David R. Green. London: Edward Arnold.

Jones, Trevor. 1983. "Residential Segregation and Ethnic Autonomy." *New Community* 11:10–22.

Jones, Trevor, and David McEvoy. 1978. "Race and Space in Cloud Cuckoo Land." *Area* 10:162–66.

Lee, Trevor R. 1977. *Race and Residence: The Concentration and Dispersal of Immigrants in London*. Oxford: Oxford University Press.

Lieberson, Stanley. 1980. *A Piece of the Pie: Black and White Immigrants Since 1880*. Berkeley, Calif.: University of California Press.

——. 1981. "An Asymmetrical Approach to Segregation." In *Ethnic Segregation in Cities*, ed. Ceri Peach, Vaughan Robinson, and Susan Smith. London: Croom Helm.

Massey, Douglas, and Nancy Denton. 1993. *American Apartheid: Segregation and the Making of the Underclass*. Cambridge, Mass.: Harvard University Press.

McAuley, Ian. 1987. *Guide to Ethnic London*. London: Michael Haag.

Mercer, John. 1989. "Asian Migrants and Residential Location in Canada." *New Community* 15:185–202.

Owen, David. 1992. *Ethnic Minorities in Great Britain*. 1991 Census Data Paper No. 1. Coventry: National Ethnic Minority Data Archive, Centre for Research in Ethnic Relations, University of Warwick.

——. 1993a. *Ethnic Minorities in Great Britain: Age and Gender Structure*. 1991 Census Statistical Paper No. 2. Coventry: National Ethnic Minority Data Archive, Centre for Research in Ethnic Relations, University of Warwick.

——. 1993b. *Ethnic Minorities in Great Britain: Economic Characteristics*. 1991 Census Statistical Paper No. 3. Coventry: National Ethnic Minority Data Archive, Centre for Research in Ethnic Relations, University of Warwick.

Peach, Ceri. 1984. "The Force of West Indian Island Identity in Britain." In *Geography and Ethnic Pluralism*, ed. Colin Clarke, David Ley, and Ceri Peach. London: George Allen & Unwin.

——. 1987. "Immigration and Segregation in Western Europe since 1945." In *Foreign Minorities in Continental European Cities*, ed. Günter Glebe and John O'Loughlin. Stuttgart: Franz Steiner.

Rhodes, Chris, and Nurun Nabi. 1992. "Brick Lane: A Village Economy in the Shadow of the City?" In *Global Finance and Urban Living*, ed. Leslie Budd and Sam Whimster. London: Routledge.

Robinson, Vaughan. 1980. "Lieberson's Isolation Index: A Case Study Evaluation." *Area* 12:307–12.

——. 1991. "Goodbye Yellow Brick Road: The Spatial Mobility and Immobility of Britain's Ethnic Population." *New Community* 17:313–30.

Shaw, Chris. 1988. "Components of Growth in the Ethnic Minority Population." *Population Trends* 52:26–30.

Smith, Susan J. 1989. *The Politics of "Race" and Residence.* Cambridge: Polity Press.

Taeuber, Karl, and Alma Taeuber. 1965. *Negroes in Cities.* Chicago, Ill.: Aldine.

Teague, Andy. 1993. "Ethnic Group: First Results from the 1991 Census." *Population Trends* 72:12–17.

Waldinger, Roger, David McEvoy, and Howard Aldrich. 1990. "Spatial Dimensions of Opportunity Structures." In *Ethnic Entrepreneurs,* ed. Roger Waldinger, Howard Aldrich, Robin Ward, and Associates. Newbury Park, Calif.: Sage.

Waterman, Stanley, and Barry Kosmin. 1987. "Residential Change in a Middle-Class Suburban Ethnic Population: A Comment." *Transactions Institute of British Geographers,* N.S. 12:107–12.

Chapter 6

Ethnicity and the Dutch Welfare State: The Case of Amsterdam

Sako Musterd and Wim Ostendorf

Ethnicity in Amsterdam

Ethnic mixes are not new to the city of Amsterdam. Because of its urban history, which is closely related to international trade, the Dutch capital has almost always contained some immigrant populations having varieties of origins and ethnic backgrounds. Until recently, however, the number of immigrating "foreigners" has been fairly modest. Except for the population of Dutch colonies overseas, the immigrants who entered the cities in the Netherlands during the first fifty years of this century were mostly either Italian ice cream sellers or Chinese restauranteurs. During some periods, the number of immigrants was even offset by the number of out-migrating people. Substantial numbers of Dutch inhabitants moved to Canada, Australia, and New Zealand during the fifties and early sixties. During the fifties, there was an influx of Indonesian immigrants after the break of the colonial relationship with Indonesia.

Apart from the World War II period, ethnicity was not an issue until the 1960s. Since then, the influx of foreigners has increased significantly and their share of the urban population has grown (fig. 6.1). Immigration managed to reduce the effects of the huge suburbanization flows out of cities like Amsterdam, and from the mid-1980s, the absolute growth of the city can be ascribed primarily to foreign immigration. There have been at least three major factors underlying recent international migration: (1) the termination

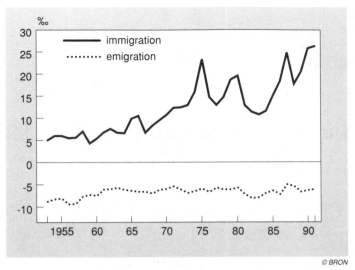

© BRON

Fig. 6.1   Immigration and Emigration (International Migration) in Amsterdam, 1953–1991

of colonial relationships, (2) the need for an extended labor force, and (3) global economic and political shifts.

Colonial Immigration

Colonial immigration to the Netherlands consists of Indonesian and, most importantly, Surinamese and Antillean populations. Colonial immigration from Surinam to the Netherlands dates from the nineteenth century. Although the ethnic composition of the Surinamese population is mixed (descendants from the slave population, mulattoes and Blacks called Creoles; contract laborers from British India called Hindustanis and from Java), until the Second World War, immigrants from Surinam were for the main part Creoles. They were not laborers, but were middle class with a strong orientation to the Netherlands, the Dutch school system (universities), and Dutch culture. Their presence was hardly noticed by Dutch society (Amersfoort and de Klerk 1986). After 1960, in a period of rapid economic growth and labor shortage, Surinamese immigration increased and became more heterogeneous in relation to social class (including the lower class) and to ethnic background (including Hindustanis). In 1975, Surinam became independent. Many Surinamese inhabitants, who possessed Dutch passports until then, chose to hold their Dutch nationality and moved to the Netherlands. The Dutch government introduced strict immigration controls in

1980, which reduced Surinamese immigration. However, migration related to family formation still goes on since marriage or cohabitation with a partner living in the Netherlands enables a person to come to the Netherlands.

Labor Force Immigration

Mediterranean immigration to the Netherlands is a typical example of labor migration from preindustrial countries to industrial countries. A shortage of labor in the Netherlands in the sixties resulted in recruitment of unskilled male laborers in Mediterranean countries, especially Turkey and Morocco. Quite naively, many Dutch thought that the "guest workers" would go back home after a while, as guests are expected to do. However, most of them decided to stay far longer, even permanently. After the oil crisis in 1973, the need for a foreign work force came to an end, but not the immigration (fig. 6.2) and the laborers started to bring over their families as well. In the early eighties, this immigration of women and children decreased steeply, suggesting the end of the process of reunification of families. But the labor migration factor and related family influx appears to be a lasting

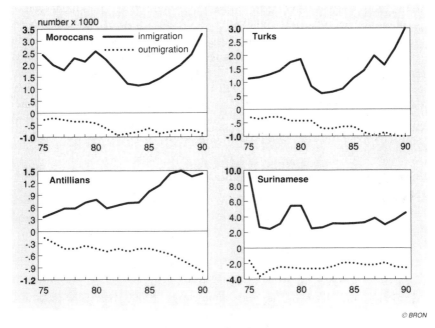

© BRON

Fig. 6.2   International Migration Balance (1975–1990) by Share of Country of Origin of the Four Most Important Countries of Origin

process. In the eighties the family-formation migration from Turkey and Morocco became much more important (Beer and Noordam 1992). Although influenced by economic fluctuations in the country of origin, as well as in the country of destination, about half of the immigrant people who entered Dutch cities during the nineties still originate in Turkey and Morocco (fig. 6.2).

Immigration Due to Global Economic and Political Shifts

In the past decade, especially at the end of the eighties and the beginning of the nineties, a third wave of immigration began to emerge. Growing numbers of political refugees from a wide array of Asian and African countries are trying to build a future in Western cities, including Amsterdam. Parallel to this development, a growing number of illegal refugees began to appear, but the actual amount is unknown. Unique events, however, sometimes provide insight as to the magnitude of this migration process. The next event is illustrative.

In October 1992, part of two blocks of apartments was destroyed in Amsterdam's Bijlmermeer district when an airplane crashed. Many illegal immigrants lived in that part of the city. Apart from the identification problem that was related to the illegal status of a number of the victims of the crash, there was another problem, that of rehousing the households who survived the disaster but could no longer live in the remaining apartments. Among them were a number of illegal households. For humanitarian reasons, the authorities decided to offer legal status to illegal inhabitants who could prove they lived in the disaster area. Although only some hundred dwellings were involved, nearly two thousand illegal immigrants applied for legal status—and these were the most legal of the illegal, it was said.

Size of the Population of Non-Dutch Origin in Amsterdam

Amsterdam always has been a very important destination for Surinamese immigrants. In 1965, half of the Surinamese population in the Netherlands lived in Amsterdam, along with some 21 percent (68,000) of people with a Surinamese or Antillean background. The Amsterdam population is less than 5 percent of the total population in the Netherlands.

In 1991, Amsterdam also had some 36,000 Moroccans, 22 percent of the Moroccan population in the Netherlands, and 26,000 Turks, 12 percent of the Turkish population in the Netherlands. Turks and Moroccans form the main part of Amsterdam's Mediterranean population. In total, on 1 January 1992, 25.2 percent of the inhabitants of Amsterdam were registered as aliens or persons of Surinamese and Antillean ethnic origin. In Rotterdam, The Hague, and Utrecht, these percentages are 21.5, 21.2, and 15.6, respectively (Muus 1992). Although only 13 percent of the total population of the Netherlands is living in one of the four largest cities, 54 percent of all aliens (mostly Turkish and Moroccan) and persons of Surinamese and Antillean ethnic origin are living there. The estimate of the number of refugees in the Netherlands on 1 January was 40,000.

Ethnic Segregation in Amsterdam

Despite the rapidly rising number of foreign immigrants, it is an interesting fact that in Amsterdam, and in other Dutch cities, there is virtually no evidence of clear or increasing spatial segregation of ethnic groups. The different categories are only moderately concentrated (fig. 6.3 and 6.4). The changes in the position of ethnic groups on the Amsterdam housing market between 1960 and 1990 can roughly be characterized as "gaining access to the Amsterdam housing stock: from lodging houses to family houses," although there are differences between the Surinamese ("being more Dutch") and the Mediterraneans (Ostendorf, Buursink, and van Englesdorp Gastelaars 1988).

A remarkable feature of the distribution of the Surinamese population within Amsterdam is the concentration in Bijlmermeer, in the southeastern part of the city. At the time of the immigration peak in the mid-1970s, just before Surinam became independent, many high-rise apartments were available in this part of the city. In an effort to combat the huge housing shortage, Amsterdam had launched a major program in which large numbers of dwellings, almost always in multistory blocks using industrial construction methods, were built in Bijlmermeer. In 1991, the area had grown to about ninety thousand inhabitants. The indigenous population was not very interested in the newly built houses, so the allocation rules for entering this segment of the housing market were relaxed drastically. Consequently, the newly arrived Surinamese families grasped this opportunity to rent new accommodations. Surinamese migrants arriving later used informal circuits to attain dwellings in that area as well.

In 1973, the Surinamese population within Amsterdam varied in socioeconomic position and type of household and was distributed over Amsterdam accordingly, although a considerable part lived in lodging houses in and around the city center. From that point, lodging houses became much less important. In 1991, the Surinamese population had to a large degree gained access to the housing stock of Amsterdam by the municipal system of housing

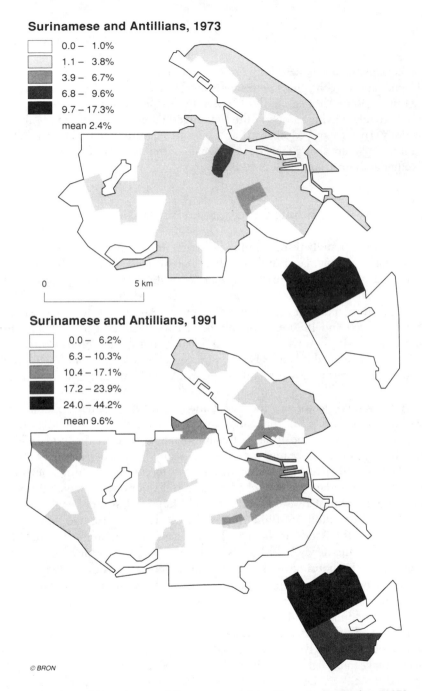

Surinamese and Antillians, 1973

- 0.0 – 1.0%
- 1.1 – 3.8%
- 3.9 – 6.7%
- 6.8 – 9.6%
- 9.7 – 17.3%
- mean 2.4%

0   5 km

Surinamese and Antillians, 1991

- 0.0 – 6.2%
- 6.3 – 10.3%
- 10.4 – 17.1%
- 17.2 – 23.9%
- 24.0 – 44.2%
- mean 9.6%

© BRON

Fig. 6.3   Spatial Distribution of Surinamese and Antilleans in Amsterdam, 1973 and 1991

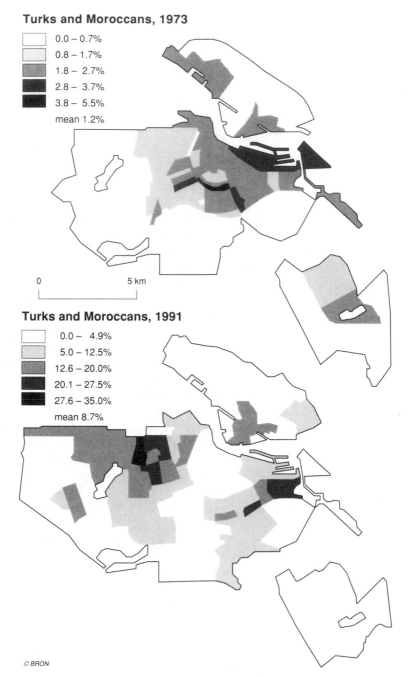

Turks and Moroccans, 1973

- 0.0 – 0.7%
- 0.8 – 1.7%
- 1.8 – 2.7%
- 2.8 – 3.7%
- 3.8 – 5.5%
- mean 1.2%

0   5 km

Turks and Moroccans, 1991

- 0.0 – 4.9%
- 5.0 – 12.5%
- 12.6 – 20.0%
- 20.1 – 27.5%
- 27.6 – 35.0%
- mean 8.7%

© BRON

Fig. 6.4   Spatial Distribution of Turks and Moroccans in Amsterdam, 1973 and 1991

allocation and was to be found in the lower quality parts of the housing stock including the zone in transition, dating from the nineteenth century, and the recently built neighborhoods at the edge of the city. In the central part of the city, where a process of gentrification is going on, the Surinamese population is losing ground.

Notwithstanding the even distribution of the Surinamese population within Amsterdam, the concentration in Bijlmermeer remains a conspicuous feature. In 1991, approximately 32 percent of the population was of Surinamese or Antillean origin. Forty-two percent of the Surinamese or Antillian population in Amsterdam was living in Bijlmermeer, an area that houses only 13 percent of the total population of the city.

The pattern of Turkish and Moroccan inhabitants within Amsterdam is far from stable. The distribution of the Turks and Moroccans shows a close relationship with the development of immigration. Here the process can accurately be labeled "from lodging houses to family houses." In 1973, the laborers were living in lodging houses in and around the center of the city without their families. The expansion of the households in later years resulted in moves to adjacent low-rent neighborhoods, with many substandard dwellings. In more recent years, the system of housing allocation has become relevant. Related to the length of stay in Amsterdam, the size of the (unified) family, and urban renewal activities in the old nineteenth century neighborhoods, the share of immigrant households that reached an adequate position on the housing allocating lists increased. Compared to the remaining population of Amsterdam, the Mediterranean families are large. The municipal system of housing allocation relates size of the family to size of the dwelling. So, more and more immigrant households are able to apply successfully for the relatively large and cheap council dwellings built from 1920 to 1960. Because of the price level, the expensive southern sector is beyond the reach of most Mediterraneans. The center of the city, which housed the total Mediterranean population in 1973, housed very few Mediterraneans in 1991.

In summary, while the relative segregation of Turks and Moroccans has not increased—the index of dissimilarity (D) has been more or less stable around .35 for almost twenty years now (Amersfoort 1992, and calculations of the authors)—the overall pattern reveals a shift from the inner city toward the more recently built areas. In other words, the development shows a shift through the concentric zones triggered by time-specific factors.

To state there is no concentration of ethnic groups at all would be too rigid, but it is quite clear that the fast increase in the number of immigrants entering Amsterdam during the past two decades did not lead to extreme segregation or polarization processes. A comparison with American cities is illuminating in this respect. In cities such as Baltimore, Atlanta, and Cleveland, which are comparable to the metropolitan area of Amsterdam in terms of size and proportion of Blacks (the comparison between Blacks in the United States and ethnic minorities in the Netherlands is often thought to be legitimate; see Schuyt 1992), the segregation indices are above .75 (Clark 1986,98–99). In Amsterdam, the index remains below .36 for Turks and Moroccans, and .34 for the Surinamese.

An important factor explaining the low level of segregation can be found in the organization of the Dutch welfare state, including special arrangements in terms of income distribution, housing, social security, subsidies, and the battle against poverty. To reach a better understanding of the spatial pattern of ethnic groups and to understand their socioeconomic position, a broader framework has to be built. Therefore, in the next section of this chapter, we will deal with the relationship between ethnicity, segregation, and poverty in the Dutch welfare state.

Dutch Welfare State

In most Western countries, the ethnic "problem" is associated with a poverty discussion and the reaction of the state to the issue of poverty. Often immigrants are poorly educated and therefore vulnerable on the labor market, which implies a weak employment position and often a weak income and housing-market position. In the United States, for example, the poverty rate among Blacks reaches about 32 percent, among Hispanics 28 percent, while the overall rate is 13.5 percent (latest U.S. Census data, in See 1991). Bearing in mind this sort of association, it is logical to put the discussion on ethnicity into the light of the issue of poverty and the welfare state. In our opinion, the core of the poverty problem is the question of whether someone's personal state isolates the person from mainstream society. The essence of poverty is the inability to maintain social contacts. In this respect, there are three key questions or aspects:

1. The distribution of affluence: Does their level of consumption of modern products allow the poor to live in dignity? This applies to housing and to income. The income should permit one to keep up with the rest of society in terms of general consumption. It should also allow one to maintain contact with that wider society (through newspapers, telephone, television, etc.).

2. The level of social segregation: Is there a high level of segregation of the poor? Many believe that strict segregation reduces contact with the remainder of society. The implications may be sought in the importance of

role models provided by successful individuals, or the maintenance of prevailing social norms, for instance.

3. The chances for social mobility: Is it possible to improve the situation? The key to coming up in the world has traditionally been a good education. Increasingly, access to suitable jobs seems to be an additional factor.

The Dutch welfare state interferes with all three key aspects of poverty: the state redistributes income, combats social segregation, and promotes social mobility. The Dutch welfare state directly addresses poverty with general (universal) programs and only indirectly touches upon ethnicity. The state developed no specific policy instruments focused on ethnicity-related problems. The main argument for this is to avoid discrimination. As an effect, stigmatization and polarization within a specific target group also are avoided.

We will first deal with poverty aspects of the Dutch policy, with special reference to the effects on the residential environment in the cities. Second, the relationship between poverty and ethnicity will be highlighted.

Redistribution of Affluence

The Dutch welfare state commands many instruments that promote the redistribution of income and guaranteed access to good-quality housing for everyone. These instruments include tax codes, social benefits (such as social security for every individual over sixty-five years old), disability benefits, unemployment benefits, and welfare payments. In addition, there are housing subsidies, both for producers and for consumers, as well as subsidies for health care, and so on (cf., Swaan 1988; Kloosterman and Lambooy 1992). The share of national income that is devoted to social programs now amounts to over 30 percent. In Great Britain it does not surpass 20 percent (EUROSTAT 1991). In addition, the average percentage of the population eligible for sickness and pension benefits is high in the Netherlands (Esping-Andersen 1990). The unemployment benefits are relatively generous in the Netherlands, too, compared with other countries (Kuttner 1984). As a consequence, the degree of income inequality is very low (fig. 6.5).

The share of social rental housing in the total stock is highest of all EU countries and the housing stock is relatively new, of good quality, and well equipped. In summary, the Dutch welfare state creates relatively modest differences between population groups in terms of possibilities to consume.

Combating Social Segregation

Income redistribution policy and the provision of social housing have been highly effective in combating social segregation in the Netherlands. In the

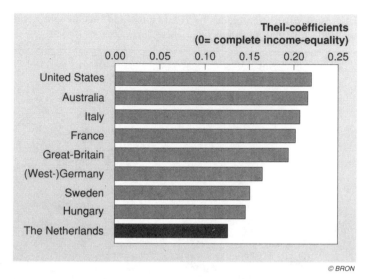

Fig. 6.5   Income Inequality, around 1986, Theil-coefficients

system of housing allocation money is only of moderate importance. Housing *needs* determine whether a household can gain access to a dwelling; the number of persons belonging to a household determines the size of the allocated dwelling. If a household cannot afford to pay the rent of the allocated dwelling, rent subsidies are available. The result is that, even within a relatively homogeneous stock, a mixture of households by income level can occur. This mixture is a policy goal for local authorities. Empirical evidence in this respect is available from a survey of the Amsterdam population. Even at the micro level, income segregation appears to be only modest, and recent processes in the city of Amsterdam do not point in a direction of a sharp polarization (table 6.1; Musterd and Ostendorf 1991).

The spatial pattern of the unemployed does not reveal any severe segregation tendency; again, the overall pattern is dispersed. The index of dissimilarity (D) for the poorly educated, nonworking population amounts to only .24. The nonworking population with a higher education is more strongly segregated; its D value is .34. This empirical evidence of the lack of spatial segregation in terms of the combination of unemployment and education characteristics is very important, because many scholars (e.g., Wilson 1987) argue that the spatial concentration of poorly educated people without a job—the "potential underclass"—may become a factor in itself to stimulate the underclass character of the people involved.

Table 6.1   Amsterdam: Households by Total Household Income and Residential
Location, 1981 and 1990 (Location Quotients, Total Area = 100)

1981 Income (1000 Dfl.):		<20	20-26	26-34	>34	n
1990 Income (1000 Dfl.):		<21	21-31	31-41	>41	n
Neighborhood/ Age						
Inner City	1981	112	84	94	74	354
	1990	115	69	83	111	417
1870-1905.	1981	106	102	77	93	693
	1990	111	107	93	65	723
1906-1944	1981	104	101	94	87	1192
	1990	98	110	93	98	1144
1945-1959	1981	98	103	94	109	233
	1990	101	103	94	95	258
1960-	1981	81	104	139	140	679
	1990	86	96	125	129	896
Amsterdam	1981 %	56.7	18.3	12.4	12.6	3152
	1990 %	49.3	22.3	11.6	16.7	3435

Source: Central Bureau of Statistics 1991. Household Surveys
1981, 1989/90. (Income classes are different in 1981 and 1990
due to inflation corrections; though not specifically meant to
compare Amsterdam figures, the classes are comparable across
years.)

Promotion of Social Mobility

Access to the Dutch educational system is very open. Virtually all of the
educational system falls under the authority of the state and the costs to the
users are very low. New job opportunities are demanding constantly higher
training, but there still is a strong correlation between the level of training
and the labor-market participation rate. In general, there is no great reason for
concern as far as the growth of the share of people with higher qualification is
concerned. In 1980, 38 percent of the cohort of fifteen-year-olds were
enrolled in the lowest type of educational training, and 26 percent attended
schools of the highest level. By 1990, both of these figures had shifted to 32
percent (SCP 1992,28). However, ethnic minorities are performing less well
than the average (SCP 1992).

Unemployment is relatively high in the Netherlands (OECD 1989) and
currently there are some 850,000 disabled persons out of a total labor force
of 7,000,000. It is generally assumed that the disability program shelters

many unemployed people. Until recently, the welfare payments for the disabled were better than for the unemployed, so many people preferred the former status and, if possible, applied for that. The figures for unemployed and disabled people in the big cities are much higher than the national figures, especially for Amsterdam. So, within the context of labor-market participation, social mobility is a serious problem for a considerable part of the Amsterdam population.

This leads to the question of how the welfare state responds to the problem of unemployment. Because the level of benefits for the unemployed and disabled is relatively high in the Netherlands, consumption needs are met. In contrast, relatively little money is spent on promoting labor-market participation and reentry of the unemployed and disabled. Because of the links between having a job and social mobility, this is important for the relatively poor and the inhabitants of foreign origin. The Dutch welfare state is dedicated toward preventing poverty in the Netherlands. However, much more attention is given to the ability to consume than to programs aiming at reentry to the labor market of the massive numbers of unemployed and disabled.

Poverty and Ethnicity in Amsterdam

The impact of the Dutch welfare state becomes clear in a city like Amsterdam. Income inequality is low, just as is segregation; the numbers of unemployed and disabled, on the other hand, are very high. Although it is a well-known fact that the employment situation and the income and housing situation of people of foreign origin are often relatively bad, it is worthwhile to review them in some detail because of the impact of the Dutch welfare state. The question is, in Amsterdam, how is poverty related to ethnicity?

Income rights for people dependent on social security are identical for every person with a legal status and are unrelated to race. So the income situation of foreigners without a job is the same as the situation for indigenous Dutch without a job. The unemployment payment may be different, however, because it depends on the former wage and the number of years worked. Furthermore, the unemployment rates differ. Controlling for education, number of wage earners per household, and number of hours worked per week, survey data of Amsterdam show a persistent difference in income between Dutch on the one hand and Turks and Moroccans on the other hand. However, the differences are relatively moderate (table 6.2).

As far as *housing* is concerned, there is formally no difference between the rights of immigrants and indigenous people. Their improved position in the housing market implies that immigrants are increasingly being housed by the

Table 6.2   Amsterdam: Total Monthly Income of Multiperson, Single-Earner Households, Headed by Persons with a Low Educational Achievement Status, Working More than 20 Hours per Week, by Country of Origin, 1987 and 1990

Income (Dfl)	Netherlands	Turkey/Morocco
1,500	3%	10%
1,500–3,000	78%	90%
> 3,000	18%	—
Number	154	48

Source: Surveys AME, Amsterdam study centre for the Metropolitan Environment, University of Amsterdam.

municipal system of housing allocation. As a consequence, the spatial segregation of categories according to ethnicity is only modest. Of the indigenous Dutch population, over 30 percent has completed higher-level secondary *education*; among the Turks and Moroccans, the share is 4 percent. Young people with an ethnic background participate at a clearly lower level in education (SCP 1992). The ethnic students in any grade are older than the Dutch students, their scores are lower, they move into the vocational forms of secondary education, and their absenteeism and drop-out rates are higher.

These differences in education do not completely explain the differences in unemployment, however. Analyses, controlling for education, language, occupation and age, show the *unemployment rate* of non-Dutch inhabitants to be twice as high as the rate for Dutch inhabitants. So, some forms of discrimination may be active. Schuyt (1992) argues that Dutch Moroccans and Turks, like the Blacks in the United States, are seen as a flexible "instrument," useful to help absorb fluctuations in the demand for labor.

Unemployment trends for Amsterdam, however, present a positive outlook (table 6.3). People who would potentially belong to the underclass (low-educated unemployed Turkish and Moroccan households) have clearly been able to improve their situation in terms of labor-market participation during the period of economic expansion from 1987 to 1990. Nevertheless, the contrasts have not been completely eradicated. New figures of unemployment since 1991, when economic decline started again, suggest that Schuyt's idea is valid.

Table 6.3 Amsterdam: Percentage of Unemployed or Disabled with Low Educational Achievement Score, by Country of Origin, 1987 and 1990

	1987	1990	Relative decline
The Netherlands	14% (n=179)	11% (n=135)	21%
Suriname/Antilles	47% (n=34)	20% (n=19)	57%
Turkey/Morocco	43% (n=62)	18% (n=31)	58%

Source: Surveys AME, Amsterdam study center for the Metropolitan Environment, University of Amsterdam.

In short, the general character of the Dutch welfare system applies to the immigrant population in Amsterdam. Although often unemployed, immigrants' consumption needs are met. The income situation for people without a job is relatively good and does not show big differences between ethnic groups. The same is true, by and large, for the housing situation. However, the employment situation of immigrants is worse compared to indigenous inhabitants. Moreover, the performance of ethnic groups in education is much weaker than that of the Dutch population. The insufficient education of ethnic groups makes them vulnerable for unemployment, in particular in periods of economic stagnation, and decreases their chances for upward social mobility. This might isolate these groups from mainstream society.

Future Expectations

The rather recent influx of large numbers of foreign migrants has not yet resulted in increased segregation between ethnic groups in Amsterdam. The special character of the Dutch welfare system is probably one of the main factors preventing sharp spatial contrasts.

Because of the influence of the Dutch welfare state, it is appropriate to deal with the ethnicity problem within the framework of the development of poverty, and the lack of possibilities for social mobility. In the preceding sections, several aspects of poverty have been distinguished: income and housing, segregation, and participation in education and the labor market. In a country like the United States, these aspects are closely related. In the Netherlands, the correlations are much lower, thanks to the instruments of the welfare state. With respect to consumption, housing opportunities, and nonsegregated housing situations, the Dutch welfare state guarantees an acceptable minimum level, irrespective of the labor-market participation. Relative poverty in the Netherlands is expressed first and foremost in the lack of a job. Yet the chance of exclusion from society through unemployment is not the same for everyone. The risk is greatest for immigrants with a low level of educational achievement. In this respect, the situation hardly differs from that in the United States (See 1991).

The absence of a perspective of upward social mobility in combination with permanent dependency on the state may result in a decrease in the level of aspiration of individuals. This might lead to the development of a so-called receptive behavior, state dependency, and as a consequence, to the emergence of an underclass (Wilson 1987). This might be labeled "the trap of the welfare state." Although the welfare state so far has been unable to increase the participation in the labor market, the fear of an underclass in the Amsterdam situation is still unfounded. Permanent dependency on the state and bleak prospects for social mobility that may induce the development of an (ethnic) underclass have not been shown thus far. The Dutch welfare state has dealt effectively with the broad redistribution of income and the prevention of segregation. As a result, there are no pronounced spatial concentrations of poverty, unemployment, or ethnic minorities.

However, Dutch society is currently facing a number of challenges with respect to these issues. The welfare state is in a crisis because present programs cost more than the state is able to supply. It appears necessary to change the focus of the welfare state from consumption to participation in the labor market. The task at hand is to increase participation in the labor market in order to maintain redistributive efforts. Related to this reconstruction are the following threats:

1. The redistribution of affluence may come under pressure. If unemployment and disability rates remain high, it will become problematic to maintain the consumption-oriented programs of income redistribution and the provision of high-quality housing. Low-income groups, and therefore ethnic groups, will feel the effects of such shifts first.

2. Spatial segregation may increase. More tasks are being relegated to the "market." With respect to housing, this has two effects. First, owner-occupied dwellings will become more prevalent. Because these are built predominantly in suburban environments, suburbanization of higher-income groups will continue. Segregation is likely to increase. Second, the function of the social rental housing sector (which accounts for 54 percent of the housing stock in Amsterdam) for the lowest-income groups will be accentuated. This will diminish the present mixture of income categories among the tenants. Residualization of social housing may be the result. Immigrants and other low-income groups will be restricted to living in this sector and therefore in the cities.

3. Social mobility is under pressure. Youngsters with an ethnic background do not perform as well in education as their indigenous Dutch counterparts. Consequently, the chance of exclusion from society through unemployment is greatest for them. The data on the development of unemployment show that the position of the foreign migrants improves as the economy grows, but the economy may stagnate. As a consequence, it is conceivable that a residual category of households might emerge with the characteristics of a permanently unemployed underclass. Moreover, the impending European integration does not provide any guarantee that low-level jobs can be retained in the Netherlands. An increasing rate of spatial

segregation will aggravate the problems of such an underclass rather than diminish them.

So far, the Dutch welfare state has been successfully avoiding the emergence of extreme contrasts in the big cities. However, recent developments seem to point in the direction that Thomas (1991) so aptly phrased in the title of his article in *Built Environment*, "The Cities Left Behind." Thomas outlines the chronic suburbanization of the middle class and the attendant concentration of poor populations. Long-term unemployment and urban racial segregation bring about social crisis in the big cities. Sometimes unemployment and segregation go hand in hand with crime, often provoked by problems related to the use of illegal drugs: "The nation declares a war on drugs and crime, yet devotes scant attention to the source of urban malaise—persistent urban poverty; ghettoization; urban isolation from affluent suburbs; and uneven regional development" (Thomas, 1991,219).

Thomas advocates economic development close to the central city, policy for welfare and social services, and programs to enhance community and family life. In other words, he demands the intervention that a welfare state can provide. So far, the Dutch welfare state has provided the answers to requests like these, but the Dutch solutions have to be revised. On the one hand, the revision will have to address the lower target levels for redistribution of incomes and fewer guarantees for suitable housing. On the other hand, it will entail more forceful intervention with respect to participation in the labor market. The directions have been charted: a decrease in dependence on the state and the promotion of individual solutions to the problems of poverty and unemployment, and therewith ethnicity. The consequences of this shift are still unclear. Will the Dutch welfare state remain successful in avoiding polarization or will the result be an increase in segregation and polarization and, as a result, exclusion of population categories from mainstream society?

References

Amersfoort, H. van. 1992. "Ethnic Residential Patterns in a Welfare State: Lessons from Amsterdam, 1970–1990." *New Community* 18(3):439–56.

Amersfoort, H. van, and L. de Klerk. 1986. "The Dynamics of Immigrant Settlement: Surinamese, Turks and Moroccans in Amsterdam 1973–1983." In *Foreign Minorities in Continental European Cities*, ed. G. Glebe and J. O'Loughlin. Stuttgart: Franz Steiner.

Beer, J. de, and R. Noordam. 1992. "Family-Formation Migration of Turks and Moroccans Now Exceeds Family Reunification." *Maandstatistiek van de bevolking* 40(Nov):6–8.

Central Bureau of Statistics. 1991. *Jaarboek inkomen en consumptie.* Den Haag: SDU uitgeeverij/CBS-publicaties.

Clark, W. A. V. 1986. "Residential Segregation in American Cities: A Review and Interpretation." *Population Research and Policy Review* 5:95–127.

Esping-Andersen, G. 1990. *The Three Worlds of Welfare Capitalism.* Cambridge: Polity Press.

EUROSTAT. 1991. *Social Protection Expenditure and Receipts, 1980–1989.* Luxembourg: EUROSTAT.

Kloosterman, R. C., and J. G. Lambooy. 1992. "The Randstad, a Welfare Region?" In *The Randstad: A Research and Policy Laboratory,* ed. F. M. Dieleman and S. Musterd. Dordrecht, Boston and London: Kluwer.

Kuttner, R. 1984. *The Economic Illusion: False Choices between Prosperity and Social Justice.* Boston: Houghton Mifflin.

Musterd, S., and W. Ostendorf. 1991. "Inkomensontwikkeling en tweetoppigheid binnen de Randstad." In *Maatschappelijke Verandering en Stedelijke Dynamiek,* ed. R. van Kampen, S. Musterd, and W. Ostendorf. Delft: Delftse Universitaire Pres.

Muus, Ph. 1992. *Migration, Minorities and Policy in the Netherlands; Recent Trends and Developments. Report for the Continuous Reporting System on Migration (SOPEMI) of the OECD.* Amsterdam: University of Amsterdam.

OECD. 1989. *Employment Outlook.* Paris.

Ostendorf, W., J. Buursink, and R. van Engelsdorp Gastelaars. 1988. *Steden. Deel 3 Atlas van Nederland.* Den Haag: Stichting Wetenschappelijke Atlas van Nederland, Staatsuitgeverij.

Schuyt, K. 1992. "Urban Poverty and Urban Renewal." Paper presented at the Conference on European Cities: Growth and Decline. The Hague

See, K. O'Sullivan. 1991. "Comments from the Special Issue Editor: Approaching Poverty in the United States." *Social Problems* 38(Nov):427–31.

Sociaal en Cultureel Planbureau (SCP). 1992. *Jongeren op de drempel van de jaren negentig.* Rijswijk: VUGA.

Swaan, A. de. 1988. *In Care of the State.* Cambridge: Polity Press.

Thomas, J. M. 1991. "The Cities Left Behind." *Built Environment* 17:218–31.

Wilson, W.J. 1987. *The Truly Disadvantaged: The Inner City, the Under-class, and Public Policy.* Chicago: University of Chicago Press.

Chapter 7

Between Integration and Marginalization: Foreign Population in the Ruhr Conurbation

Günter Thieme and Hans Dieter Laux

Germany has always refused to be considered as an immigration country although it has been the destination of large numbers of immigrants for a long time. Within the context of theoretical concepts on assimilation and marginalization, the analyses in this chapter examine integration of the foreign population into German society. Our specific focus is on immigrants within the cities of the Ruhr. The Ruhr area has been the heartland of German industrialization, it still is the largest conurbation of the country, and it has had a long history of immigration flows since the middle of the nineteenth century.

The chapter begins with a short review of immigration to Germany after 1949, then turns to a brief characterization of the recent economic changes in the Ruhr area and the development and spatial distribution of its foreign population. This is followed by a discussion of the concepts of assimilation and marginalization that leads to the identification of three broad dimensions of immigrant status: demographic structures, employment characteristics, and educational attainment. Specific measures of each of these dimensions are then utilized to assess integration of foreign populations in the Ruhr area. The conclusion discusses future prospects of foreign population in Germany and state policies of immigration and naturalization.

Immigration to Germany after 1949

In contrast to the former German Democratic Republic (GDR), the Federal Republic of Germany (FRG) has been a country with massive immigration since its foundation in 1949. Between 1950 and 1990, West Germany had a net immigration gain of more than 8.5 million people, which equals nearly two-thirds of the total population increase (Laux 1993, 198). Until the end of the 1950s these immigrants were predominantly expellees and refugees from the former German territories in Eastern Europe and from the GDR. After the Berlin Wall was built in 1961, immigration from East Germany was totally cut off from the FRG's booming labor market, a situation that led to a sharp increase in migration from other countries. Based on intergovernmental agreements between Germany and several Mediterranean countries, workers were first hired in Italy, Greece, and Spain.

After the economic recession of 1966–67, labor migrants from Yugoslavia and, above all, from Turkey became the most numerous groups of foreigners (Blotevogel, Müller-ter Jung, and Wood 1993,86ff.). In Germany, these persons euphemistically were called *Gastarbeiter* (guestworkers), which means that their stay was intended to be a temporary affair only. Indeed, in the very beginning, most of the foreign workers considered themselves as temporary migrants or sojourners. In 1973, 11.9 percent of the entire workforce was made up of foreigners, a share that has never again been reached. In the same year, cessation of recruitment for persons from non-EU countries ended this first stage of expansion. In spite of significantly reducing the number of employed foreigners, the halt in recruitment did not lead to the expected decrease of total foreign population. On the contrary, a structural change in the composition of foreign population occurred because in response to the policy of family reunification introduced by the German authorities, an increasing number of workers decided to bring their families to join them.

Until the middle of the 1980s, the international migration to Germany was dominated by the traditional labor migrants from the Mediterranean countries oscillating according to cycles of economic development. Since that time, however, two additional groups of immigrants have become increasingly important: (1) applicants for political asylum who were attracted by the economic opportunities and the liberal asylum regulation of the German constitution, and (2) *Aussiedler* (ethnic Germans) from eastern European countries (Kemper 1993). After the breakdown of the socialist system in eastern and southeastern Europe, these immigration flows dramatically rose to a maximum in 1992. Within the period from 1989 to 1992, the reunified Germany as a whole experienced a net migration gain of some 2.6 million people, half of them ethnic Germans who are not counted as "foreigners." In relative terms, this figure even surpassed the immigration rates of traditional immigration countries such as the United States and Canada.

Due to new regulations concerning the admission of ethnic Germans and a restrictive change of the asylum law in 1993, however, the numbers of immigrants significantly dropped after that year. The total number of foreigners in Germany had risen to an unprecedented level of 6.5 million persons, or 8.0 percent of the total population, at the end of 1992. In spite of the influx of new groups of immigrants, the socioeconomic and demographic structures of foreign population in Germany are still dominated by the traditional guestworkers and their families. Therefore, the following analyses will mainly focus on this group.

Before turning to the case study, a short explanation of the term foreigner should be given. In Germany, all persons without the legal status of a German citizen are considered and counted as foreigners. In contrast to countries where the "ius soli" is the legal basis of acquiring citizenship, being a German does not depend on the length of residence or on whether a person was born in Germany, but primarily on ethnic origin and ancestry ("ius sanguinis"). Consequently, no statistical information on race, ethnic origin or ancestry is available for all those who are or have become German citizens.

Changing Economic Structures

In the following analysis, the Ruhr area is defined as the territory of the *Kommunalverband Ruhrgebiet* comprising eleven *Kreisfreie Städte* and four *Landkreise* (fig. 7.1). This region, which at the end of 1992 had a total population of almost 5.4 million people, has been traditionally known as the largest conurbation and the most powerful industrial area in Germany, shaped by smokestack industries such as coal mining and iron and steel industries. This image, which originated from the economic booms of the late nineteenth century and the first decades after the Second World War, no longer corresponds with the real situation. Since the 1960s, the Ruhr area has been confronted by a sequence of severe economic crises leading to a fundamental restructuring of the economy (Dege 1991; Dege and Kerkemeyer 1993) and suffered from a permanent decrease of population mainly caused by migration losses (fig. 7.2). Since the end of the 1980s, however, a certain recovery has occurred, predominantly based on the influx of non-German population. Considering the development of the total labor force, this general trend becomes even more apparent. Between 1965 and 1985 the Ruhr conurbation lost more than 400,000 jobs, a decrease of almost 18 percent. In the same period, the rate of unemployment rose from virtually zero to 14.2

Fig. 7.1 The Ruhr Conurbation within the Federal Republic of Germany

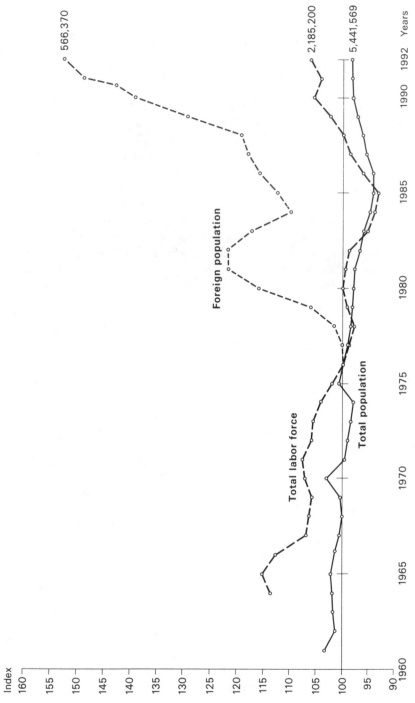

Fig. 7.2 Ruhr Area: Selected Indicators of Population and Employment (1976 = 100) (Kommunalverband Ruhrgebiet: Städte- und Kreisstatistik Ruhrgebiet, various years)

percent. The increase of about 250,000 jobs since 1985 is a sign of economic change and recovery.

Some additional indicators characterize the process of restructuring in the Ruhr area. The number of persons employed in mining and manufacturing decreased from roughly 1.4 million in 1965 to about 950,000 in 1991. This loss has been overwhelmingly caused by the dramatic decline of the mining and iron and steel industries. In the middle of the 1960s, these two traditional sectors still occupied more than 21 percent of the total labor force, a figure that dropped to 8.2 percent in 1991. This decrease was compensated by a significant upswing of the service sector during the last two decades. In spite of this development, the Ruhr conurbation must be considered as an economic region that is still marked by a comparatively strong position of the manufacturing sector. As a result of the process of economic restructuring, the manufacturing sector is more and more characterized by technologically advanced branches like environmental technology, which can be considered as one of the leading sectors of the fifth Kondratieff cycle starting in the eighties.

Development and Regional Distribution of Foreign Population

Compared to other metropolitan areas, especially in southern Germany, the development and composition of the foreign population in the Ruhr area displays the following characteristics: (1) the immigration of foreign workers and their families started somewhat later (Giese 1978); (2) the proportion of foreigners has never reached the values of cities such as München, Stuttgart, Frankfurt, or Köln, which have 15 to 20 percent of foreign population (O'Loughlin 1985); and (3) the composition of the foreign population in the Ruhr conurbation is marked by a strong predominance of persons of Turkish nationality (Bähr and Gans 1987).

Figure 7.2 shows the growth of the foreign population in the Ruhr area since 1976, the year after which detailed data on foreigners became available for smaller regional units. At this time, almost 372,000 persons, 7 percent of the total population, were counted as foreigners. In spite of the 1973 halt in recruitment for foreign labor, the number of non-German inhabitants rose to an all-time high in 1982. After a temporary decrease, a strong upswing of foreign population has taken place since the end of the 1980s, leading to a share of 10.4 percent in 1992. In contrast to the labor-oriented immigration from Mediterranean countries, the most recent increase of foreigners in the Ruhr conurbation is largely due to the asylum seekers and refugees particularly from eastern and southeastern Europe. Moreover, the natural growth attributable to the comparatively young foreign population already living in Germany is a remarkable component of the population growth. In 1992 nearly 19 percent of all births in the Ruhr area were from non-German parents and the natural increase of the foreign population amounted to more than ten thousand as compared to a natural loss among the German population of more than fifteen thousand.

The Turks make up the largest proportion of guestworkers in the Ruhr area (fig. 7.3). Between 1976 and 1992, their share rose from 43.0 to 45.7 percent, as compared to a figure of 30.3 percent for Germany as a whole in 1991. This increase is largely attributable to the natural growth of the Turkish population already living in Germany. In the Ruhr area, the immigrants from the former Yugoslavia come second; their remarkable rise during recent years is due to the flow of refugees from Croatia and Bosnia. In contrast, the Italians, Greeks, and Spaniards show an absolute decline in population between 1976 and 1992, indicating a significant remigration to their respec-

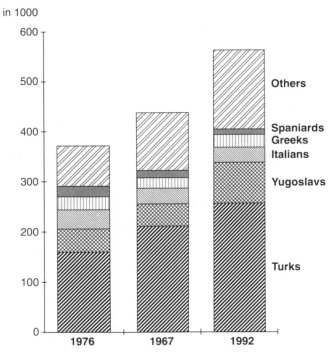

Fig. 7.3   Ruhr Area: Foreign Population by Nationality, 1976–1992
(Kommunalverband Ruhrgebiet: Städte- und Kreisstatistik Ruhrgebiet, various years)

tive home countries. Finally, the increasing number of "other nationalities" is due both to the immigration of asylum seekers and a growing share of highly educated and qualified migrants particularly from the countries of the European Union.

The total foreign population as well as the different nationalities are unevenly distributed across the cities and counties of the Ruhr area (fig. 7.4). The highest shares of foreigners can be found in cities having employment available in mining or steel and iron industries, such as Duisburg, Gelsenkirchen, and Hagen. In contrast, the service center of the Ruhr, the city of Essen, has a rather low percentage of foreigners. The association between economic structure and foreign population is even closer when the distribution of Turks is considered. Turks are concentrated in the northern parts of the Ruhr area where the mining and heavy industries are located. It is interesting to note that these strongholds of Turkish population in the Ruhr area coincide with the favorite destination areas of the large immigration flows of Poles during the last decades of the nineteenth century (Klessmann 1987).

Theoretical Considerations on the Integration of Foreigners in Germany

The immigration of various ethnic groups to Germany, at different time periods and with different legal statuses, has contributed to the phenomenon of ethnic stratification which is well known in countries with a long tradition of immigration (Heckmann 1992, 91ff.). The basic meaning of this term is that social status and positions in society are not only assigned by educational attainment, occupational qualification, or property, but also by criteria such as race, religion, and nationality. In Germany, the preconditions for ethnic stratification have been existent since the beginnings of the recruitment of foreign migrants because a specific underprivileged position in the labor market was provided for this "imported" workforce.

In the course of time, an increasing differentiation of immigrant population groups took place in Germany. The majority of the foreign population continued as a less-powerful part of the society, disadvantaged and discriminated against in many ways; but there also developed certain subgroups of foreign population that cannot be defined by their ethnic status alone. This combination of ethnic and class affiliation has a major influence on group formation and group consciousness. Gordon (1978) introduced the term *ethclass* for such social milieus or subsocieties that distinguish themselves by their nationality, class position, urban or rural way of life, and regional background. In the context of our study, this means that in the Ruhr area

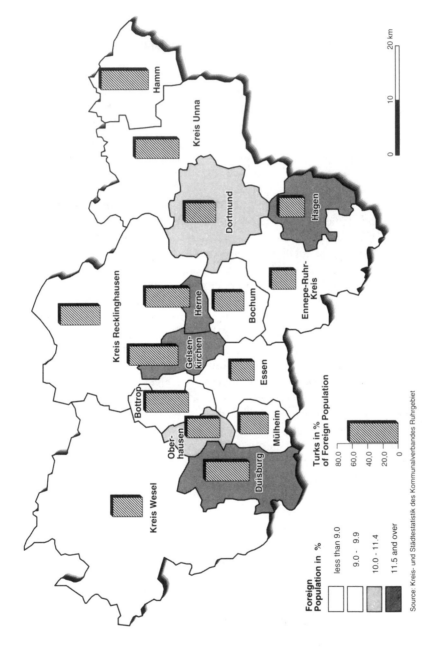

Source: Kreis- und Städtestatistik des Kommunalverbandes Ruhrgebiet

Fig. 7.4 Ruhr Area: Foreign Population, 1992 (Kommunalverband Ruhrgebiet: Städte- und Kreisstatistik Ruhrgebiet, various years)

there have developed subgroups such as the Turkish skilled workers, the Greek owners of small businesses, the semiskilled Moroccan laborers, and the Romanian asylum seekers. When these groups no longer perceive themselves as sojourners, the problem of their assimilation and integration into the German host society becomes increasingly urgent.

In his classic study *Assimilation in American Life*, Gordon distinguishes seven different types or stages of assimilation (1964, 71). Characteristically, cultural assimilation, or acculturation is the first step of this process. The crucial stage of the whole assimilation process, however, is structural assimilation, that is, large-scale entrance into cliques, clubs, and institutions of the host society on the primary-group level, normally combined with intermarriage and the absence of prejudice and discrimination toward the immigrant group. Thus, an ethnically egalitarian social structure appears to be the implicit objective of Gordon's approach.

It is evident that substantial parts of the foreign population in Germany, especially the Turks as the largest group, are far from having attained structural assimilation. Whereas many "material" aspects of the host country's culture tend to be rapidly accepted by most of the foreign immigrants, the situation is different from the "immaterial" aspects of religion, norms, and values. Here, ethnic minorities usually are much more resistant toward the influences of the majority culture (Heckmann 1992, 183).

In contrast to approaches emphasizing the assimilation process, theories of marginalization (Park 1928; Stonequist 1937) focus on the fact that many immigrants are forced to live in two different or even antagonistic cultures. Modifying the classical theory, Heckmann does not concentrate on "marginal man" as a type of personality but introduces the concept of marginal positions in society. Typically, in these positions group affiliations are uncertain or unclear. In the German context, this means that the situation of the first-generation and, particularly, second-generation immigrants is characterized by the loss of ties to the culture of the home country through partial assimilation and also a lack of acceptance in the host society. Often different forces of socialization are effective at home or at school, in the family or at the workplace. In the majority of cases, the immigrants have not become naturalized citizens although their permanent residences have always been in the host country.

In order to find empirical support for the conflicting theories of either integration or marginalization, various studies have investigated the relationship between variables such as length of stay, segregation, interethnic contacts and ethnic identification (Esser 1981), or language competence, educational attainment, age at immigration, and concentration of foreigners in residential areas (Esser 1982). Within the structural approach used in this study, three major sets of aggregate indicators are utilized to measure the degree of integration of the various foreign population groups in the Ruhr area. These are (1) demographic structures, (2) employment characteristics, and (3) educational attainment.

Demographic Characteristics

Basic demographic measures can be important indicators of the immigration history and the growth potential of particular populations. As a first step, the analysis of the sex and age composition of different nationalities proves to be instructive. A good example is the city of Duisburg, one of the remaining centers of heavy industry and the place with the highest percentage of foreign population in the Ruhr area.

The age pyramids of Duisburg's German, Italian, and Turkish populations in 1987 contrast significantly (fig. 7.5). The German population is characterized by a small base, a bulge formed by the baby-boom generation of the 1960s, the birth losses attributable to the Second World War and the early postwar period, and finally the large surplus of women caused both by an excess male mortality and the deaths from the two world wars. The Italians, an example of the first wave of immigrants to Germany, have a strong surplus of males, particularly in the later years of their working age. In sharp contrast to this, the age distribution of Italian women appears to be more "normal." The narrow base of the pyramid is very similar to the German population. The imbalance between the sexes indicates, however, that this is not a stable population that has come to stay permanently. Indeed, the rate of remigration is high among the Italian immigrants to Germany: between 75 and 90 percent depending on the year of immigration went back to Italy within eight to nine years (Kreutz 1990, 51). Moreover, the economic development of Italy during the last two decades certainly has eased the pressure to make one's fortune abroad. The decline of the Italian population already mentioned above (fig. 7.3) gives support to this interpretation.

The population structure of the Turks in Duisburg is remarkably different. On the one hand, there are very few people older than sixty years because the Turks were among the most recent immigrants coming to Germany. There is a considerable surplus of males among the Turkish inhabitants older than forty who had been recruited as temporary workers and in most cases had come without bringing their families. The sex ratio is more balanced for the younger age groups, containing more people who were born in Germany. In addition, after recruitment ceased in 1973, Turkish immigrants in principle were only allowed to enter the country for reasons of family reunification,

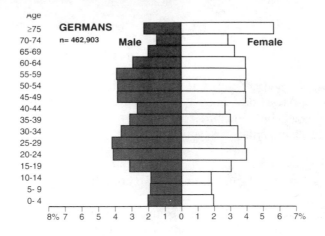

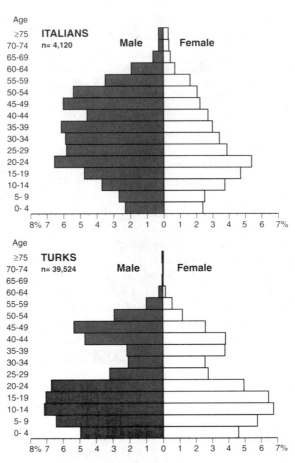

Fig. 7.5   City of Duisburg: Population Pyramids for Selected Nationalities, 1987
(Population census 1987, unpublished material)

a measure that increased the number of wives joining their husbands abroad. In contrast to the Italian or Spanish immigrants, the rate of remigration has always been rather low, another indication that the term *Gastarbeiter* (guestworker), which is widely used in Germany, is grossly wrong—at least for the Turkish population—because a substantial proportion has abandoned the plan of ever returning to their home country.

The shrinking base of the Turkish pyramid suggests declining fertility. By the end of the period 1975 to 1985, the total fertility rate (TFR) of most nationalities (table 7.1) was equal to or lower than that of the German population (1.28). Even the fertility of Turkish women, which had been rather high in 1975, was only slightly above replacement level in 1985. This apparent trend of convergence between the generative behavior of immigrants and German nationals can be seen as an indicator of at least partial adaptation and assimilation to the value system and social norms of the host society.

Another important indicator is the duration of stay in Germany. The Spaniards, Italians, and Greeks are the groups with the highest percentage of persons living in Germany for more than twenty years (table 7.2). While the majority of these immigrants from the European Mediterranean countries remigrated after only a few years, a significant portion decided to stay in Germany. Moreover, it must be taken into account that among the persons staying less than twenty years, there is a large number of children born to parents who have been living in Germany for a long time. This is particularly true for the Turkish population. Referring to their age pyramid (fig. 7.5) the comparatively high share of persons with a stay of less than twenty years must be contributed to an above-average fertility level as well as to the general process of family reunification and family formation. Among the Turks there is an increasing number of second- and third-generation "immigrants" who

Table 7.1   Total Fertility Rates of Immigrants in Germany, 1975 and 1985

Nationality	1975	1985
Greeks	2.84	1.25
Italians	2.34	1.53
Spaniards	2.00	1.24
Yugoslavs	2.15	1.40
Turks	4.30	2.41

Source: OECD Migration Data Base.

Table 7.2   **Ruhr Area: Duration of Stay of Foreign Populations, 1992**

Nationality	Less than 10 years (%)	10 to 20 years (%)	More than 20 years (%)
Greeks	29.1	20.9	50.0
Italians	22.1	26.5	51.4
Spaniards	11.0	20.3	68.7
Yugoslavs	55.9	21.3	22.8
Turks	31.4	46.2	22.4

Source: Statistisches Landesamt Nordrhein-Westfalen (unpublished material).

were born in Germany. In contrast to this, the short stay of the Yugoslavs is mainly the result of the recent influx of refugees and asylum seekers.

Household structure is an additional distinguishing feature of foreign populations (fig. 7.6). In Germany, the Ruhr conurbation is not among the

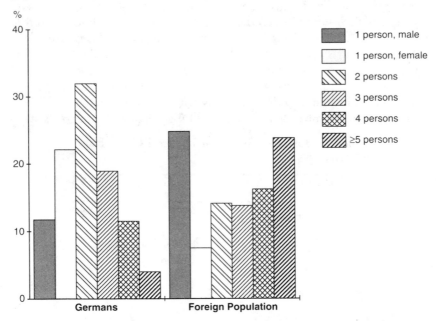

Fig. 7.6   Ruhr Area: Households by Size, 1987 (Population census 1987, unpublished material)

pioneers of diversified family forms and household types which are found in the more socially progressive service metropolises such as München, Frankfurt, Hamburg, or Berlin. Nevertheless, among the German population, the number of one-person households (particularly females) exceeds all other household sizes. There is a continuous decline in the number of households with increasing household size. The situation is totally different from the foreign population (for which, unfortunately, the figures cannot be broken down to different nationalities). Here we find a bipolar distribution of households with the first maximum for male one-person households and a second maximum for households with five or more persons. One-person and even two-person households of foreigners frequently are binational households, meaning the parents or one parent lives abroad while the children and, possibly, grandparents stay at home. The large households of foreigners can be explained by a large number of children or by the presence of non-family members.

Employment Characteristics

Among all socioeconomic variables, labor-force participation and employment structure undoubtedly are among the most important indicators of integration into the host society. Massive labor migration into Germany started in the 1960s when German employers were eager to compensate the increasing lack of labor force caused by a strong economic boom, and the building of the Berlin Wall. The large majority of these migrants came from Mediterranean countries. In Germany, they predominantly took on unskilled or semiskilled blue collar jobs that were increasingly rejected and abandoned by the German labor force. From this point of view, the labor migrants can be described as an "industrial reserve army."

The foreign labor force in the Ruhr area is concentrated in a small number of industries (table 7.3). More than 65 percent of non-German employees can be found in energy and mining, manufacturing, and construction, the industries most severely affected by the process of economic restructuring. In contrast to this, the branches of the service sector show a proportion of foreigners generally below average. The position of foreigners in the German labor market has changed little during the last ten years. There continues to be a strong concentration in the less-attractive, low-paid, and insecure segments of the labor market, and foreigners undoubtedly are among the groups most vulnerable in times of economic recession or restructuring. The unemployment rate dramatically summarizes this marginal position. In the

Table 7.3   **Ruhr Area: Foreign Labor Force by Industry, 1991**

Industry	Foreign component of total labor force(%)	Component of foreign labor force(%)
Agriculture, forestry	8.3	0.7
Energy, mining	14.9	15.6
Manufacturing	9.6	40.9
Construction	9.6	8.6
Retail trade, wholesale trade	3.8	7.3
Transport, communication	5.7	3.8
Finance, insurance	0.8	0.4
Other services	7.0	19.4
Public service, administration	3.2	3.4
Total	7.7	100.0

Source: Kommunalverband Ruhrgebiet: Städte- und Kreisstatistik Ruhrgebiet 1992.

Ruhr area in December 1993, the rate was 24.1 percent for foreigners compared to 12.7 percent for the total population.

One aspect of increasing importance is the phenomenon of self-employment among foreigners in Germany. Although self-employment and the foundation of small businesses have not played a role comparable to that of various ethnic groups in the United States, in 1985 some 140,000 foreigners in Germany were self-employed (including their supporting family members). There is a strong concentration in a few business types. In a sample study of Turkish enterprises in the three Ruhr cities of Essen, Dortmund, and Duisburg, more than 40 percent of the businesses were groceries. Restaurants came next with 21 percent followed by tailors with 10.5 percent (Zentrum für Türkeistudien 1989, 47). Most of these businesses are not restricted to ethnic enclaves and therefore are making some progress toward leaving the niche economy. While this is by no means a general trend, the increasing number of ethnic businesses can be interpreted as a step of assimilation into the German society.

Variations in labor-force participation also characterize the foreign population of Germany (table 7.4). Even considering the influence of contrasting age structures, there is a striking contrast between the Greeks, Italians, and Yugoslavs on the one hand and the Turks on the other hand. Thus, the extremely low employment rate of the Turkish women can be interpreted as a consequence of the traditional family pattern and the social position of women typical of an Islamic society. This observation may also serve as an indicator of the numerous barriers to assimilation and integration still existing among the Turkish population. In contrast, the Yugoslavs, Italians, and Greeks show a behavior that seems to be very similar to the German population. In particular, the Greeks have been quite successful in entering the female labor market, thus indicating a comparatively high socioeco-nomic achievement.

Educational Attainment

The socioeconomic status of most of the foreign population is rather low, even though the situation varies among the different foreign groups. There is general agreement that education is the most important factor influencing the degree of acculturation and that an improved educational attainment can open the door to social mobility and increase the chances of achieving a higher socioeconomic status. A recent sample study of Turkish fathers and sons in the state of Nordrhein-Westfalen, whose core region is the Ruhr area, showed that educational attainment is closely related to the degree of

Table 7.4 Ruhr Area: Labor Force Participation Rate by Nationality, 1987

Nationality	Labor force as % of total population		
	total	male	female
Germans	43.8	59.2	30.1
Greeks	53.6	66.1	39.4
Italians	57.9	72.9	34.3
Yugoslavs	53.1	68.0	33.7
Turks	35.0	53.2	13.8

Source: Population Census 1987 (unpublished material).

integration into the host society (Schultze 1991, 424). The continuation of a poorer standard of education will ensure that disadvantage or even marginality will be passed from one generation to the next.

German schools are run and, particularly, financed by the *Länder* (states), not by the federal authorities. School attendance is compulsory from the age of six to fifteen. Apart from special schools for the physically or mentally handicapped, there is no distinction of school types in the first four years (elementary school). After that, there is, in most cases, a subdivision into three types of schools: the *Hauptschule*, which a majority of students attend for another six years before becoming blue-collar workers; the *Gymnasium*, which after another nine years qualifies one for going to a university; the *Realschule*, which is in between the other two types. Recently, there has been a tendency toward a comprehensive school system (*Gesamtschule*), especially in strongholds of the Social Democrats such as the Ruhr area.

In 1993, the types of schools attended varied between the different nationalities (fig. 7.7). The proportion of students attending the *Grundschule* (elementary school) is primarily influenced by the age structure and conse-

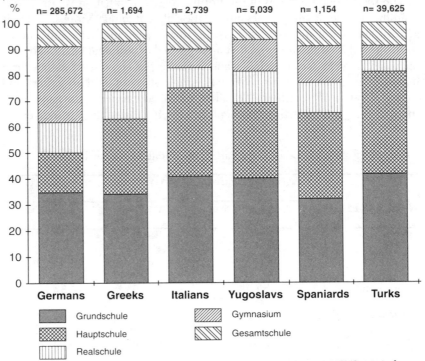

Fig. 7.7   Ruhr Area: Students by Nationality and School Type, 1993 (Statistisches Landesamt Nordrhein-Westfalen, unpublished material)

quently the fertility level of a specific population. These rates are very low among the Spaniards and the Greeks, a reflection of the low fertility of these population groups. When we proceed to the proportion of students in *Hauptschulen*, the least prestigious of all secondary schools, significant differences emerge. Whereas less than 10 percent of Germans attend this type of school, almost 27 percent of the Turks and more than 30 percent of the students from the former Yugoslavia are to be found in these schools, which have seen a rapid decline of importance among the German majority. The contrary is true for the upper level of secondary schools, the *Gymnasium*: the proportion of Germans (25 percent) is much larger than the percentage of Turks and Italians qualifying to attend this more prestigious school. Among the groups of foreign population, the Greeks appear to have the highest aspirations toward educational qualification.

Examination of changing school attendance patterns provides additional insight. For this purpose the percentage shares of the three traditional types of secondary schools (adding up to 100 percent) are plotted for six selected nationalities (fig. 7.8). A clear disparity continues to exist between German children and the children of foreign immigrants, but some groups definitely have caught up. Whereas in 1979, Greeks, Italians, and Yugoslavs had a proportion of about 80 percent of the students attending the lowest level of secondary school, and the Turks had even more, this situation has changed considerably within less than fifteen years. Particularly the Greeks, but also the Spaniards, have been quite successful in reaching a higher level of educational qualification. The Turks still are the group with the greatest handicap.

Attending a certain type of school, however, does not necessarily imply successful completion. In the survey on Turkish social mobility (Schultze 1991), over 40 percent of the second generation had not even completed a basic general education (*Hauptschulabschluß*). Such a low level of qualification almost inevitably will restrict future employment to the unskilled or semiskilled segment of the labor market. This in turn may lead to feelings of resignation and frustration. Even in a region like the Ruhr where processes of immigration and assimilation have a continuous tradition, acculturation and social integration do not come automatically—educational qualification and vocational training must be used as tools to stimulate these processes.

Prospects and Policies

Are there distinct trends toward integration or even assimilation of foreign groups, parts of which have been in the Ruhr region for several decades now,

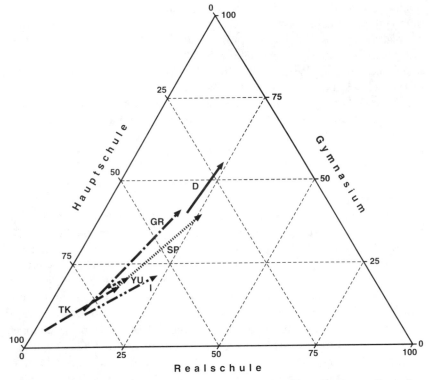

Fig. 7.8   Cities in the Ruhr Area: Secondary School Students by Nationality and
School Type, 1979 and 1993 (Statistisches Landesamt Nordrhein-Westfalen,
unpublished material)

or is the foreign population still characterized by a marginal position in the
German society?

Obviously, there cannot be a simple answer to such a complicated
question—the differences between and within the various ethnic groups of
foreigners simply are too great. Some tendencies and trends emerge, however.
On the one hand, there are clearly visible signs of acculturation, especially
with regard to material aspects of culture. Even some important behavioral
attitudes such as generative behavior or attitudes toward saving and acquisi-
tion of housing property (Zentrum für Türkeistudien 1989, 2ff.) appear to
have changed considerably. Much less change has occurred in other, more
fundamental aspects of norms and values, especially among the largest
foreign group, the Turks, whose Muslim religion makes integration into the
social system of the host country more difficult.

Considering structural assimilation, only limited progress can be seen so far. Foreigners, no matter whether first or second generation, still have a marginal position in the labor market and suffer a much higher risk of unemployment than the rest of the population. Also, there continue to exist large disparities in educational attainment and qualification although remarkable progress has been made by some nationalities. Moreover, there is still considerable residential segregation between the native population and most of the immigrant groups, although the indices are much lower compared to case studies in the United States. In summary, there seems to be more evidence for the marginalization theory than for successful integration and structural assimilation.

What consequences could exist for state policies in such a situation? Germany has always claimed not to be an immigration country, but in reality there has been an extraordinarily strong immigration to the Federal Republic of Germany since its foundation in 1949. Considering the long tradition of foreign immigration to Germany (Bade 1991), it will be necessary to develop a responsible immigration legislation. Leaving all other causes apart, the demographic aging process alone will require substantial labor immigration to Germany after the turn of the century (Schmid and Chruscz 1994, 38ff.; Fijalkowski 1994, 188).

The second intensively and controversially discussed issue is the amendment of German naturalization legislation. The original law of 1913 emphasizes the so-called *ius sanguinis*, the right of the blood. This means that citizenship is based on ethnic origin. As a consequence, Germany has had, until recently, a very restrictive naturalization system in which foreigners were not legally entitled to become German citizens even if they had lived in the country for many years or were born in Germany. Since 1990, this legislation has gradually been changed. Today, young foreigners between ages fifteen and twenty-three, resident in Germany for at least eight years, and other foreign persons living in Germany for at least fifteen years are entitled to become German citizens. In all other cases, naturalization still is very much a matter of discretion. In recent years the numbers of naturalizations, excluding ethnic Germans, have increased (27,000 in 1991 compared with an average of 14,000 during the years 1984–87), but these are still very low figures in comparison with other European countries such as the Netherlands or Sweden (Hullen and Schulz 1993–94, 23). Increasingly, however, it is argued that the process of integration not only implies that immigrants are prepared to accept the basic values and constitutional principles of the host country, it also requires that the host society be willing to accept the foreigners without demanding complete assimilation. This also implies that social integration must be combined with legal integration,

162 Günter Thieme and Hans Dieter Laux

that is, a substantial improvement of the legal position of immigrants (Wollenschläger 1994, 206ff.).

Xenophobic excesses cannot be prevented by the fact that immigrants become naturalized citizens, but citizenship is a precondition for an improved legal and social status. Thus, an immigration law as well as additional reforms of naturalization legislation will be necessary parts of facing and accepting the realities of international migratory movements in Germany (Cohn-Bendit and Schmid 1992, 328ff.) and at the same time be tools to regulate the flows of immigrants.

References

Bade, Klaus J., ed. 1991. *Deutsche im Ausland—Fremde in Deutschland. Migration in Geschichte und Gegenwart.* München: C.H. Beck.

Bähr, Jürgen, and Paul Gans. 1987. "Development of the German and Foreign Population in the Larger Cities of the Federal Republic of Germany Since 1970." In *Foreign Minorities in Continental European Cities*, ed. Günther Glebe and John O'Loughlin. Stuttgart: Franz Steiner.

Blotevogel, Hans Heinrich, Ursula Müller-ter Jung, and Gerald Wood. 1993. "From Itinerant Worker to Immigrant? The Geography of Guestworkers in Germany." In *Mass Migrations in Europe. The Legacy and the Future*, ed. Russell King. London: Belhaven.

Cohn-Bendit, Daniel, and Thomas Schmid. 1992. *Heimat Babylon. Das Wagnis der multikulturellen Demokratie.* Hamburg: Hoffmann und Campe.

Dege, Wilfried. 1991. "Das Ruhrgebiet—eine Industrieregion im Wandel." In *Industriegeographie der Bundesrepublik Deutschland und Frankreichs in den 1980er Jahren*, ed. Wolfgang Brücher, Reinhold Grotz, and Alfred Pletsch. Studien zur Schulbuchforschung 70:75–95.

Dege, Wilfried, and Sabine Kerkemeyer. 1993. "Der wirtschaftliche Wandel im Ruhrgebiet in den 80er Jahren." *Geographische Rundschau* 45:503–9.

Esser, Hartmut. 1981. "Aufenthaltsdauer und Eingliederung von Wandern. Zur theoretischen Interpretation soziologischer 'Variablen.' " *Zeitschrift für Soziologie* 10:76–97.

———. 1982. "Sozialräumliche Bedingungen der sprachlichen Assimilation von Arbeitsmigranten." *Zeitschrift für Soziologie* 11:279–306.

Fijalkowski, Jürgen. 1994. "Zuwanderung und Ausländerfeindlichkeit—Handlungsmöglichkeiten der Politik." In *Migration und Ausländerfeind-*

lichkeit, ed. Gernot Böhme, Rabindra Chakraborty and Frank Weiler. Darmstadt: Wissenschaftliche Buchgesellschaft.

Giese, Ernst. 1978. "Räumliche Diffusion ausländischer Arbeitnehmer in der Bundesrepublik Deutschland 1960–1976." *Die Erde* 109:92–100.

Gordon, Milton M. 1964. *Assimilation in American Life: The Role of Race, Religion, and National Origin.* New York: Oxford University Press.

———. 1978. *Human Nature, Class, and Ethnicity.* New York: Oxford University Press.

Heckmann, Friedrich. 1992. *Ethnische Minderheiten, Volk und Nation. Soziologie inter-ethnischer Beziehungen.* Stuttgart: Ferdinand Enke.

Hullen, Gerd, and Reiner Schulz. 1993–94. "Bericht 1993 zur demographischen Lage in Deutschland." *Zeitschrift für Bevölkerungswissenschaft* 19:3–70.

Kemper, Franz-Josef. 1993. "New Trends in Mass Migration in Germany." *Mass Migrations in Europe: The Legacy and the Future,* ed. Russell King. London: Belhaven.

Klessmann, Christoph. 1987. "Long-Distance Migration, Integration and Segregation of an Ethnic Minority in Industrial Germany: the Case of the 'Ruhr-Poles.' " In *Population, Labour and Migration in the 19th- and 20th-Century Germany,* ed. Klaus J. Bade. Leamington Spa et al.: Berg.

Kreutz, Henrik. 1990. "Europäische Integration, Weltoffenheit und nationale Identität. Wie deutsch ist die Bundesrepublik? Wie deutsch soll sie sein?" In *Zu viele Fremde im Land?,* ed. Paul Bocklet. Düsseldorf: Patmos.

Laux, Hans Dieter. 1993. "Grundzüge der Bevölkerungsentwicklung in den beiden deutschen Staaten bis zur Wiedervereinigung." In *Bevölkerung und Raum,* ed. Dieter Börsch. Handbuch des Geographieunterrichts, Vol. 2. Köln: Aulis.

O'Loughlin, John. 1985. "The Geographic Distribution of Foreigners in West Germany." *Regional Studies* 19:365–77.

Park, Robert E. 1928. "Human Migration and the Marginal Man." *American Journal of Sociology* 33:881–93.

Richmond, Anthony H. 1988. *Immigration and Ethnic Conflict.* London.

Schmid, Josef, and Detlef Chruscz. 1994. "Demographische Untersuchung zur Frage eines Einwanderungsbedarfs in der Europäischen Union." *Forum Demographie und Politik* 5:18–45.

Schultze, Günther. 1991. "Der berufliche und soziale Eingliederungsprozeß der ersten und zweiten Generation türkischer Arbeitnehmer in Nordrhein-Westfalen." *Informationen zur Raumentwicklung* 7/8:421–427.

Şen, Faruk, and Andreas Goldberg. 1994. *Türken in Deutschland: Leben zwischen zwei Kulturen*. München: C.H. Beck.

Stonequist, Everett V. 1937. *The Marginal Man: A Study in Personality and Culture Conflict*. New York: Russell & Russell.

Wollenschläger, Michael. 1994. "Migrationspolitik und Zuwanderungsrecht, Illegalität und Legalisierung, Integration und Staatsangehörigkeitsrecht." In *Das Manifest der 60. Deutschland und die Einwanderung*, ed. Klaus J. Bade. München: C.H. Beck.

Zentrum für Türkeistudien, ed. 1989. *Türkische Unternehmensgründungen— von der Nische zum Markt? Ergebnisse der MAGS-Untersuchung bei türkischen Selbständigen in Dortmund, Duisburg und Essen*. Studien und Arbeiten des Zentrums für Türkeistudien 5. Opladen: Leske & Budrich.

Chapter 8

Between Melting Pot and Ethnic Fragmentation: Historical and Recent Immigration to Vienna

Heinz Fassmann and Rainer Münz

In the nineteenth and early twentieth centuries, Vienna was an important European metropolis. Elites came to the capital of the Austro-Hungarian Empire, as did laborers from the eastern parts of Europe. After 1918, Vienna lost importance, attractiveness, and inhabitants. However, since the late 1970s, there have been distinct signs of change. Vienna and its historical inner city have become attractive once more as a business site, a holiday destination, and a place to live. This has led to immigration from within Austria and from abroad. The consequences of this new wave of immigration are already visible: a renewed housing shortage and political and social conflicts directly linked to the large number of labor immigrants in certain areas.

In this chapter, we elaborate on three different topics: (1) how many migrants are in Vienna, the source of Vienna's immigrants, and how this has changed; (2) where immigrants are placed in the labor and housing markets, and how immigrants are spread across the city in 1991; and (3) what kinds of integration (or nonintegration) exist, and which political perspectives are relevant to an ethnically pluralist society in the city. Data utilized in this chapter are primarily based on the censuses of 1857 through 1991, and on a survey of place of birth and migration from the microcensus of 1988.

Changing Ethnic Composition of the Viennese Population

The ethnic and cultural mix of the populations of the great European metropolises is the result of their historical growth, even if more remote descendants of the immigrants refute this and with it their own origins. Welsh, Scots, and Irish came to London, followed later by people from the British colonies overseas. Until the Second World War, Berlin was the center of attraction for people from the eastern parts of the German Empire, Poles, and people from the Baltics, and it probably will remain so in the future. In the nineteenth century, people were also attracted to Vienna from all parts of the Habsburg Empire and beyond. The city "burst at the seams."

The Historical Pattern

In 1790, the population of Vienna, including its suburbs, was approximately 200,000. By 1860, it had reached no more than 500,000, but by 1910 it exceeded two million. The average annual population increase was about 15,000 between 1850 and 1914. In the late nineteenth and early twentieth centuries, Vienna was by far the most attractive city in the Austrian part of the empire (Fassmann 1986). Immigration changed both the social structure and the geographic origins of the Viennese population, and the "real" Viennese were actually in the minority. In 1880 (table 8.1), over 60 percent of the people living in the Austrian capital had been born outside the city itself. By 1910, their share was still 51 percent. In 1900, more than a quarter of the Viennese population were immigrants from Bohemia, Moravia, and the Austrian part of Silesia, and almost a tenth of the population were born in another European country: in Hungary (under constitutional law the provinces of the Hungarian Crown were considered "foreign" after 1867), Germany, and Italy. In 1900, only a small share of the population came from the German-speaking alpine provinces of the Austro-Hungarian Empire.

Development of the Viennese Population after 1918

After the fall of the Habsburg Empire, immigration into the former imperial capital came to a halt. Many migrants, notably Czechs and Poles, went back to their countries of origin, which had become sovereign states in 1918. The population of Vienna began to shrink from its 1914 population of 2.1 million. In 1923, Vienna had 1.87 million inhabitants, and those born outside the city still made up the majority (table 8.2). At the beginning of the 1930s, about a fifth of the population came from Bohemia and Moravia and some 15 percent from lower Austria.

The political situation during the 1930s—civil war, authoritarian regime (1934–38), "Anschluß" to Nazi Germany—accelerated the fall in the population of Vienna. About 200,000 Viennese either went into exile, had to flee, or were deported into concentration camps and murdered. In 1945–46, only

Table 8.1   Vienna: Origins of Population by Place of Birth, 1857–1910

	1857[a] abs.	%	1880 abs.	%	1890 abs.	%	1900 abs.	%	1910 abs.	%
Vienna	205,531	43.8	271,429	38.5	610,062	44.7	777,105	46.4	991,157	48.8
Alpine provinces[b]	88,000	18.7	131,694	18.7	206,774	15.1	250,857	15.0	301,275	14.8
Bohemia, Moravia, Silesia	105,353	22.4	201,251	28.6	378,074	27.7	438,695	26.2	499,272	24.6
Galicia, Bukovina	3,417	0.7	13,577	1.9	24,163	1.8	36,763	2.2	47,115	2.3
Provinces Austrian part of Empire	1,492	0.3	3,874	0.5	7,757	0.6	8,958	0.5	9,841	0.5
Hungarian crown lands[c]	23,547	5.0	54,128	7.7	100,666	7.4				
German States/German Empire	22,780	4.9	20,142	2.9	25,515	1.9				
Other foreign countries[d]	3,093	0.7	8,661	1.2	11,537	0.8	162,579	9.7	182,761	9.0
Total	469,221	100.0	704,756	100.0	1,364,548	100.0	1,674,957	100.0	2,031,421	100.0

Source: Calculations based on John and Lichtblau 1990.
[a]Unknown in 1857: 16,008 or 3.4 percent.
[b]Carinthia, Lower and Upper Austria, Salzburg, Styria (including Lower Styria = Slovenia), Tyrol (including Trento and Bolzano), Vorarlberg; 1857: including Krain, Görz, Gradisca, Dalmatia, Istria, and Trieste.
[c]Today's Hungary, Slovakia, Banat, Transsylvania, Croatia, Slavonia, Burgenland and Fiume/Rijeka.
[d]Since 1900: Hungary, the German Empire and other foreign countries not separately shown.

Table 8.2 Vienna: Population by Place of Birth, 1923–1988

	1923 abs.	%	1934 abs.	%	1951 abs.	%	1971 abs.	%	1988 abs.	%
Vienna	1,004,301	53.8	1,077,102	57.5	1,134,192	64.2	1,054,192	65.3	932,697	62.9
Other Austrian provinces	304,737	16.3	349,133	18.6	329,086	18.6	312,563	19.4	332,153	22.4
Foreign countries	556,742	29.9	447,895	23.9	302,824	17.2	247,490	15.3	217,975	14.7
Total	1,865,780	100.0	1,874,130	100.0	1,766,102	100.0	1,614,841	100.0	1,482,825	100.0

Source: Estimates based on John and Lichtblau 1990; 1988 data are projections from the Austrian microcensus February 1988.

a few exiles and Nazi victims returned to Vienna. The immigrants of the early postwar years were primarily new refugees and people expelled from Eastern Europe, but also "displaced persons" who ended up in Austria more or less by chance. After the beginning of the Cold War and the establishment of the Iron Curtain, hundreds of thousands of Eastern European refugees left their home countries. This emigration had several peaks in the crisis periods of communist rule (Hungary 1956, Czechoslovakia 1968, Poland 1980–81, GDR 1989). Many of these refugees were temporary migrants to Vienna who sooner or later became residents of Germany, the United States, Canada, Australia, or South Africa.

In 1951 Vienna had 1.77 million inhabitants, of whom almost two-thirds were born in the capital (table 8.2). By 1971, the population had fallen to 1.61 million and by the mid-1980s to as low as 1.5 million. The three main reasons for this decline were the low birth rate, the continuous process of suburbanization that led to an exodus of young adults to the surrounding small cities and villages, and the decreasing influx of people from Austria's other federal provinces. Both suburbanization and reduced immigration can be interpreted as indicators of the fact that since the 1950s the attractiveness of Vienna had been declining.

Recent Immigration

In the second half of the twentieth century, the people born in Vienna formed a clear majority of the population, exceeding 60 percent in each census year (table 8.2), despite the influx of refugees from Eastern Europe and of labor migrants from the former Yugoslavia and Turkey. At the end of the 1980s, only 37 percent of Viennese had been born outside of the city: about 332,000 came from other Austrian provinces and about 218,000 from abroad (table 8.3).

The question of how many "immigrants" actually live in Vienna is not easy to answer statistically. The figure depends on the methodology of the survey or the administrative database used, and on the definition of "immigrant." The microcensus refers to the population's place of birth, whereas the population register and the 1991 census refer to nationality. Vienna's population register suggests that on 1 January 1991, 206,003 foreigners were living in Vienna. The national census of 1991 indicates a lower figure (196,625). In 1993, the proportion of foreigners living in Vienna was 12.8 percent, which is considerably lower than in comparable European cities (Munich: 20 percent, Frankfurt: 27 percent, Zurich: 20 percent).

The official figure does not include the unknown number of unregistered foreigners living in Vienna. Estimates vary from 50,000 to 100,000 illegal

Table 8.3 Vienna: The Nine Most Important Countries of Origin by Place of Birth (1988) or Nationality (1988 and 1991)

Country of origin	Microcensus (place of birth) 1988		Population register (nationality) 1988		Population register (nationality) 1991	
	abs.	%	abs.	%	abs.	%
Former Yugoslavia	57,886	30.8	61,410	38.1	91,447	44.4
Former Czechoslovakia	33,898	18.0	1,742	1.1	4,062	2.0
Germany	20,663	11.0	7,238	4.5	9,321	4.5
Turkey	(13,428)	(7.1)	33,907	21.1	46,858	22.7
Poland	(12,967)	(6.9)	8,867	5.5	15,891	7.7
Hungary	(8,933)	(4.7)	2,526	1.6	5,159	2.5
Romania	(4,934)	(2.6)	387	0.2	3,060	1.5
Italy	(4,483)	(2.4)	1,589	1.0	2,086	1.0
CIS	(2,762)	(1.5)	390	0.2	1,116	0.5
Total	218,000	100.0	160,710	100.0	206,003	100.0

Sources: Austrian microcensus 1988; Viennese population register; author's calculations. *Note*: The relative random sampling error is about 20 percent in the case of the frequencies shown in brackets. The actual figure can thus deviate substantially from the sampling figures. This should be taken into account when interpreting the figures.

immigrants and the Viennese police quote a figure of 90,000 to 100,000. Included in this, however, are quite a large number of "working tourists," who only live and work in Vienna temporarily or irregularly but not on a permanent basis.

Of the approximately 218,000 Viennese (both Austrians and foreign nationals) who were born outside Austria in 1988, almost one-third came from former Yugoslavia and one-sixth from the Czech Republic. A further tenth had immigrated from Germany. The proportions of immigrants from Turkey, Poland, Hungary, Romania, Slovakia, and Italy (including numerous South Tyroleans) were even smaller.

The year 1988 was the last before the start of a considerable wave of immigration caused by the fall of the Iron Curtain. The population register shows an increase in the foreign population of more than 28 percent for the period between 1988 and 1991. This corresponds to an increase of nearly 10 percent a year (table 8.3). The 1991 census indicates an increase of 83,000 foreigners (73.4 percent) in Vienna compared to the 1981 census.

Where naturalization is rapid, the statistics show a considerably higher number of immigrants from a particular country than of nationals of that country. In general this indicates historical and cultural affinities between the country of origin and the country of destination. In the case of Vienna, this is true for immigrants from Germany, the Czech Republic, and Slovakia. Where naturalization is delayed, or where there is only a slight tendency to take up Austrian nationality, the number of nationals of a particular country of origin remains high. This is true both for immigrants who came recently and for immigrant groups with high fertility. By law, children of immigrants born in Vienna receive the nationality of their parents, since Austria does not automatically grant citizenship to all children born on its soil.

With regard to the geographical origins of immigrants, there is a wide gap between the public perception and empirical findings. Most Viennese would estimate the proportion of Turks, Romanians, and immigrants from the former Yugoslavia to be much higher than it actually is. People who came to Austria as displaced persons immediately after World War II or as refugees from Hungary (1956), the former Czechoslovakia (1968–69), or Poland (1980–81) either emigrated later to Germany, the United States, Canada, Australia, or South Africa, or integrated quickly. The latter have, in general, become Austrian citizens, and in most cases it is only the surname that indicates their origins.

In contrast, the labor migrants recruited by Austria since the mid-1960s and the refugees and asylum seekers of the 1980s and early 1990s are by no means fully integrated into Viennese society. Many of them are linguistically, culturally, and socially marginalized. Thus, labor immigrants, refugees, and asylum-seekers are more visible than other immigrants. They are noticed particularly in public places like parks, playgrounds, schools, daily markets, and public transport. In conjunction with already existing fears and prejudices, this selective awareness leads to a collective dramatization of the actual extent of the phenomenon.

Residential Segregation

The last wave of immigration to Vienna coincided with a shift in the basic philosophy of urban planning. In the 1980s, primacy was given to the revitalization of the inner city while new housing projects and other developments at the urban fringe were sharply reduced. This led to a restructuring of the housing market. Badly equipped but reasonably priced small flats were modernized. They came back onto the market in smaller numbers, but with more comfort and at considerably higher prices. Ironically, this process of gentrification—leading to a considerable boom in this segment of the housing market—was partly subsidized by public funds while hardly any social housing was created. Although from the mid-1980s the demand for flats rose strongly in line with demographic trends, Vienna experienced a shortage of both cheap, older flats and new council flats.

This led to a sharp increase in rents and to a marginalization of those immigrants on the housing market who came during the 1980s and early 1990s. It also led to an increasing ethnic segregation within the city. Such segregation endangers the future social integration of immigrants and potentially increases the level of social tensions.

Today immigrants from former Yugoslavia and Turkey, the traditional labor migrants and their families, have by far the worst living conditions in Vienna (table 8.4). Only 15 percent of them live in luxury or standard quality flats (types A and B), about 56 percent have toilets in their flats but no bathroom (type D), and 18 percent live in flats with no sanitation whatsoever (type E). In contrast, about 90 percent of the native Viennese population and almost 85 percent of the immigrants from other Austrian provinces, Western Europe, and overseas live in luxury or standard quality flats (types A and B). Today about 85 percent of all flats in Vienna are classified as luxury or standard quality.

Another indicator of the marginal position of ex-Yugoslavs and Turkish labor migrants is their small average living space coupled with only slightly lower than average rent per living space (table 8.4). They pay excessive rents for small, poorly equipped flats outside fashionable residential areas. The comparison also shows the privileged situation of many Western European

Table 8.4   Vienna: Housing Situation of Resident Population and Immigrants, 1988

Type of flat	Born in Vienna %	Immigrants from other parts of Austria %	Immigrants from Turkey and former Yugoslavia %	Immigrants from other foreign countries %	Total %
Category A (%)	64.4	55.3	4.2	57.5	58.9
Category B (%)	25.6	29.9	11.8	25.3	25.8
Category C (%)	3.7	5.0	10.1	7.0	4.6
Category D + E (%)	6.3	9.7	73.8	9.2	10.7
Total (%)	100.0	100.0	100.0	100.0	100.0
Living space per head in m²	32.9	33.0	15.0	35.3	32.1
Rent costs per m² living space (AS per month)	32.0	32.3	29.3	36.1	32.4

Sources: Austrian microcensus February 1988; author's calculations.

and overseas immigrants to Vienna. Both their living space per head and their monthly rents are above the Viennese average.

More than 90 percent of all labor migrants from former Yugoslavia and Turkey live in old, small, and often overcrowded flats. There is no prospect for a rapid change of this situation, for all foreigners in Vienna are denied access to council flats and other subsidized housing whereas about 40 percent of Vienna's blue collar-workers (and their families) holding Austrian citizenship are living in subsidized flats.

In many cases, discrimination on the labor market, economic and social marginality, and bad housing conditions are interlinked. Despite excessive rents, labor migrants from the former Yugoslavia, Turkey and East-Central Europe undoubtedly try to minimize costs. They rent cheap, substandard flats to avoid larger investments or redemption payments. In most cases this is not the result of just a shortage of money but also of the expectation of a limited period of residence in Vienna. Instead of investing a larger part of the income to improve living conditions in Vienna, they prefer to acquire easily transportable consumer durables or to build or extend houses in their countries of origin. The strategies of ex-Yugoslavs, Turks, and other labor migrants are similar in this respect to those of many commuters coming from the surrounding Austrian provinces of Lower Austria, Styria, and Burgenland.

As a result of their marginalization in the housing market, people from the former Yugoslavia, Turkey and East-Central Europe are concentrated in districts with a large proportion of houses built during the nineteenth and early twentieth centuries (1815–1914). Fifty percent of all foreigners (1991 census) live in six of the twenty-three Viennese districts (Leopoldstadt, Favoriten, Ottakring, Rudolfsheim-Fünfhaus, Brigittenau, and Landstraße). In 1981, 50 percent of the foreigners were still spread over seven districts. During the 1980s, the dissimilarity index (D) rose from .19 to .21 revealing a slight increase in ethnic segregation. This process becomes more evident if smaller statistical areas are taken into account.

Figures 8.1 and 8.2 show the share of foreigners among the Vienna population in 1981 and 1991. The changes are evident: In 1991, the spatial distribution of buildings dating from the early 1870s is almost identical with the distribution of the foreign population. Additionally, there are the former village centers of the suburbs south and east of the inner city. There, too, foreigners can manage to get short leases at mostly exorbitant prices in run-down buildings, just before these are torn down or revitalized.

This process has led to a growing segregation between the foreigners and the Austrian population from 1981 to 1991. The Austrian population has increased in the districts and areas with a growing share of modern buildings

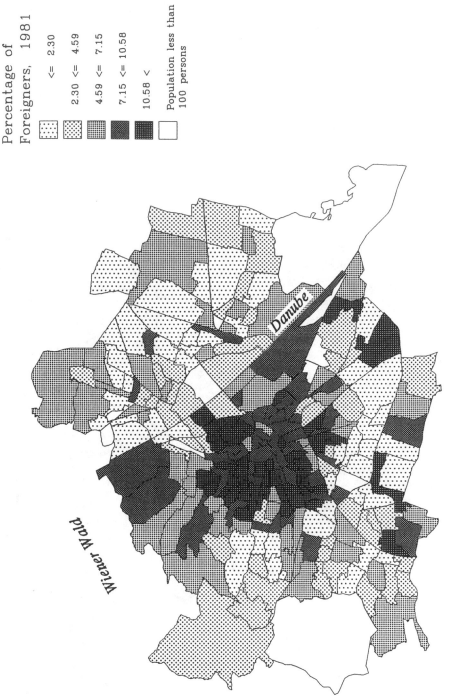

Percentage of
Foreigners, 1981

- <= 2.30
- 2.30 <= 4.59
- 4.59 <= 7.15
- 7.15 <= 10.58
- 10.58 <

Population less than
100 persons

Wiener Wald

Danube

Fig. 8.1 Vienna: Proportion of Foreigners, 1981 (Population Census 1981; map by Ursula Reeger, ISR: software: MERCATOR, Stefan Klein)

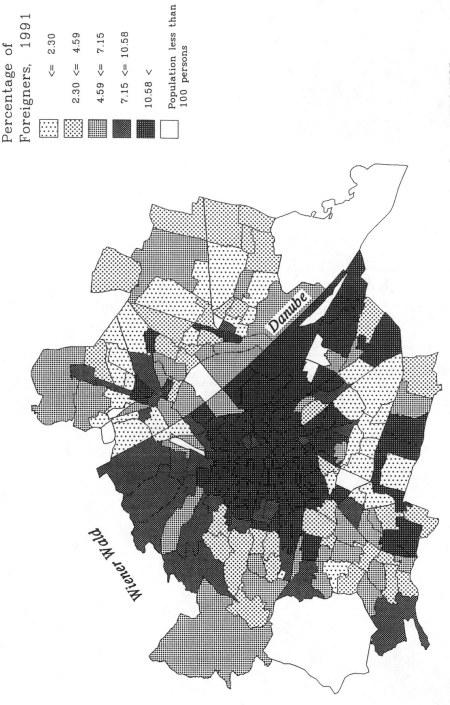

Percentage of
Foreigners, 1991

    <= 2.30

2.30 <= 4.59

4.59 <= 7.15

7.15 <= 10.58

10.58 <

Population less than
100 persons

Wiener Wald

Danube

Fig. 8.2 Vienna: Proportion of Foreigners, 1991 (Population Census 1991; map by Ursula Reeger, ISR: software: MERCATOR, Stefan Klein)

and social housing east of the city, beyond the Danube, in the south and west, and along the slopes of the Wiener Wald, but has decreased in the central districts. Exactly the opposite was the case for the foreign population; there was a strong increase in the inner city, especially in traffic-intense and noisy areas, and only a small increase in the suburbs.

The limitation to particular sectors of the housing market leads to a heavy spatial concentration that has intensified with increased immigration. This leads to further problems that play a central role in the public debate and directly trigger the empirically unfounded prejudice that Vienna is flooded with immigrants. Despite the relatively small share of foreigners in Vienna, the concentration of pupils whose mother tongue is not German in compulsory schools (primary and secondary schools) and the perceived concentration of foreigners in public places in these parts of the city seem to indicate the contrary.

Segregation in the Labor Market

The existing regime of work permits for non-EU immigrants that restrict a change of the employer, along with limited job opportunities for foreigners, highly reduces the spatial mobility of most immigrants not holding Austrian citizenship. Therefore, the spatial distribution of natives and foreigners is closely connected with their occupational positions.

In Vienna, most of the labor migrants from the former Yugoslavia and Turkey were recruited during the periods of high economic growth at the end of the 1960s and of the 1980s. They took low-wage jobs and positions vacated by locals and postwar immigrants. The present socioeconomic situation of these immigrants shows that most of them were not upwardly mobile. In general, immigrants from the former Yugoslavia and Turkey neither made a career within the companies they were working for nor were able to gain entry to privileged segments of the labor market. Even though at the end of the 1980s over 50 percent of them had been in Austria for more than ten years, 80 percent of them were still employed as unskilled or semiskilled workers (table 8.5). Less than 10 percent of them had reached positions as skilled workers or foremen and most other positions remained inaccessible.

Thus, the typical immigrants of the 1960s, 1970s, and 1980s are still not well integrated into the job market in Vienna. Immigrants to Vienna from ex-Yugoslavia and Turkey not only have poorer chances of being promoted but also are heavily concentrated in a small number of sectors of the economy. They are particularly overrepresented in Vienna's building trade, tourism, catering, domestic service, and personal social services (table 8.6).

Table 8.5 Vienna: Occupational Status of Resident Population and Immigrants, 1988

Occupational status	Born in Vienna %	Immigrants from other parts of Austria %	Immigrants from Turkey %	Immigrants from former Yugoslavia %	Total
Unskilled worker	9.3	9.2	55.7	11.6	12.2
Semiskilled worker	7.7	13.7	24.4	12.3	10.7
Skilled worker	12.1	12.8	9.5	9.5	11.9
Manual workers (total)	29.1	35.7	89.6	33.4	34.8
Lower-level employee	23.9	22.8	8.0	21.7	22.5
Middle-level employee	19.0	16.3	1.9	13.3	16.8
Higher-level employee	20.0	19.0	0.6	22.3	18.8
Employees, civil servants (total)	62.9	58.1	10.5	57.3	58.1
Self-employed	7.9	6.4	0.0	9.5	7.1
Total	100.0	100.0	100.0	100.0	100.0

Source: Austrian microcensus February 1988; author's calculations.

Table 8.6 Vienna: Occupational Position of Resident Population and Immigrants by Sector, 1988

Sector of economy	Born in Vienna %	Immigrants from other parts of Austria %	Immigrants from Turkey %	Immigrants from former Yugoslavia %	Total %
Primary sector (total)	1.4	1.1	2.0	1.3	1.8
Consumer goods industry	3.0	4.6	5.3	7.2	4.0
Basic industry	3.9	4.5	4.4	3.9	4.1
Finishing industry	14.4	13.4	15.4	12.0	14.0
Building industry	5.3	7.5	11.3	1.9	6.1
Secondary sector (total)	26.6	30.0	36.4	25.0	28.2
Catering, accommodation	3.2	1.6	5.2	9.6	3.5
Trade, transport	26.3	22.2	18.4	27.1	24.6
Economic services	11.5	10.8	2.7	8.3	10.3
Public services	22.6	27.2	9.1	20.1	22.6
Personal services	7.4	7.1	26.2	8.4	8.9
Tertiary sector (total)	72.0	68.9	61.6	73.5	69.9
Total	100.0	100.0	100.0	100.0	100.0

Source: Austrian microcensus February 1988; author's calculations.

In these sectors, the work often involves small wages, low prestige, physical risks, and unfavorable working conditions (e.g., working outdoors, cleaning, unclearly defined working hours, and excessive overtime). These sectors are also subject to business cycle and seasonal fluctuations that render permanent employment unlikely. The fact that these positions are primarily filled by foreign labor in Vienna (and elsewhere in Western Europe) also permits the maintenance of such unattractive working conditions.

In Vienna, immigrants from Asia, Africa, and Western Europe occupy special positions. Many have succeeded in establishing themselves in specific niches of the Viennese labor market and the urban economy. An indicator of this is the fact that these immigrants from Western Europe and overseas are more often self-employed (about 10 percent) than all other groups. This is especially true in the catering industry. Immigrants from Africa and Asia have also established themselves in trade and transport (e.g. as newspaper vendors or as traders on Vienna's daily and weekly markets) as well as in those public sectors open to them (especially the health service). Central and Western European immigrants (particularly from Germany, but also from Poland, the Czech Republic, Slovakia, and Hungary) are also to be found in these sectors.

The high proportion of labor migrants from Western Europe and overseas employed in higher and top positions shows that today—for the first time since the end of the Austro-Hungarian Empire—an elite has started to immigrate to Vienna. There is no longer a one-way Austrian brain-drain toward Western Europe and North America. Vienna has become more attractive for immigrants from Western Europe and overseas. This is partly due to the much-increased number of representatives and offices of foreign and multinational firms using Vienna as a geographic base to develop markets in Central and Eastern Europe, and also the presence of a number of international organizations (e.g., UNIDO, IAEO, UNRWA).

Models of Living Together: Multiculturalism, Integration, Assimilation, or Social Divisions

It is possible to formulate theoretically and to observe empirically various models describing how natives and immigrants could live together. The two important dimensions are economic/social integration and cultural assimilation. By combining both dimensions, there are four types of models of living together (table 8.7). On the one end, there is perfect integration of immigrants into the receiving society. In this case, one can observe a total economic and social integration of foreigners into the receiving society (e.g.,

Table 8.7   Types of Immigrant Societies

	total cultural assimilation of immigrants into the host society:	no cultural assimilation of immigrants into the host society:
total economical and social integration of immigrants:	(1) Society of resident and successful assimilees "melting-pot"	(3) functioning multicultural society
no economical and social integration of immigrants:	(4) society of resident inhabitants and assimilees who are unsuccessful or who suffer strong discrimination	(2) two-thirds society split along ethnic lines; "fragmentation"

through total assimilation, type 1). On the other end, there is a "two-thirds" society split along ethnic lines (type 2), with economic or social integration and no cultural assimilation of immigrants. Type 3 describes a functioning multicultural society. This is defined by economic and social integration but little assimilation of immigrants into the host society. Type 4 is only theoretically possible. It is a society of resident inhabitants and foreigners who are equally unsuccessful but totally assimilated among one another.

Various types of integration or fragmentation are linked to specific patterns of spatial distribution of foreigners. In cases of assimilation, the homes of immigrants are usually spread over different residential areas. The opposite is the case in an ethnically divided society. In many cases concentration phenomena are a sign of the exclusion of individual groups of immigrants. Neither total assimilation nor the other extreme, the development of ethnic ghettos, lead to lasting changes in the cultural and ethnic self-image of the receiving society.

Has Vienna Ever Been a Melting Pot?

The late nineteenth century, when net immigration was high, offers some historical context to the understanding of the present situation in Vienna. By the turn of the century, the "native Viennese" had become a statistical minority in their own hometown. In those days, immigration and the extension of the city kept a lasting economic boom going. In two waves, 1860–1873 and 1890–1914, major parts of the urban infrastructure were rebuilt and both public buildings and housing blocks were built in the grand style. The quality ranged from aristocratic and bourgeois palaces to small flats with varying degrees of sanitary facilities.

The concentration of newly built, small, cheap, substandard flats in the urban development areas of that time and the building of reliable and efficient public transport systems (tramway, subway, local railway) increased the pace of the spatial segregation of the local and immigrant populations. New ghettos soon emerged. The Jewish immigrants from Galicia, Bukowina, and eastern Hungary mostly settled in the second district (Leopoldstadt); the immigrants from Bohemia and Moravia were concentrated in the southern (tenth to twelfth) and western (fifteenth to seventeenth) districts and in Floridsdorf (twenty-first district).

In reference to a similar phenomenon in the United States, the Vienna of the turn of the century is often referred to as a "melting pot" (John and Lichtblau 1990). This metaphor implies that immigrants of different origins, with different cultural, ethnic, and linguistic backgrounds, would not disappear without a trace into the culture of the receiving society but would interact, allowing for the gradual emergence of a new culture. In the case of Vienna, this was probably only true to a very limited extent.

After 1850, even mass immigration from various parts of the Austro-Hungarian Empire did not lead to the buildup of any lasting non-German-speaking ethnic minorities in Vienna. By 1900, total assimilation already was the dominant political and cultural model of the day. To speak fluent German became more and more important. For higher career posts, even conversion to Roman Catholicism was required. Gustav Mahler, who wanted to become director of the state opera, was a prominent example of such a conversion. This assimilation pressure left its traces in the census results. From decade to decade, a shrinking proportion of Vienna's inhabitants professed to speaking the language of their country of origin—be it Czech, Polish, Hungarian, or Croat. One could conclude that by giving up their national or linguistic identities, Slav immigrants paid the price for their entry to Viennese society. In contrast, Jewish immigrants were not even given the same chance to assimilate. In the course of the twentieth century most of them were forced to emigrate, were expelled, or were murdered. This applied even if they spoke perfect German, had fought for Austria in World War I, or were baptized.

It is Viennese cuisine that most clearly shows traces of the immigration of the nineteenth and twentieth centuries: jam- or chocolate-filled pancakes ("Palatschinken"), goulash and meat-filled cabbage rolls, various sausages ("Debreziner," "Krainer," "Krakauer," "Polnische"), "Powidl" (thick plum jam), and all kinds of dumplings. It tells us more, however, about the origins of the women working in the kitchens in private households and restaurants than about the noble and bourgeois families for whom they were cooking. Jewish Vienna has disappeared almost without a trace. The children and grandchildren of Slav immigrants, on the other hand, are fully integrated and German-speaking, and for the most part see themselves as "true" Austrians. Only the surname still bears witness to their origins and even the spelling has often been Germanized as the Czech, Hungarian, or Croat way of writing family names disappeared. Sometimes the name was even changed, an unmistakable sign of overassimilation. Prominent and less-prominent examples abound: Vesely became Wessely, Vlcek became Wiltschek, and Vaclavik became Waldheim (and at a later stage even Austria's president). All of this contradicts the attractive image of the melting pot, an often-cited cliché that presents Vienna as a successful mixture of various cultures of origin (see John and Lichtblau 1990).

Unplanned Immigration

Another type of relations between nationals and immigrants arose through the "unplanned immigration" of the 1960s and 1970s when foreign labor from the former Yugoslavia, Turkey (and later also from east-central Europe) was recruited. In contrast to the immigrants of 1860–1914 and 1945–1950, most of these migrants did not come to Vienna with the intention of settling for good.

The original idea was to recruit labor migrants and seasonal workers for a limited period. That is why they were called *Gastarbeiter* (guestworkers). The plan was to send them back home sooner or later and to replace them by new foreign labor ("rotational model"). However, only half of the foreign labor recruited by Austria between 1965 and 1985 did return to the respective countries of origin. The rotational model failed: recruited foreign workers got married, gave birth to children, and decided to stay in Austria. In many cases, other family members followed the "pioneer generation." Therefore, today the term guestworker is partly euphemistic, partly also deceptive. Many of the so-called guestworkers have been living in Vienna for decades or were even born here. Although the majority of the pioneer generation did not intend to immigrate for good, it gradually became interested in staying. Those Austrian firms that employed labor migrants were also interested in their staying. Any rotation would have involved new recruitment and new training costs for the firms.

Although they have been living in Austria for a long time, most labor migrants have retained their foreign citizenship. Therefore, they have no voting rights, they cannot be elected—not as members of Parliament, or provincial or local assemblies or as shop stewards—they cannot become civil servants, and they are not allowed to rent council flats. More restrictive legal provisions apply to them than to the native population and under certain circumstances, they can be expelled and sent back to their countries of origin. This all leads to insecurity regarding the nature and length of their stay in Vienna and forces many labor migrants and their dependents to lead an ambivalent way of life. On the one hand, many keep the door to their home country open, while on the other hand they would also like to establish themselves permanently in Vienna (Lichtenberger and Fassmann 1987).

To some extent, labor migrants from former Yugoslavia, Turkey, and east-central Europe live in two worlds or simply between two worlds. Very often this leads to their dividing the place of residence as many labor migrants own, build, or renovate houses in their country of origin. These houses are a symbol of their material success but also can be seen as an investment for their often-deferred return home. In this way, substantial resources flow to the peripheries of east-central Europe, the Balkans, and Turkey. Investment capital is tied up there in real estate that very often can neither be exploited commercially nor sold at suitable prices. Today this is particularly true for immigrants from the crisis and war-torn areas of Croatia, Bosnia-Herzegovina, Kosovo, and East Anatolia who can neither make use of their family homes nor sell them.

New Immigration and New Perspectives

In the nineteenth and the early twentieth centuries, Vienna was one of the most attractive and fastest growing metropolises of Europe. Thereafter, it lost importance, attractiveness, and population. Since the late 1970s, there have been clear signs of a changing trend. As a location, as a holiday destination, but also as a place to live, Vienna is becoming attractive again. It has become fashionable to live in the inner city and the trend toward migration to the suburbs appears to have been halted. At the same time, a large number of immigrants are coming to Vienna both from other parts of Austria and from abroad. The fall of the Iron Curtain has further accelerated this development. Vienna is not unique: the same can be said for Berlin, Hamburg, and Frankfurt, but also for Prague and Budapest.

The new attractiveness of the central European metropolises need not become a disadvantage for urban society. All the same, most of the native population would like to be more isolated from immigrants from abroad. Yet the age structure of the urban population, the low fertility of the couples living in the city, the future workforce requirements of the urban economy, and the geopolitical position of European metropolises make any complete strategies of separation appear illusory. Cities like Vienna, Berlin, Hamburg, and Stockholm, as well as Prague and Budapest, will continue to be attractive destinations for immigrants.

Although some labor migrants of the 1960s and 1970s will sooner or later return to their countries of origin, the majority will stay and become part of the Viennese society on a permanent basis without fundamentally changing its character. They will become integrated in the Viennese working class and confronted with its resentments and prejudices. As was already the case with the Slav immigrants of the nineteenth century, the price of this integration will probably be the loss of their ethnic identity. However, the less-secure legal position of these labor migrants and their split existence still act both as an objective and a subjective obstacle to their social integration. For the immigrants and their children, assimilation may at first glance appear advantageous. It reduces social discrimination in daily life and improves the chances of making progress at work. However, whether or not the city as a whole benefits from total assimilation is less certain.

Following these suggestions, a city like Vienna need by no means give up its social and cultural identity. On the other hand, this identity must not be looked upon as being static. Municipal policy must do its share by creating a framework to cope with exploitation of new immigrants on the labor market, with unacceptable living conditions, and with the marginalization of entire groups. The slogan must be: social and spatial integration instead of ghetto building; municipal citizenship/denizenship instead of no political rights. This would mean an opening of the segmented housing market, more social housing, measures against ghetto building, and the opportunity for political participation by granting political rights also to those who decide to live in Vienna and to integrate into Austrian society.

References

Fassmann, Heinz. 1986. "Migration in Österreich: 1850–1900. Migrations-tröme innerhalb der Monarchie und Struktur der Zuwanderung nach Wien." *Demographische Informationen*. Institut für Demographie der Österreichischen Akademie der Wissenschaften:22–36.

John, Michael, and Albert Lichtblau. 1990. *Schmelztiegel Wien—einst und jetzt: Zur Geschichte und Gegenwart von Zuwanderung und Minderheiten. Aufsätze, Quellen, Kommentare.* Wien and Köln: Böhlau.

Lichtenberger, Elisabeth, and Heinz Fassmann. 1987. "Guestworkers—Life in two Societies." In *Foreign Minorities in Continental European Cities*, ed. Günther Glebe and John O'Loughlin. Stuttgart: Franz Steiner.

Chapter 9

Immigrants in Milan: Gender and Household Strategies

Felicitas Hillmann

Recent migration to Italy and to Milan from the third world is part of a broader "feminization of global migration" (Camus-Jaquez 1990,144). Immigrant women do not fit the stereotype of being largely passive, their fate determined more-or-less exclusively by the success or failure of the man—husband, father or brother—to whom they are attached, as was the case in the European "Gastarbeitersystem" (Castles 1987). Emerging in Italy and other countries is a household-oriented migration process that involves female migrants as leading players. Indeed, in many parts of Italy, the immigration process began with female migrants. Furthermore, the problems and opportunities faced by female migrants are very different from those faced by male migrants going to the same destination.

Many authors have emphasized that migration is not a gender-indifferent process and introduced gender as an analytical category in their research. Theoretical models of explanation started with the "threefold" and "fourfold oppression of women." Women face oppression as immigrants on account of race, class, and gender; and are further oppressed by how they perceive themselves (Kosack 1976; Morokvasic and Wilpert 1983). Some authors have emphasized the importance of female migrant workers in the international division of labor and the process of globalization (Sassen 1989; Potts 1990). In recent years, there has been a shift to more complex and less-global models that focus on structural and individual determinants embedded in their cultural context (see Morokvasic 1983; Lim 1990; Boyd 1989; Radcliffe 1990; Chant and Radcliffe 1992). Female migrants do not belong only to the

187

category of the "widowed," "separated," or "divorced" women, as it is often assumed in the literature. There is also a substantial proportion of married women who migrate to Italy independently (Andall 1992,42). Here seems to be at work what Morokvasic (1993,461) calls the "changing landscape of migration": we can no longer speak of overwhelmingly male-dominated migratory patterns.

The purpose of this chapter is to describe and analyze the population of legal and illegal immigrants in Milan, with special emphasis on female immigrants from the third world and the role of gender in the international migration process. I will first characterize the main patterns of recent immigration to Italy, nationally and regionally, and to Milan in particular. Then I will focus on the situation of female immigrants, with special regard to employment, housing, and assistance issues, in contrast to male immigrants. Finally, I will report results of detailed qualitative research on the household strategies utilized by female immigrants from three countries: the Philippines, Peru, and Somalia.

Recent Immigration to Italy

Like other Mediterranean countries, in the 1980s Italy moved from being a country of emigration to a country of immigration. According to data made available by ISTAT (National Bureau of Statistics) in December 1992, more than 925,000 permits to stay had been issued, representing the number of legal immigrants. Eighty-four percent of these permits were issued to foreigners from non-European Union countries. The six most numerous immigrant groups (table 9.1) were from Morocco, Tunisia, the Philippines, the former Yugoslavia, Albania, and Senegal. Eighteen countries each sent at least ten thousand migrants to Italy. This new immigration can be described in terms of several general features:

1. "Push-factors" have grown in significance compared to "pull-factors" as an explanation for immigration. It is more and more the case that people emigrate in order to escape harsh economic, political, and environmental conditions at home and not because of a perception that Italy welcomes guestworkers. Indeed, the rate of unemployment in Italy has been increasing, while the immigration policies in Italy (as in other Western countries) have correspondingly become more and more restrictive.

2. The ethnic and national composition of the recent immigration to Italy is highly heterogeneous compared to the more homogeneous forms of labor-migration of the 1960s. Although the percentage of foreigners with respect to the total population, at 1.5 percent, is still low compared to other European

Table 9.1   Italy and Province of Milan: Number of Residency Permits Issued, 1992 and 1993

Nationality	Italy (31 Dec. 1992)	Province of Milan (31 March 1993)
Morocco	95,741	11,613
Tunisia	62,112	3,654
Philippines	44,155	9,733
Former Yugoslavia	39,020	2,853
Albania	28,628	2,031
Senegal	27,572	2,377
Egypt	23,515	10,183
China	21,417	5,386
Poland	21,221	1,163
Brazil	18,751	3,046
Sri Lanka	17,242	2,612
Romania	16,446	1,833
Somalia	14,973	2,465
Argentina	14,871	1,957
Ghana	14,216	561
India	13,382	887
Ethiopia	13,001	2,857
Iran	11,139	1,472
Pakistan	7,850	1,292
Peru	7,493	1,790
Total	925,172	122,179

Source: Ministero Affari Esteri; Questura di Milano; Murer 1993.

countries, the rate of immigration in Italy has shown a rapid increase in the last ten years. Meanwhile, it is possible to distinguish the more traditional groups, Eritreans, Moroccans, Filipinos, Egyptians, and Chinese from the more recent groups including Sri Lankans, Peruvians, and Poles.

3. All existing literature, and other relevant sources of information, indicate significant illegal immigration. Estimates oscillate between 10 and 20 percent of all immigrants, while some studies put the number of illegal immigrants as high as 35 percent (CESPE 1990). The means of illegal entry to Italy are various and often depend on the particular group involved. Some people are thought to enter Italy with the illegal help of travel agencies in the countries of origin. The favorite route is to enter Italy by train, by taxi, or on foot from Switzerland or Austria after first having entered Western Europe from airports in Prague or Budapest. Although shipping controls have

recently become more vigilant, North Africans are thought to have come via container ships.

4. "Reverse" migration has contributed significantly to the numbers. Countries that were once *targets* of emigration from Italy have turned into *sources* of emigration. This is often the case when parents or grandparents who once left Italy have maintained familial and legal ties. This process is especially true of Latin America, where a majority of reverse migrants come from Argentina.

5. Immigration from third world countries includes a high percentage of female migrants coming alone. Migration from Islamic countries (Morocco, Tunisia, Pakistan, etc.) is dominated by male immigrants, with the noteworthy exception of Somalia. Large numbers of female migrants, on the other hand, come from Catholic countries such as the Philippines and several Latin American countries. Immigration from other countries (including Sri Lanka) is more gender-balanced.

A lack of political consensus concerning immigration has created an atmosphere of confusion in both policy formulation and enforcement. Despite the introduction of the Immigration Legalization Law 39 in 1990, a clear statement of the rights of the immigrants does not exist. The application of the law often appears inconsistent, if not chaotic. One result is that a large part of providing assistance to immigrants has been left to the church and other volunteer organizations to cope with the best they can.

Regional Immigration Patterns

Immigration to Italy displays regional patterns that reflect the diversity of regional economies. Especially important to immigrants is the informal economy (black market), which is estimated to be about 30 percent of the total economy (Venturini 1991, 100). Dividing the immigrant labor market by sex and ethnic group, a general picture of regional differentiation is described below.

Despite its chronically high unemployment rate, the South of Italy is home to 18.6 percent of all immigrants (ISTAT 1992). Many immigrants there are seasonal laborers and return to their home countries for the off-season (especially those whose home countries are nearby). Some also move cyclically to metropolitan centers, especially in the North, where work is plentiful and wages higher. Over 35 percent of immigrants live in the center of the country, where many have found work in the private tertiary labor market, as restaurant employees, watchmen, and doorkeepers, or in small-scale industry. For male African immigrants street hawking is an important source of income. The North, where 45 percent of all immigrants live, offers work for immigrants on the lowest levels of the labor market in large-scale industry, in construction, and in the restaurant business. Street hawking is also common.

This regional sketch is based almost entirely on male immigration. Female immigrants, irrespective of age or special skills they might possess, are incorporated in the domestic services sector with few exceptions. While on the surface this may seem like a more agreeable setting, it is far more restrictive in terms of social mobility. For instance, nearly all job-placement and training programs, sponsored by the EU or the Italian state, are directed toward men.

Immigration to Milan

Milan, in the North of Italy, is the capital of the Lombardy region. Metropolitan Milan, with over 1.4 million inhabitants, is part of the industrial triangle along with Genoa and Turin and is the seat of a majority of Italy's private finance and administrative agencies. Although the area is Italy's most industrialized, the infrastructure is thought to be weakening. There were sizable layoffs at all of Milan's larger factories in 1992. Nonetheless, the 5.5 percent unemployment rate in Milan in 1990 was the lowest in Italy (Bianchini 1991,24). Compared to the rest of Italy, Milan has a greater than average percentage of workers employed in the chemical industry, engineering, electromechanics and electronics, and in the financial and business-service sectors. It has less than the national average employed in agriculture, construction, and public administration. Social services in metropolitan Milan are comparatively well funded although deficiencies are seen in such sectors as elder-care and walk-in medical services.

One of Milan's main problems is the emergence of social exclusion and homelessness. About 12 percent of Milan's residents are classified as poor, and social inequality and polarization is thought to be increasing (Zajczyk and Mingione 1993,67ff.). Owing to housing scarcity, market prices have risen considerably over the last ten years, which, along with an overburdened city administration, has produced an elevated vulnerability within some social groups (Tosi 1993,19).

Since World War II, Milan has been an important migrant destination. In the 1950s and 1960s, large flows of immigrants came from rural Lombardy and Veneto, and from the southern regions such as Puglia, Sicily, Campania, and Sardinia. The peak of this interregional immigration was reached in 1958–63 and was directly connected to labor demand in Lombardian industry. Then, immigrants were mostly young men (many of them illiterate) whose goal was to improve their families' economic conditions, but first they had to overcome the precarious living conditions in the city. These migrants prestructured the institutional framework for today's immigrants. For instance, the language schools that once served the needs of illiterate Italians are today attended by foreign immigrants with little knowledge of Italian.

Until 1979, the majority of non-Italian immigrants were from other West European or industrialized countries. Since then, 75 percent of all immigrants have come from Eastern Europe or the third world (Osservatorio del Mercato di Lavoro 1991, 5). While immigration from countries of the third world crystallized as a *fait social* around 1980 its beginnings reach back to the late 1960s.

The initial flow of third world immigration to Milan was composed of two main groups. The first group is that of young men from North Africa (the so-called *marocchini*, or *vu cumprà*) who would carry with them products for sale in Italy. These immigrants tended to stay only temporarily, returning to their home countries after their goods had been sold. The second, less-visible group, consisted of women who came to Italy from the former Italian colonies of Eritrea (Ethiopia) and Somalia to work as domestic workers. Church institutions took an active role in organizing this form of immigration from Catholic (or proselytized) countries. In the early 1970s, immigration from third world countries to Milan was predominantly female and its numbers moderate. It was only in the mid-eighties that immigration flows from other countries began to add to the presence of foreigners.

Today, the ethnic and national composition of immigrants to Milan is highly diverse, representing eighty-four separate nationalities, and with males outnumbering females. As of November 1992, 40 percent of all third world immigrants in the metropolitan area were female. In some national groups, however, women represent the overwhelming majority, including El Salvador, Brazil, Peru, the Philippines, China, Ethiopia, and Somalia.

By March 1993, the Questura (the county immigration authority) registered a total of 122,179 permits to stay issued to foreigners in Milan (table 9.1) of whom 65 percent were immigrants from third world countries (Murer 1993). About 51,000 registered foreigners (not counting illegal immigrants) reside in Milan. A 1993 estimate of illegal migrants for metropolitan Milan put their number at 25 to 35 percent of the total immigrant population. Most are thought to come from Latin America, especially Peru; Eastern Europe, especially Yugoslavia; and African countries including Egypt, Ethiopia, Senegal, Guinea, Ivory Coast, Morocco, Algeria, and Tunisia (Synergia 1992). The voluntary medical services organization, NAGA, reports that it treats about 1,500 illegal immigrants monthly and that the number of illegal female immigrants from Latin America working as domestic workers is increasing (*La Repubblica* 1993,7).

Third world immigrants are mostly young: 62 percent are between the ages of twenty-one and forty, 18 percent are younger than twenty, and 20 percent are between forty-one and sixty. Immigrants from Egypt and China, having the highest rate of family reunification, are the only groups showing a well-balanced age structure. Those countries whose immigrants to Milan are almost exclusively male are the least well balanced in terms of age. For instance, only 2 percent of the Senegalese immigrants are younger than twenty and no Senegalese immigrant is older than sixty. On the whole there are extremely few immigrants from third world countries older than sixty. This is not true for immigrants from developed countries.

Gendered Immigrant Patterns in Milan

The Milan immigrant community, which includes large numbers of female immigrants, can only be understood by emphasizing the role of gender in the migration process. Among factors in Milan that are particularly sensitive to gender are labor, housing, and access to social assistance. They are briefly reviewed here.

Gendered Labor

The overwhelming majority of third world immigrants work in conditions representing the lowest rank in the Italian economy. The jobs they hold are often tedious, sometimes dangerous, and usually low paid. It is work that many researchers believe Italians refuse to do (Macioti and Pugliese 1990). In addition, many immigrants work in the black market. According to a recent comprehensive survey on immigration in Milan (IRER-OETAMM 1991), job availability for immigrants is strikingly determined by sex: the range of employment opportunities for men includes thirty-nine different occupations. For women it is only twenty-seven occupations, with 95 percent of the women concentrated in only ten occupations. In general, immigrant men work as construction laborers, as low-level employees in the chemical industry, or as street hawkers. This results in immigrant men being very visible in Italian society. Male immigrants—excluding Filipinos, Sri Lankans, and Mauritians—seldom work as domestic workers, with the exception of some chauffeurs.

In contrast, nearly all female immigrants, regardless of their skills, are domestic workers. They work in the household as nurses, as assistants for the elderly, as baby-sitters, as cleaners, and so on. Some immigrant women work in cleaning cooperatives, and a few get jobs as nurses in private hospitals. Unlike their male counterparts, immigrant women are not visible in Italian society, even though a higher proportion of them are working. Over 16 percent of female immigrants report being unemployed compared to 21 percent of male immigrants (IRER-OETAMM 1991).

Gendered Housing

Even though only 3.6 percent of Milan's total population is composed of foreigners, Milan's most prestigious zone, Centro Storico, recorded the highest percentage of foreigners, 6.9 percent in 1992. This invites the question as to why the highest percentage of immigrants is to be found in the area where the highest rents are paid. Immigrant women are far more likely to live in Centro Storico than immigrant men, who are more likely to reside in Milan's more peripheral zones (fig. 9.1). This striking difference in place of residence reflects the data concerning job availability. More women are registered in the Centro Storico because they work as domestic workers and live with their employers.

When these data are compared with corresponding data gathered by one of Milan's most important NGO assistance agencies, the Segreteria per gli Esteri, we get a completely different distribution of foreigners in Milan. The 6.9 percent in the Centro Storico drop to 2 percent and the districts Sud and Est emerge with the highest density of foreigners. This discrepancy is easily explained by the fact that the official data on residence take account only of those immigrants who are legal and who have registered their place of residence.

Because most immigrants live in single housing units separated from one another, no ethnic districts exist. Immigration adds to an already burdened housing market. According to IRER-OETAMM (1991), 70 percent of all immigrants consider housing, after employment, their biggest problem. Nearly 50 percent of all immigrants live in transient or substandard conditions, usually sharing living space (hotel rooms, dormitories, garages, vacant buildings) with others of their own nationality. For a further 12 percent it is not possible to judge: "accommodation with the employer" is not a qualitative item and "other type of accommodation" is unlikely to be privileged housing. In the early 1990s, there was a significant number of dwellings squatted by immigrants.

As women working as domestic workers usually live in the homes of their employers, many are forced to find alternative weekend housing. On the whole, living-in conforms well with their intentions as immigrants: they find

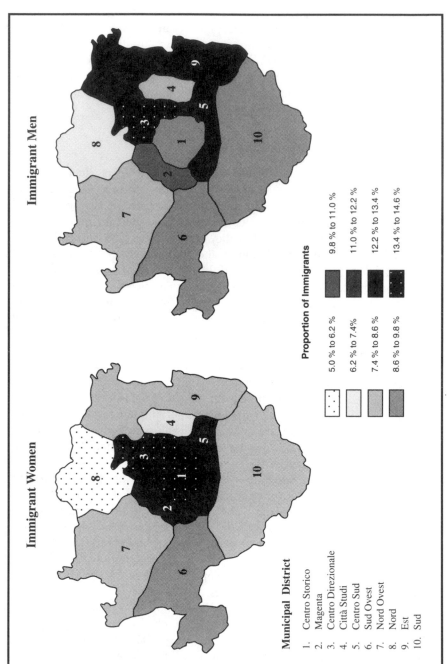

Immigrant Women

Immigrant Men

Municipal District

1. Centro Storico
2. Magenta
3. Centro Direzionale
4. Città Studi
5. Centro Sud
6. Sud Ovest
7. Nord Ovest
8. Nord
9. Est
10. Sud

Proportion of Immigrants

5.0 % to 6.2 %   9.8 % to 11.0 %

6.2 % to 7.4 %   11.0 % to 12.2 %

7.4 % to 8.6 %   12.2 % to 13.4 %

8.6 % to 9.8 %   13.4 % to 14.6 %

Fig. 9.1   Housing of Third World Immigrants in Milan, 1990, by Gender

work and housing at the same time, and because of the reduced costs of living are soon able to send money home, so fulfilling their migration purpose. Some immigrant women work part-time as domestic workers and rent apartments with other women in the same situation. Women-centered forms of cohabitation seem to emerge mainly in the case of married immigrants.

Gendered Immigrant Assistance

The Plan for Immigration first proposed in spring 1992, of which the main objective ostensibly was to eliminate the social problems associated with immigration, has been largely unsuccessful. One primary goal was to send the message to all illegal immigrants "that they can expect no form of positive future in their adopted country, that they will always be subject to exploitation in employment, and that if found by the authorities they will be deported without delay" (Comune di Milano 1992,58). A second primary goal was to clear the squatted immigrant dwellings, and then create "receiving" centers for immigrants. The second part of this policy was only partially carried out before the Department for Immigration was abolished in fall 1992. The result of moving the immigrants has been a spatial shift of immigrant settlements to other areas.

Since fall 1992, immigration policy has become the responsibility of the General Social Assistance Department, which has little capacity to improve the situation. The Catholic Church, the biggest of the volunteer associations trying to render assistance, recently appealed to the Italian government not to discharge all social responsibility to private associations. Dormitories, run by the church or by cooperatives (and partly publicly financed) are already overcrowded.

The social assistance structure in Milan makes few provisions for female immigrants. There are no official shelters. Assistance structures (about 40 percent of which are run by the Catholic Church or by private organizations) provide about 2,150 beds, of which only 62 beds are available for women (see Zanfrini 1992). In 1992, these centers fell far short of satisfying demand. Therefore, many women have to rely on private resources to cope with the lack of housing. Many women develop and maintain social networks of friends and relatives. Having relatives alone, however, seems not to be enough to avoid housing problems. In 1990 almost 60 percent of the women who found temporary accommodation at a church-run shelter reported having relatives in Milan. Very few women resort to living on the street (as some men do) which again adds to their invisibility. Women who are turned away by a receiving shelter and who have neither friends nor relatives to provide accommodation, nor money enough to stay at a hotel, are often forced into direct or indirect forms of prostitution.

In summary, female immigrants who come alone to Italy must contend with a gendered assistance structure that does not adequately recognize their presence. The work they do often leaves them vulnerable because it isolates them, and they may become visible only in a moment of crisis. Since formal institutions such as trade unions hardly reach them, social problems become privatized. This vulnerability of females is exacerbated by an Italian society that is more comfortable with keeping immigrants invisible, or, in any case, avoiding "negative visibility." Even though non-European immigration to Italy was initially female, one still cannot find an official center in Milan to attend to the special needs of immigrant women (and their children).

Most vulnerable are those women who have immigrated illegally and who depend entirely on the goodwill of their employers. Immigrant women depend far more than immigrant men on their social networks and on private structures for assistance. One experienced social worker observed, "the immigrant women have developed social networks to a greater extent than the men because of their need for security." This need for security promotes invisibility, and invisibility reinforces the view that the social problem does not exist.

Household Strategies of Female Migrants

In order to understand the particular situation of female immigrants at the destination, it is necessary to examine the social and familial context in which the migration decision was made. For this detailed analysis, I draw upon my interviews with about one hundred immigrant women, many of them illegal, complemented by church assistance records and field observations. Altogether, eighty interviews had been recorded and handwritten notes were made during twenty interviews.

My findings indicate that few women emigrate from the third world to Milan without maintaining an active role in a larger social context, normally consisting of the household unit in the native country. Thus, any comprehensive analysis has to take into account the structural situation in the native country. Hardships are often faced by these households, including push factors like unemployment, insufficient wage levels, and war, leading to the migration decision. The decision to migrate is strategic and the geographic destinations of emigration differ according to sex. The decision also reflects a broader household logic rather than individual goals, with regular financial remittances often being one of the goals. As a result, many women have become parts of "transnational households," usually following household decisions made to satisfy short-term needs. Explaining these strategies only in terms of rational longer-term economic behavior would be misleading.

Household strategies are defined here as "actions directed at balancing the household resources, the consumption needs, and the alternatives for productive activity" (Boyd 1989,645). The concept of household strategies is part of the more general research on family economies (Hareven 1978). MacDonald and MacDonald (1964) showed that kinship and friendship ties are crucial factors in the migration process. Hugo (1981) broadened the context further by showing the importance of village and ethnic ties in the migration process. My aim in what follows is to show how household strategies underlie the migration process in the case of women. There exist different household strategies for different ethnic and national groups. I will focus on three national groups that figure prominently in Milan, female immigrants from the Philippines, Peru, and Somalia.

Philippine Women

Milan has been a target of a continuous immigration flow from the Philippines since 1975. Initially, Catholic agencies encouraged women willing to emigrate by offering them temporary formal work contracts for Italy. Today the church no longer has an active role in connecting the immigrants. Instead, illegal passageways to Italy and Milan are arranged by travel agencies, which demand anywhere from five thousand to eight thousand dollars (US). Many women immigrants from the Philippines are highly skilled and belong to the working poor before leaving the Philippines. They usually have clear ideas about the utility of emigrating. One of the most common objectives of these women is to reach the point of being able to send money back home in order to finance a better upbringing and education for their children. One longer-term objective is to save enough money to start a business at home as a way of providing security for their old age. Many of these women previously have been domestic workers in Hong Kong and Arabian countries; others decided to move away after having worked in the Philippines for many years.

Imelda, fifty years old, has lived in Milan for five years since giving up her job in the Philippines. She describes her decision to emigrate as follows:

My children are grown-up and it's very expensive to take them into courses for education. And I'm very particular about supporting their study with more money because I would like them to study in one of the favored classes in school. That is my dream for my children: that they will be lawyers. It is expensive for me to buy them shoes and clothes and pay for the car. I decided to earn here and to send my money; it was to be put into some business and then after two years more I will return to my country. So I have a security for my old age, too.

Some Philippine women do not choose to emigrate to Italy per se, rather they are looking for a place to work. As the interview with Imelda demonstrates, the household strategies are clear and well organized. While the percentage of illegal Philippine immigrants is high, most illegal immigrants are not concerned with their legal status. Their perception of their illegal status turns out to be quite realistic given the current circumstances in Italy. Here is a typical statement: "No, I'm not afraid of control or things like that. You know, my belief is: as long as I do not violate any rules or laws in Italy, there is no reason for them to make disturbances of me."

Peruvian Women

Peruvians have come to Italy mainly in the last two years. The percentage of these immigrants who are women and illegal is very high. In spring 1992, Italy tried to stem Peruvian immigration by introducing a highly restrictive visa policy. The high percentage of illegal Peruvian immigrants continues in part because of the strong migration chains they have built up in the past, and also because of the harsh political and socioeconomic conditions in Peru that have followed the introduction of the IMF's structural adjustment program (Alvarado 1991). In 1991, the number of families living in poverty was placed at 89 percent. Many households finance the emigration of a single female member by selling off major appliances. As Linda, twenty-three years old, reports: "The television, almost the house, the stereo set, with this I bought the passage." Formal means of financing emigration, such as borrowing the money from a bank, are normally avoided. Other sources of finance include severance pay, or savings, especially when the women have already worked for a number of years.

Financial support has also been internationalized coming mainly from relatives and friends living abroad. There is also resource pooling in the case of professional groups, such as nurses. It is more often young girls from families with many children who are sent, or who decide to contribute to the income of the family at home. They come to represent the "hope of the family." Most Peruvian women say that their migration project is temporary and that they would like to return home as soon as the situation in Peru improves. Until then, remittances sent home are used for raising the children they left behind or for their family, including parents, sisters and brothers.

Many of the Peruvian immigrant women were living in Peru as working heads-of-household before leaving their children with their mothers out of necessity and emigrating to Italy. They choose Italy because they think of it as a country where one can easily gain entry, and, not unrelated to this, because of the already high number of Peruvians in Italy. Again, illegality does not seem to be a concern as is exemplified in this response to the issue: "I'm convinced that I don't mean trouble to nobody, that I earn my money in an honest way. I buy my ticket for riding on the public services. I do everything respecting the order. Surely I would prefer to be legally here one day."

Somalian Women

Somalia is the only Islamic country from which female immigrants outnumber males. Emigration of Somali women to Italy began in the 1970s as Italians returned home from the former colony bringing their domestic workers with them. A second wave of female immigrants entered Italy in the late 1980s. In the early 1990s, after the civil war in Somalia had created such desperate conditions, more males joined this wave.

In most cases the war in Somalia was the main reason for emigrating or for remaining away from home. Compared to Peruvian and Philippine women, the Somalian women who came before 1992 (thus excluding refugees) constituted a rather homogeneous group. Very few were older than thirty when they entered Italy. Another common feature was the absence of a father at home. For those Somalian women, the migration project is seen as a temporary opportunity, both to avoid unemployment, and—given the deteriorating conditions at home—to help out those family members left behind. Many of these women thought that they would be able to continue their studies upon returning home. Khadija's story is typical. Born in 1968, she came to Naples in 1988, then moved to Milan, and is now sending money to her family in Mogadishu: "There are still three brothers and two sisters in Somalia and none of them have a job. Now I don't know how they survive. Another brother stays as a refugee in Finland. I came here four years ago and then I could not go back because of the war. At first I succeeded in helping my family."

Another reason, which Khadija also mentions, as to why Somalian women stay in Italy and the men do not, has a cultural background. According to Somali custom, men do not share in domestic work and thus do not regard it as a source of income for themselves even in Italy. Somalian men outnumber Somalian women in applying for refugee status in northern Europe. When asked why she did not go to another country like her brothers in search of refugee status, a Somalian woman who had been working as a domestic in Milan for three years answered: "And who feeds the family at home?" This seems to indicate that the task of sustaining the family during this period of crisis has emerged as the women's responsibility. All the Somalian women I spoke with who were able, sent money home—even those who had been living in Milan illegally for a long time. The Somalian community has established informal courier networks that allow them to send money home and to get news about their families. The money is usually brought personally to Somalia via Kenya or Djibouti. The courier usually commutes every two months to Africa, even in times of war.

Outlook

Italy offers two main advantages for many third world immigrants. First it offers a modest demand for menial labor (work the Italians themselves reject), especially in the black market and in the domestic services sector. The latter factor tends to increase the flow of female immigrants. Second, it is relatively easy to get into the country illegally and to stay there. The immigrants in the Italian domestic services sector are thought to play a complementary role with respect to the local labor force (Andall 1992; Macioti and Pugliese 1990). However, the economic crisis in Italy in the early 1990s also shows that in times of recession the domestic labor sector is attractive to the Italian labor force again. To the immigrants are left mostly the illegal (and therefore unstable and poorly paid) jobs.

The gendered labor market and the Italian assistance structures tend to keep the immigrant women invisible. Nearly all shelters and all job training programs, most of them financed by the EU, are directed toward men. Because of the immigration policy that tends to eliminate the "negative visibility," and the little visibility of female migrants working as domestic workers, those female immigrants are not perceived to be a social problem. Therefore, female migrants are forced to develop and maintain strong private social networks much more than men. The Catholic Church plays a leading role here, granting paternalistic help to female migrants.

The case study shows how those household strategies are transnational and gendered. They are gendered because of their targets: Somalian male migrants choose other countries to go to more than Somalian women do. They are gendered also because of their social and cultural impact: Peruvian and Philippine migrants often reported that they had been the working head of the household and that they left their children to their mother or another responsible female. Supplementary household strategies often are internationalized. Girl friends or colleagues staying abroad finance the expatriating of the newcomers.

From the perspective of the illegal female migrants, illegality is relatively unimportant. They do not even perceive themselves as illegal because they understand illegality to be equal to criminal offense. As long as they do not commit any crime—so they say—they do not feel illegal. They do act in the logic of a household decision and they know very well about the responsibilities they have assumed by going away. Their role in Italy is much more determined by the events in their home countries than by Italian immigration policy. They typically are responding to short-term needs of the family that do not necessarily follow a rational, long-term economic logic.

We can also tentatively conclude that two phenomena that meet at the local level—the attempts of the Italian government to stem immigration and the tendency of illegal immigrants to organize with the help of internationalized household strategies—are closely interrelated. With more rigid attempts on the part of the authorities to stem the flow of migrants, illegal immigration did not stop. However, at least in the case of the Philippines, the price of illegal passage increased.

References

Alvarado, Jorge Bernedo. 1991. "The Vital Adjustment." In *Peru Solidarity Forum*. Lima: Parroquia San Juan Bautista.

Andall, Jacqueline. 1992. "Women Migrant Workers in Italy." *Women's Studies International Forum* 15:41–48.

Bianchini, Franco. 1991. *Urbanisation and the Function of Cities in the European Community*. City case study Milan. Kent: University of Kent.

Boyd, Monica. 1989. "Family and Personal Networks in International Migration." *International Migration Review* 23:638–70.

Camus-Jacquez, Geneviève. 1990. "Refugee Women—the Forgotten Majority." In *Refugees and International Relations*, ed. Gil Loescher. Oxford: Clarendon Press.

Castles, Stephen. 1987. *Migration und Rassismus in Westeuropa*. Berlin: Express-Edition.

CESPE, ed. 1990. *Flussi migratori e ricerca sociale in Italia*. Rome: Papers 1.

Chant, Sylvia, and Sarah A. Radcliffe. 1992. *Gender and Migration in Developing Countries*. London and New York: Belhaven.

Comune di Milano. 1991. *Aspetti strutturali della popolazione straniera a Milano*. Bollettino 27. Milan: Tavola.

————. 1992. *Piano per l'immigrazione*. Milan: Assessore Diego Masi. Mimeo.

Hareven, Tamara. 1978. *Transitions: The Family and the Lifecourse in Historical Perspective*. New York: Academic Press.

Hugo, Graeme. 1981. "Village Community Ties, Village Norms, and Social and Ethnic Networks." In *Migration Decision Making*, ed. G. F. de Jong. New York: Pergamon.

IRER-OETAMM (Istituto di Ricerca della Lombardia and Osservatorio Economico-Territoriale dell'Area Milanese), ed. 1991. *L'immigrazione straniera extracomunitaria nella realtà metropolitana milanese*. Milan.

ISTAT (Istituto Nazionale di Statistica). 1992. "La presenza straniera in Italia." *Notiziario ISTAT*, 4 April, Rome.

Kosack, Godula. 1976. "Migrant Women: The Move to Western Europe—a Step Towards Emancipation?" *Race and Class* 17:369–79.

Lim, Lin Lean. 1990. "The Status of Women in International Migrations." Paper presented at the UN-Expert Meeting on International Migration and the Status of the Female Migrants, 27–30 March, San Miniato (Italy).

MacDonald, John S. and Leatrice D. MacDonald. 1964. "Chain Migration, Ethnic Neighborhood Formation and Social Networks." *Milbank Memorial Fund Quarterly* 42: 82–97.

Macioti, Maria, and Enrico Pugliese. 1990. *Gli immigrati in Italia*. Bari: Laterza.

Morokvasic, Mirjana. 1983. "Why Do Women Migrate?" *Studi Emigrazione/Etudes Migrations* 70:131–41.

————. 1993. " 'In And Out' of the Labour Market: Immigrant and Minority Women in Europe." *New Community* 19:459–83.

Morokvasic, Mirjana, and Czarina Wilpert. 1983. *Bedingungen und Folgen internationaler Migration*. Berlin: Technische Universitaet Berlin.

Murer, Bruno. 1993. *Rapporto sull'immigrazione a Milano*. Milan: Comune di Milano, Centro Stranieri.

Osservatorio del Mercato di Lavoro. 1991. *Immigrazione straniera in Lombardia*. Milan: Regione Lombardia.

Potts, Lydia. 1990. *The World Labour Market*. London: Zed Books.

Radcliffe, Sarah A. 1990. "Ethnicity, Patriarchy, and Incorporation Into the Nation: Female Migrants as Domestic Servants in Peru." *Environment and Planning D, Society and Space* 8:229–49.

La Repubblica, 9 June 1993, 7.

Sassen, Saskia. 1989. *The Mobility of Labour and Capital*. Cambridge: Cambridge University Press.

Synergia, ed. 1992. *Profilo statistico-sociologico sull'immigrazione in Italia ed elaborazione di una stima sulla clandestinità a Milano*. Milan.

Tosi, Antonio. 1993. *Immigrati e senza casa*. Milan: Franco Angeli.

Venturini, Alessandra. 1991. "Immigration et marché du travail en Italie." *Revue Européenne des Migrations Internationales* 7:97–113.

Zajczyk, Francesca, and Enzo Mingione. 1993. "Le nuove povertá urbane in Italia." *Inchiesta* 97/98:63–80.

Zanfrini, Laura. 1992. *Il ritratto della solidarietà: le iniziative del privato sociale per l'accoglienza degli stranieri a Milano*. Quaderni ISMU 5. Milan.

Chapter 10

Foreign Immigrants in Madrid

*Mana J. Aguilera Arilla, Aurora Garcia Ballesteros,
M. Pilar Gonzalez Yanci, P. Pumares Fernandez, and
Vicente Rodríguez Rodríguez*

Spain, up to the seventies, was a nation of high emigration. In recent years, it has become a population receiver country and the number of immigrants is growing (Colectivo I.O.E. 1987; Gozalvez Perez 1990). Although in 1992 Spain had fewer immigrants than many other European countries, there were more than half a million, or 1.2 percent of its total population. Nevertheless, the number of Spanish emigrants is still important (Izquierdo 1992).

Two broad groups of immigrants are found in Spain: (1) settled and "regular" immigrants, registered together with the native population, and (2) nonregistered immigrants. Most of the nonregistered immigrants arrive illegally in the country as they do not fulfill the requirements of the Ley sobre Derechos y Libertades de los Extranjeros of 1985 (Law on Aliens). Most come from Morocco and Black African nations. Due to the strategic location of Spain between Africa and the European Union, many migrants simply cross the Straits of Gibraltar. Others come across the Portuguese border, through other European countries, or arrive at the international border at Madrid airport. Some of these illegal aliens have regularized their situation through processes established by the Spanish authorities, while others remain clandestine and are subject to exploitation and other difficulties. Even among regularized aliens, some become clandestine once again when they lose their jobs.

Like other immigration receiving countries, Spain has started taking measures to prevent a massive flow of immigration that the labor market cannot absorb. The measures started with the Law on Aliens, then two regularization processes were introduced (in 1985–86 and again in 1991), and today an admission quota is being discussed.

Within this framework, we will analyze in this chapter some aspects of alien immigration in Madrid. First, the geographical distribution of registered immigrants in Madrid and some metropolitan municipalities is described. We use the information given by the Padrón de Habitantes (List of Inhabitants) of 1986, updated in 1990, and by the Census of 1991. Next we analyze the demographic and socioeconomic features of registered immigrants using 1986 and 1990 data. Third, we summarize a study of immigrants who have entered into the regularization processes. The fourth part assesses the social impact that nonregistered immigrants have on Madrid's population, as well as the attitudes toward immigrants possessed by that population. The study ends with some future prospects regarding alien immigration in Spain.

Evolution and Distribution of Immigrant Population

Although the region of Madrid is one of the main immigration-receiving centers in Spain, the number of immigrants is low relative to other European cities that have traditionally received immigrants. Thus, according to the Padrón de Habitantes of 1986, the 46,237 registered aliens (1 percent of the entire population) who lived in the region, increased to 59,000 aliens (1.2 percent) in 1991. This was an increase of 27 percent in five years (Aguilera, Gonzalez Yanci, and Rodriguez 1991). The number of nonregistered aliens is much higher, but is difficult to measure. Only when we obtain some additional detailed information from the regularization process will we be able to assess their numbers.

The origin of registered immigrants is diverse. The largest groups come from European and South American countries (a third in each case), the others are North Americans, Asians, and Africans, in that order. The last two groups have increased most during recent years. Countries such as Argentina, Portugal, United States, Morocco, the Philippines, France, and Chile contribute the largest percentages. There is a female prevalence among European, American, and Asian aliens, in contrast to the prevalence of African males. Illegal aliens mainly come from Morocco, the Dominican Republic, Peru, the Philippines, Argentina, Chile, Poland—countries that have suffered from demographic, political, and social pressures.

The distribution of immigrants by origin within the urban region of Madrid is related to the characteristics of the immigrant population as well as the social conditions. Some increases in segregation have been observed with the urban development of Madrid (and that of the aureole of municipalities form the metropolitan area). This was caused in part by the various activities delegated to the different municipalities and partly owing to demographic and socieconomic factors that underlie residential segregation.

Within the city, districts with high immigrant populations are situated in the center and northwest. The lowest immigrant populations are in areas farthest away from the center to the south, which have the highest socioeconomic status. The general distributive pattern within Madrid defines a central space with a high volume of immigrants, and peripheral areas that contain small numbers (fig. 10.1), a fact that has not changed basically from 1986 to 1991. The foreign population from North America and the EU is located in the center and north of the city, in the areas with higher social and economic standing (fig. 10.2). African and South American aliens live in the south of the city (as well as in some northern and central peripheral areas), in areas possessing lower quality of life. The other immigrants do not show a clear distributive pattern but are located mostly in peripheral areas.

Outside the city, in some western and northeastern municipalities, the number of immigrants was over 2 percent in 1991 compared to a little over 1 percent in the city. The south and west parts of the metropolitan area are the favorite location of (observed) illegal immigrants. Rural municipalities receive very few immigrants.

General Characteristics of Immigrants

Age and Gender Structures

The immigrant population of Madrid has a different age and sex composition than that of the native population (fig. 10.3). The foreign population has a prevalence of adults (more than 70 percent of the total) and lower rates of dependency and masculinity than the native population. Most immigrant groups have more females than males in their adult populations.

Immigrants are located according to the economic means available to them and the standard of living in the district. In those areas with the highest socioeconomic rank, the pyramid of immigrants is more aged, which is similar to Madrid. Here the population is composed primarily of Europeans and Americans. The foreign population tends to be younger in those districts where there is a younger native population and with fewer economic resources, mainly in the south of the city. The origins of these immigrants are some of the less-developed countries in Latin America, Europe, and Asia.

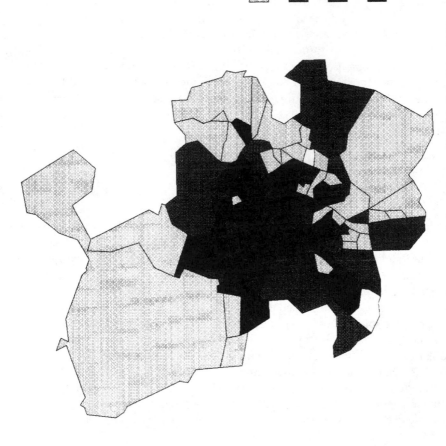

% immigrants in Madrid

0.01 to 0.28

0.28 to 0.59

0.59 to 1.14

1 14 to 3.5

Fig. 10.1 Foreign Population in Madrid and Surrounding Municipalities, 1991

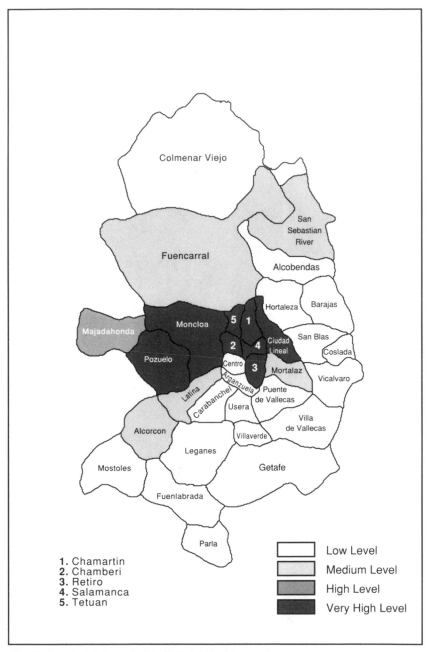

Colmenar Viejo

San
Sebastian
River

Alcobendas

Fuencarral

Hortaleza   Barajas

Majadahonda

Moncloa   **5** **1**

Pozuelo

Ciudad
Lineal

San Blas

Coslada

2   **4**

Centro   **3**   Mortalaz

Vicalvaro

Arganzuela

Latina

Puente
de Vallecas

Carabanchel

Usera

Villa
de Vallecas

Alcorcon

Villaverde

Mostoles

Leganes

Getafe

Fuenlabrada

Parla

1. Chamartin
2. Chamberi
3. Retiro
4. Salamanca
5. Tetuan

Low Level

Medium Level

High Level

Very High Level

Fig. 10.2   Social Areas in Madrid and the Metropolitan Area

CITY OF MADRID, 1986

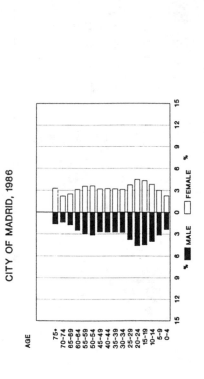

FOREIGN POPULATION IN MADRID

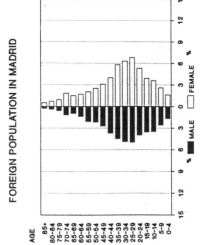

EUROPEANS IN MADRID

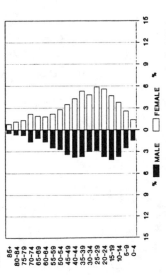

ASIANS IN MADRID

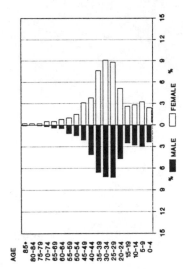

Fig. 10.3   Age and Sex Pyramids, Madrid, 1986

Socioeconomic Characteristics

Our analyses of socioeconomic indicators utilize academic (education) level, employment level, and occupation and type of company in which foreign immigrants work. For these we use the categories established by the National Institute of Statistics.

According to academic level, foreign immigrants have a rather low educational standard (more than 50 percent have not passed primary school). There is a clear spatial contrast (fig. 10.4): the foreigners with low educational attainment (illiterates and those without formal education) tend to live in the districts and municipalities with low social rank, especially in the south (Figure 10.2). These represent 25.5 percent of the total, compared to 15.3 percent who are graduates and live in the areas with high social rank. On the whole, academic level decreases on moving from the city outward to the metropolitan area.

Academic level also varies according to sex and origin. Women are more numerous among the illiterates and those without formal education, as are Africans and Asians. Europeans, Americans, and Latin Americans have the highest percentages of graduates.

In the employment activity rates, foreigners display higher values than those of the native population, always surpassing 40 percent both in the city and in the metropolitan municipalities. The male activity rate exceeds that of females, both because of the difficulties that women experience in getting a formal job and for social and cultural reasons deriving from varying origins of foreigners. As a general rule, the highest activity rates are to be found among aliens from less-developed countries.

Workers, students, and housewives represent more than 75 percent of the immigrant population. Significant numbers of retired people are found only among American and European immigrants, while among Africans, Asians, and Latin Americans this group is very small. There is a greater concentration of working immigrants in the north of Madrid. In the south, we find more people who are unemployed and more first-time job hunters.

Information about occupation and industry is not fully comprehensive because many of the low-socioeconomic-level foreigners do not declare their occupation, often because of a low level of education, lack of a specific profession, or the temporary nature of their job. Of all those who declared their profession, the main characteristics included prevalence of technicians and managers and a concentration in the financial sector found among Europeans and Americans; and a prevalence of workers in hotels, trade, construction, or private services found among immigrants from Africa, Latin America, and Asia. The familiar spatial dichotomy is seen again with the

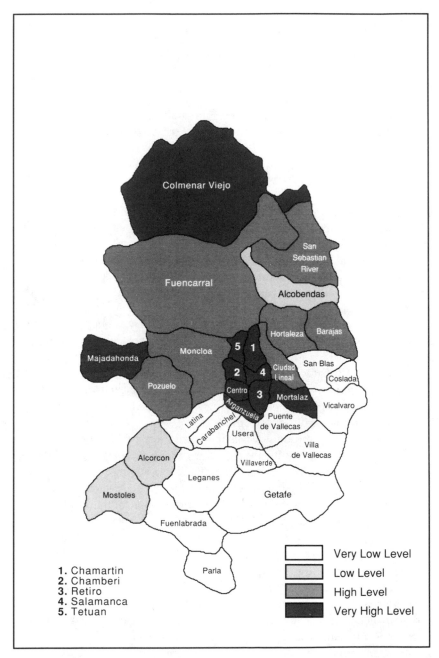

1. Chamartin
2. Chamberi
3. Retiro
4. Salamanca
5. Tetuan

Very Low Level
Low Level
High Level
Very High Level

Fig. 10.4   Foreign Immigrant Academic Level

northern districts and municipalities having the highest percentages of higher level professionals and the southern ones having workers with lower qualifications (fig. 10.5).

The Regularization Process

From June to December 1991, an exceptional process of alien regularization took place in Spain. It was instituted mainly as a result of the creation of a high number of illegal immigrants since the first regularization process in 1985–86, and to the prospect of a single European market. The process, with a total of 127,004 applications (compared to fewer than 40,000 in the first process), has had significant consequences for Spanish immigration.

The information obtained from this process provides some reliable information on the number of aliens in the workforce. Previously, the official numbers showed a clear tendency toward highly qualified foreigners from Western countries (Izquierdo 1992), while the size characteristics of other groups was poorly understood, partly because of their irregularity.

The regularization process confirms the new role of Spain as an immigration-receiving country. It sheds new light on the qualitative change in immigrant populations, showing increases among Africans, Poles, Chinese, and Filipinos in addition to the largest group, Moroccans, who represented 44 percent of the applications—almost four times the number of legal Moroccans. Madrid's area is the main receiving center for these immigrants, with 31.5 percent of the applications.

Figure 10.6 compares the origin, citizenship, and occupation of previously regularized immigrants with those who were regularized in 1991. Among alien workers who had been regularized by 1991, there is a prevalence of middle- or high-status occupations, taken up basically by people of the EU, North Americans, and Argentinians. Also relevant are qualification services performed by Filipinos, Chinese, Moroccans, and Portuguese.

Figure 10.6 also shows the origins and occupations of aliens whose regularization was decided in 1991, approximately two-thirds of the total granted. The service sector predominates, but the percentage of high- to middle-qualification jobs is just 14.2, while low-qualification jobs (mainly household positions) reach up to 53.9 percent, performed mainly by Moroccans, Dominican women, Peruvians, Chinese, Filipinos, and Portuguese. Construction jobs here have a greater relative importance than among previously regularized aliens. In this sector, workers come especially from Morocco, Peru, and Poland.

It could be said that foreign employment mirrors Madrid's most dynamic

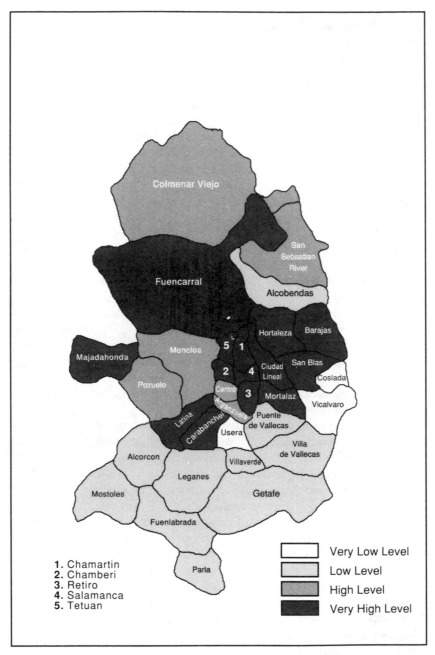

1. Chamartin
2. Chamberi
3. Retiro
4. Salamanca
5. Tetuan

Very Low Level
Low Level
High Level
Very High Level

Fig. 10.5 Profession of Greater or Lesser Rank for Foreign Immigrants

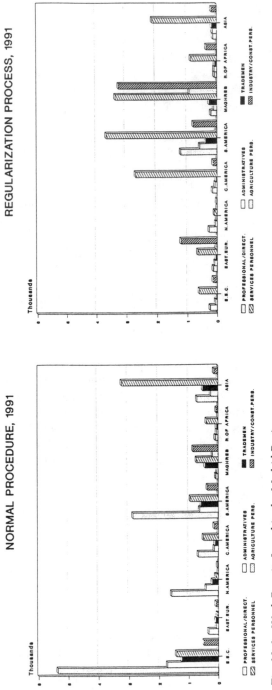

Fig. 10.6 Work Permits Issued in the Madrid Region

economic sectors. As a financial center and the main receiver of multinational companies, it has an important percentage of highly qualified workers, usually from Western nations, who do not have the problems of regularizing their situation. On the other hand, linked to these sectors, low-qualified, labor-intensive services appear that take advantage of the flexibility of other immigrants.

The precarious situation of low-skill immigrants makes it much harder for them to achieve a legal position through the normal process. The construction sector serves as a good example: There was a huge demand from 1986 to 1991, so aliens concentrated in the small companies that might not be concerned about the legal situation of their workers. On the other hand, the bigger companies, working on large projects, hired Spaniards. Manufacturing also has refrained from hiring foreign workers, due partly to heavy trade-union pressures.

Social Impact of the Ethnic-Cultural Diversification of Immigration

Simultaneously with the increasing number of immigrants, the ethnic, cultural, and socioeconomic diversity of Madrid has increased. At present, the foreigners arriving from the third world and the countries of the former socialist Europe are proportionally more numerous. As a result Madrid's immigrant community has changed from being "invisible," that is, having a similar ethnic and cultural background as natives, to being visible. The new economic immigrants suffer from a host of problems and their cultural and behavior patterns provoke diverse reactions. Many of the evils in Madrid's society are attributed to them, including such problems as unemployment and lack of safety.

We have used qualitative surveys from the Center for Research of Social Reality (CIRES 1992), in order to detect the impact that this immigration is having on Madrid's society. The interview part of the research had overcome the problem of the language barrier with many of the immigrants. Yet, these interviews have been the only means of learning the opinion that immigrants hold regarding the attitudes of Madrid's society toward them, and also of detecting which of the problems they feel are most important.

The problems that affect the immigrants of Madrid, apart from the most generic ones related to labor conditions or job insecurity, are the lack of housing and schooling for the second-generation immigrants. (The number of children of immigrants is estimated to be between three thousand and ten thousand depending on the source.)

The problem of housing is significant in a city like Madrid where there are still pockets of poor housing occupied by marginalized families in deteriorating neighborhoods. These include housing projects that were built in the sixties and were used at that time by immigrants from other areas of Spain (Pumares 1993). It is noteworthy, however, that some of these building complexes have been remodeled. Upon their arrival, immigrants must live in hostels set up by nongovernmental organizations (NGOs), in slums that are not in habitable condition, or in apartments in marginalized areas. This makes their integration into society quite difficult and also generates a negative image among Madrid's residents. At the same time, a significant number of Madrid's residents have had to emigrate from the capital because of the high cost of real estate. Thus, housing is perceived as a problem by many.

In the surveys taken by CIRES, we do not detect a strong negative reaction toward the immigrant population on the part of Madrid's residents. On a scale from 0 ("I don't mind having an immigrant as a neighbor") to 10 ("It would really bother me to have an immigrant as a neighbor"), the average rating was 2.5. However, it is not possible to discern whether this is a true attitude or an answer conditioned by the fact that in reality there is only a small chance that the persons asked would ever have such neighbors, considering the current small number of immigrants. One must take into account that three-fourths of those interviewed confirmed that immigrants did not live in their neighborhoods.

News and testimonies from the immigrants themselves, especially from the Moroccans and Black Africans, paint a different picture. They sense a general rejection by Madrid's residents toward some immigrants. They also specifically cite refusals to rent apartments and higher housing deposits than those for the autochthonous population. Housing, per se, is not as severe a problem for the large numbers of women who work as live-in maids and enjoy a bedroom with good hygienic conditions. This comfort does not come without cost, howewer, because their work does not allow them to live with their husbands and children.

With respect to schooling, official sources estimate that 3,000 immigrant children are in nonpaying schools in the Madrid area (2,371 in public schools and 600 in subsidized schools). The majority attend schools in the periphery, which would seem to indicate that in the last few years immigrants are settling in the neighborhoods of lowest standards of living.

Schooling for the second generation of immigrants is basic for their integration, but it presents many problems. More than half the children going to school initially speak no Spanish. Their cultural backgrounds are as heterogeneous as their countries of origin: Morocco, Chile, Poland. The educational authorities only provided twenty centers in a few districts and municipalities with support staff and additional teachers to deal with the problem. This slow and limited response on the part of the government officials is due to the fact that they believe they are dealing with a relatively new phenomenon. In addition, because it is difficult to plan for the needs of the immigrants, since many of the immigrant families are only here temporarily, the government tends to concentrate its efforts in those areas where there are larger pockets of immigrants.

Attitude of Residents toward Immigrants

In a recent colloquium held in Madrid on racism, xenophobia, and cultural diversity, it was concluded that presently it is not possible to determine whether Spanish society in general, and Madrid's residents in particular, have racist attitudes toward immigrants, because of the immigrants' recent arrival and still scant numbers. Nevertheless, one does detect some worrisome attitudes. In a recent survey, taken by the Centro de Investigaciones Sociológicas (CIS), a third of the Spaniards interviewed said they would not deny votes to a political party with a racist platform. Along these lines, some small right-wing and skinhead groups have sprayed antiimmigrant slogans in various districts in both the center of Madrid and in the periphery. The slogans are directed especially at the immigrants most rejected who are addressed as "moros" (moors), "niggers" (negros), and "sudacas" (South Americans). At the same time, all the surveys confirm that, although Spanish society proclaims that it is not racist, there has always existed a rejection of certain ethnic, cultural, and economic collectives, especially Gypsies and Moroccans. For this reason, it is possible that this attitude will spread to the new immigrant groups having different ethnic and cultural profiles, especially to the Black Africans.

The number of people who think that the proportion of immigrants is excessive is only 20 percent. Many respondents agreed with statements such as "citizens of every country should have the right to settle in any country without any type of limitations." However, when the economic factor is introduced, one finds a significant backing for phrases like "workers from other countries should only be admitted when there are no Spaniards who can fill their jobs." The most negative Spanish attitudes come from those groups with the lowest socioeconomic conditions. In addition, a significant percentage of the population would like to limit the immigration of North Africans, Black Africans, and to a lesser degree, South Americans. This attitude is especially manifest among adults between fifty and sixty-four years of age who consider themselves right-wing and who have a lower educational and socioeconomic level. However, more than half of the people interviewed were in favor of integrating these three groups of immigrants, especially the Latin Americans since they have a cultural affinity with this group. Only one-third of the people interviewed were in favor of having the immigrants return to their country of origin.

All sections of the population feel that the lack of employment and the cultural differences are the largest problems facing integration. This sentiment runs deeper than a mere xenophobic and racist attitude, although in the majority of cases it is difficult to dissociate the latter from the economic and cultural attitudes. This points to another area of study, the association that Spaniards might make between the immigrants and the important problems in Spain and Madrid: unemployment, lower wages, more delinquent crime, and so on. On this issue, there is no majority opinion. Only one-quarter of those residents interviewed believe that immigrants have contributed to the decrease in wages, and one-third thinks that they have increased delinquency. Fewer than half believe that immigrants have influenced the rise of unemployment.

In Madrid, there are not the same social tensions between Spaniards and immigrants as there are in other European cities. Nevertheless, as the visible number of immigrants is rising, some strains of racism and xenophobia begin to emerge. Immigrants have been blamed for robberies, violence, drugs, and various crimes, and this process causes more rejection. The immigrants perceive the attitudes of the Spaniards toward them in different ways: some of them think that racism exists, but others believe that the situation is much better than in other European countries.

Overall, Madrid's society has still not fully realized the change that is taking place. This explains why there is only a small minority that is clearly racist, and another minority clearly committed to helping immigrants in their integration. Meanwhile, the majority of society waits. And the only way to keep this majority from leaning toward the racist and xenophobic minority is to promote authentic public policies for immigration, policies that will avoid the formation of ghettos and will promote and facilitate the means for raising the economic and cultural level of the immigrants.

Prospects for the Future

Immigration is a recent development in Spain and, therefore, in the urban region of Madrid. Madrid's society is becoming aware, little by little, of the resulting changes and of the problems that arise from the new visible immigrants.

According to the polls, up until now just a minority of the population is clearly racist. At the same time, only a small fraction of the population collaborates in the solidarity and supporting networks that try to ease the immigrants' integration. The social majority is still waiting (Gimenez 1993), but it is becoming more aware that racism is growing and that we need to take measures to prevent attacks on immigrants. The new penal code proposes a hardening of penalties for racist and xenophobic crimes as a means of fighting this type of behavior.

According to a poll by Demoscopia, taken on 11–15 December 1992 for the newspaper *El Pais*, 54 percent of the population think racism and alien rejection has grown, 31 percent think it is the same, and only 11 percent think it has decreased. The majority of the population feels that racism and the rejection of aliens in Spain is the same (31 percent) or stronger (29 percent) than in other EU countries. That same poll asked what measures the government should take in relation to immigrants already in Spain. A vast majority (84 percent), larger by 10 percent than the previous year, thinks they should be helped to regularize their situation. However, 6 percent are in favor of making them return to their home countries.

Even more troublesome is the attitude taken toward the alien workers coming to Spain. It is a critical period for Spain's labor market since unemployment keeps an ascending curve and, as we have seen, part of the population thinks immigrants compete for their own jobs. In the poll, there are two different groups: 10 percent favor closing the borders to immigration completely, while 26 percent think there must be a policy of open borders. It is worth pointing out that the percentage of immigration rejectors is stable, while the percentage of open-borders supporters has increased by four points.

A growing majority (62 percent versus 58 percent in 1991) declares itself for a setting of quotas. Everything stresses the need for the authorities to set immigration policies. Local and regional authorities as well as the central administration are designing some initiatives. Local and regional authorities have, for example, a policy for the integration of immigrants' children in the schools, and even a policy for adult education to facilitate their faster integration in the Spanish society. In relation to housing, a problem for many immigrants, there are agreements with several Madrid municipalities to build permanent houses in place of present marginal settlements.

At the level of the central administration, there are two basic initiatives that have increased the controversy among the immigrant associations or their supporters. On the one hand is the modification of the Ley de Asilo y Refugio (Law on Asylum) of 1984 to homogenize it with the legislation of other EU countries. Once the law is put into effect, only people persecuted in their own countries will be admitted as refugees, according to the definition in the Covenant of Geneva. Therefore, the entrance right for every seeker of asylum in Spain will be abolished to avoid admitting economic immigrants under that figure. This law is important for Madrid since, of the twelve thousand people who have claimed sanctuary in Spain, 85 percent concentrate in the city.

Second, in keeping with decisions made at the European Conference on Uncontrolled Migrations, measures are being taken to control the entrance of immigrants coming, mostly, from Africa. The Spanish government has subscribed agreements with Morocco, either for the return of aliens coming into Spain through that country or for a stricter control of the Straits of Gibraltar and the vigilance of the Spanish coasts.

Finally, a Ley de Cuotas (Quota Act) considering the real capacity of the Spanish labor market to absorb foreign workers is under discussion. The Ministry of Labor has assessed the twenty thousand jobs open to immigrants in 1993, most of them household and temporary agricultural positions. The plan would also take measures to prevent temporary immigrants from staying in Spain illegally. Madrid's regional authorities are prepared to receive just three thousand new immigrants, mostly for household jobs. This amount is very low, as the authorities acknowledge, if we consider past immigration rates.

Everything seems to indicate that Spain is turning into the southern champion for the European fortress, to prevent a wave of African immigrants from joining the wave coming from Eastern Europe. The key problem is still there: the need to define an EU immigration policy clearly stating entrance regulations and to organize proceedings for immigrants; but help is most urgent in the economic and social development of the immigrating countries.

References

Aguilera, M.J., M.P. Gonzalez Yanci, and V. Rodriguez. 1991. "Los inmigrantes extranjeros en el municipio de Madrid." *Actas de las III Jornadas de Población Española*. Málaga: Excma.

CIRES. 1992. *La realidad social en España*. Madrid: Fundación BBV y Caja Madrid.

Colectivo I.O.E. 1987 "Los inmigrantes en España." *Revista de Estudios Sociales y de Sociología Aplicada* 66:376.

Gimenez, C. 1993. *El Desafío de la Inmigración*. Madrid: Consejería de Integración Social.

Gozalvez Perez, V. 1990. "El reciente incremento de la población extranjera en España y su incidencia laboral." *Investigaciones Geográficas* 8:7–36.

Izquierdo Escribano, A. 1992. *La inmigración en España 1980–1990.* Madrid: Ministerio de Trabajo y Seguridad Social.

Pumares, P. 1993. "La Inmigración Marroquí en la Comunidad de Madrid." In *El Desafío de la Inmigración.* Madrid.

Chapter 11

Ethnic Change in Late-Apartheid South African Cities

Jürgen Bähr and Ulrich Jürgens

Ethnic conflicts have intensified all over the world since the beginning of the 1990s, and they increasingly involve violence. South Africa is only one of many regional examples in which population groups of varying skin color, language, or cultural background are vying for political and economic power and dominance.

Particular issues arise when different ethnic groups live together in cities. From an early date, urban ethnicity and sociospatial processes have attracted the interest of social scientists. As early as the 1920s, the school of "social ecology" identified segregation of residential areas along racial and ethnic lines. One model, that of invasion and succession, interprets segregation in terms of sociospatial competition of different population groups for the same area (Park, Burgess, and McKenzie 1925). In their analyses, Shevky, Williams, and Bell also emphasized that residential segregation, whether voluntary or forced by society through discriminatory measures, is one of the most important factors underlying the overall sociospatial differentiation of urban populations (Shevky and Bell 1955). As a rule the term *segregation* has been associated with negative connotations, whereas *integration* or *assimilation* is viewed positively.

Such theories and concepts can only be applied to South Africa with certain reservations. Above all, we must remember that for a long time the government prevented the assimilation of Blacks (i.e., Africans, Indians, and Coloreds) into the mainstream culture of the socially dominant White population group and that residential integration was explicitly blocked by legal measures. Since the abolition of apartheid in 1991, these regulations and restrictions are no longer in force, but too little time has passed for exact analyses and final prognoses. In this chapter, we will report on the early experiences in the postapartheid phase, basing our analysis first on general social indicators and then on the development in individual residential areas. Our urban analyses focus on the Johannesburg and Durban metropolitan areas.

Sociopolitical Change in South Africa

The sociopolitical upheavals and the trend toward greater democracy all over the world in the past few years have not failed to have an effect on South Africa. The socialist block has slowly fallen apart since the middle of the 1980s, and more rapidly since 1989, thanks to perestroika and glasnost. In the process, South Africa has been able to liberate itself from stereotypical ways of thinking in terms of East and West. Domestic policy is no longer subordinated to foreign policy, which was traditionally governed by the fear of "Black" encirclement and aimed at warding off "communist" influence on "White" South Africa. The objective now is to direct intrasocietal change so as to guarantee that all population groups will be able to participate democratically in society, in the economy, and particularly in politics. Within the Convention for a Democratic South Africa (CODESA) representatives of the most varied political groups had been preparing a new constitution since December 1991, which came in force after the first free elections for all population groups in April 1994.

The Preapartheid Phase and the Heyday of Apartheid

The dimensions of this most recent social change can only be fully appreciated against the background of the long tradition of racial hostility and segregation. Until the end of the nineteenth century, informal regulations and customs sufficed to uphold the colonial superiority-inferiority system between Whites and non-Whites. It was the high spatial concentration of population in the new cities of the Witwatersrand following the discovery and exploitation of the rich mineral resources that increasingly led to legal discrimination. In contrast to the patriarchal, personified master-servant relationship in the agrarian society of the period prior to 1870, the anonymity of industrial society required that the master and his orders be at least vigorously supported by the (White) lawmakers, if not completely replaced by them.

Control mechanisms and sanctions, which were generally aimed at the non-White population groups, were concerned with their spatial and social mobility. Pass laws, job reservation, the introduction of the migratory labor system and migration laws, plus the setting up of locations and townships are examples. After 1948, when the apartheid policy became the official state doctrine, such regimentation was formulated more and more rigidly and the appropriate laws were implemented. The main pillars of apartheid policy after 1950 were the Population Registration Act, which by classifying the population into Whites, Blacks, and Coloreds (originally also including Indians) made it possible to enforce segregation, and the Group Areas Act, which prescribed residential segregation of the population groups defined according to skin color and language. The enforcement of the legal regulations led to the forced relocation of hundreds of thousands of persons, arrests, and high social costs. In order to finance the mechanisms of apartheid, costs also increased for White taxpayers. Violent domestic conflicts occurred and the international boycott movement against South Africa was established.

The Phase of Reform-Apartheid, 1976 to 1991

In contrast to the former East Block states, in South Africa the process of change has been evolutionary rather than revolutionary. After the Soweto uprising in 1976, the White government attempted to integrate the non-White population majority into the White-dominated social structures by reforming the apartheid system. This strategy, which attempted to maintain White privileges, was only partially successful, however. The administration of F. W. de Klerk, which began in 1989, sought to totally abolish apartheid laws.

Until 1989, legislation concentrated on liberalizing economic apartheid and making it more flexible (through repeal of job reservation and influx controls) and on abolishing certain forms of racial segregation in the social area that caused particular offense on the international scene, petty apartheid. As a result of the natural population development and the brain drain to foreign countries in certain professions (SAIRR 1992, 8ff.), it was no longer possible to fill high-qualification jobs exclusively with members of the White population, as had traditionally been done. In its basic features, the state-run school system continued to be segregated until the beginning of 1993, the exception being a few mixed-race schools started in the spring of 1991. Nevertheless, multiracial private schools existed; universities had been opened to all racial groups; and private enterprises offered on-the-job training programs. These brought forth a non-White middle class whose lifestyle is modeled on that of Europeans.

It was primarily this group that tried to avoid the problems of overcrowded housing, poor transportation and services, and violence in the townships by moving into residential areas that had previously been reserved for Whites. Mixed-race residential areas (so-called grey areas) developed particularly in the inner-city areas of Johannesburg and Durban. These functioned as ports of entry for further non-White migration from townships all over the country (Jürgens 1991).

To legalize de facto violations of the law, the legislature agreed to introduce so-called free trading areas in 1984 and free settlement or open areas in 1988, in extension of the Group Areas Act. To meet economic needs on the one hand and residential needs on the other, mixed-race areas were proclaimed.

President P. W. Botha was overthrown by his own party in 1989. This and the changing domestic conditions opened the way to radical societal changes, whose implications depart from the apartheid system. Representative measures are the repeal of the Social Amenities Act in October 1990 and the abolition of the Group Areas Act and the Population Registration Act in July 1991.

Urban Development in South Africa up to the Beginning of the 1990s

The implementation of the apartheid city by means of influx controls, forced resettlement, and an extensive bureaucratic apparatus was repeatedly challenged by the non-White majority of the population with "defiance acts." Nevertheless, for a long time the powers upholding the state were determined to practice racial segregation even in the face of international threats. After the end of the 1970s this political will weakened. The goal was to co-opt Coloreds and Indians into the tricameral parliamentary system introduced in 1983, which was dominated by the White group. Although the abolition of apartheid laws was being discussed, new group areas continued to be set up until the end of 1990. *The Star* (4 September 1990) of Johannesburg proclaimed: "Shock over new Indian group area."

The system of apartheid failed because urban development was much more dynamic than the governing legal system. Despite the introduction of free trading and free settlement areas, the apartheid laws could not be made flexible enough to keep pace. The population was becoming increasingly mobile, both spatially and socially. As a consequence, residential and job structures fit less and less to the apartheid regulations.

Population Structures

The figures on the population of the different groups in South Africa show that the percentage of Whites has dropped continuously since the 1920s (table 11.1). The number of Whites decreased from 21.6 percent of the total population in 1904 to 14.4 percent in 1990. This development is particularly pronounced in large cities, including Johannesburg (table 11.2). Durban seems to be an exception, but this is attributable to the fact that the Black townships are generally classified as part of the homeland KwaZulu, thus concealing the relative decline of the White population in the official statistics (Table 11.2).

Two contrary types of population dynamics exist parallel to each other in South Africa. One, which is typical of first world countries, applies mainly to the White population and is characterized by a high percentage of old people, low numbers of children, low dependency ratios (the number of members in a household divided by the number of its members in employment), and small households. On the other side, third world characteristics apply not only in the homelands, but also in the non-White townships: a high percentage of young population and large households (Keenan 1988) (table 11.3).

Although inflation, economic stagnation, high unemployment rates, and personal danger due to criminality and political violence should discourage people from moving into the cities (Keenan 1988, 42; Karcher 1990), the growth of the townships is undiminished. The Black South African population that is potentially ready to move into the cities from the rural areas of the erstwhile White South Africa and the homelands has by no means been exhausted with an urbanization rate of 40 percent and an assumed natural population growth of 3 percent (Hattingh 1988, 8; Republic of South Africa 1989, 88). For the year 2000, an urbanization rate of only 41 percent is projected for Blacks, but 95 percent for Asians, 79 percent for Coloreds, and 92 percent for Whites (*Natal Witness*, 10 April 1991). Considerable deviations from the official projections on population are evident in the figures of the Urban Foundation South Africa, which considers 53 percent of the Black population urbanized in 1985 and projects 69 percent in 2010 (fig. 11.1).

Residential Structures

The original goal of the government, to separate members of the Black population groups from the White region by establishing homelands, kept the government from supporting construction of formal housing in the townships. On the one hand, the government had little interest in improving the residential circumstances. On the other hand, Black private initiative was discouraged, because, until 1986, the apartheid laws did not allow Blacks to acquire property, and as a rule they were unable to present any self-financing. As a result there is today a tremendous shortage of housing. Most heavily

Table 11.1 South Africa: Population Development by Race Group, 1904–1990 (population in thousands)

	Whites	%	Coloreds	Asians	Blacks	Total
1904	1,117	21.6	445	122	3,490	5,174
1911	1,276	21.4	525	152	4,019	5,972
1921	1,521	22.0	545	163	4,697	6,926
1936	2,003	20.9	769	220	6,596	9,588
1946	2,372	20.8	928	285	7,830	11,415
1951	2,642	20.8	1,103	367	8,560	12,672
1960	3,088	19.3	1,509	477	10,928	16,002
1970	3,773	17.3	2,051	630	15,340	21,794
1980	4,390	14.9	2,620	796	21,685	29,491
1985	4,843	14.4	2,941	882	24,916	33,582
1990	5,471	14.4	3,319	1,013	28,248	38,051

Sources: Republic of South Africa 1990,1.6; Development Bank of Southern Africa 1991,20–24.
Note: 1904–1970: Results of population censuses; 1980 and 1985: Results of population censuses adjusted for undercount; 1990: Projection on the basis of the population census of 1980 and 1985: The figures for 1980, 1985, and 1990 include the "independent" homelands.

Table 11.2 Johannesburg and Durban: Population Groups

	Whites %	Coloreds %	Asians %	Blacks %	Total (000s)
Johannesburg Metropolitan Area					
1946[a]	51.8	3.6	2.6	42.1	618
1970[b]	34.4	6.0	2.8	56.9	1,442
1985[c]	32.0	7.6	3.6	56.8	1,610
1991[c]	28.1	6.8	3.4	61.6	1,916
Durban Metropolitan Area[d]					
1946[e]	34.4	3.2	31.5	30.9	340
1970[f]	29.1	5.6	65.3		750
1985[c]	31.4	6.1	50.0	12.5	982
1991[c]	28.8	5.7	50.6	14.8	1,137

[a]*The Star*, ed. 1987. [b]Schneider and Wiese 1983.
[c]Republic of South Africa (1986a; 1986b; 1992a; 1992b): figures for 1985 not adjusted for undercount.
[d]In the 1960s and 1970s the border between the White Durban metropolitan area and the Black homeland KwaZulu was removed several times. As a result, Black townships and so-called Black spots were incorporated with their population into KwaZulu, thus concealing the relative decline of the White population in the Durban area.
[e]Praechter 1961,49. [f]Van den Berghe 1971,42.

Table 11.3 Soweto: Population Indicators for Selected Townships

Township	Dependency ratio	Aged ≥ 50 %	Aged ≤ 11 %	Average household size	Time
Moroka	2.9-3.3	11.9-7.7	30.2-18.1	n.a.	1978-85
Phiri	3.2-4.3	8.7-7.2	28.6-25.9	7.9-7.3	1981-85
White City	3.4-5.1	10.1-8.7	32.3-30.3	6.2-6.2	1981-85

Source: Keenan 1988, 43.

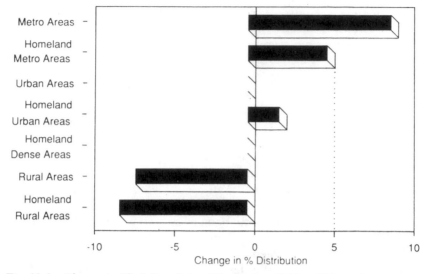

Fig. 11.1   Change in Black Population Distribution, 1985 to 2010 (Urban Foundation, 1991b)

affected are Blacks, but also affected are Indians and Coloreds and increasingly poor Whites who are seeking affordable flats (*Sunday Star*, 23 February 1991; *Weekly Mail* 8–14 May 1992). The latter group ("the desperate Whites") has been increasing in size rapidly since the repeal of job reservation and particularly of the Group Areas Act. They face competition from non-Whites for space in the formerly White inner cities. Historically known as the clientele of militant and extreme rightist White parties, poor Whites are important to the political future of South Africa and to proponents of apartheid (van Niekerk 1991). The South African Urban Foundation assumes a figure of 200,000 poor Whites (*International Herald Tribune*, 15 October 1991).

Taking the present population growth rate into account, projections show that more than 330,000 housing units for the lower-income groups will be needed annually over the next ten years to fill the housing gap all over the country (Shill 1993). Estimates of the South African Housing Trust for a sixteen month period in 1988–1989 show only 9,200 finished houses, however, and 19,350 lots provided with services (*Sunday Tribune*, 17 September 1989). The gap between supply and demand on the housing market is thus continuously widening.

In the past decade, both illegal and informal solutions to the housing supply have therefore become more and more important. In violation of the provisions of the Group Areas Act, which until its repeal in July 1991 reserved residential areas for individual population groups, non-Whites increasingly moved into vacant flats in White residential areas (Pickard-Cambridge 1988; Rule 1989; Bähr and Jürgens 1990). The increasing Africanization of the living atmosphere ("At street level . . . downtown Johannesburg seems more like Abidjan than any European metropolis" Contreras 1991, 18) governs the reality of the future South African city, but also the perception of Whites, who view this as a "third world takeover" (*Die Patriot*, 21 June 1989).

Numerically much more important as a housing alternative are informal forms of living and house construction, including squatter settlements, and also "people on the pavement." Particularly affected are the non-White townships and the peri-urban zone of the large cities, but increasingly vacant downtown areas, parking lots, parks, and overgrown undeveloped land in the formerly White cities as well (see Bernstein 1989). Estimates by the Urban Foundation for 1990 indicate that approximately 2.26 million Blacks live in informal housing units in the Pretoria-Witwatersrand-Vereeniging (PWV) area alone (Urban Foundation 1991a, 7). According to projections based on the 1991 census, in the country as a whole as many as seven million squatters live in urban areas. The proportion of Blacks living in squatter camps and informal residential structures has risen from 3.9 percent in 1985 to 17.3 percent in 1991 (*Cape Times*, 30 April 1992).

The shacks are by no means a homogeneous housing type. Boaden (1990, 80) distinguishes thirty-five different types of informal residential areas in Durban alone. Illegal squatter settlements or ones that are at best tacitly accepted, alternate with officially proclaimed and financed site-and-service schemes. Free-standing shacks exist alongside so-called backyard shacks and outbuildings, which residents of formal housing in the township either tolerate or sublet for a fee. Hence, depending on the social background of the population, the physical environment, the historical development, and land-ownership conditions, shack areas can vary greatly in physiognomy, in the precariousness of their existence, and in the social harmony among their inhabitants (Boaden and Taylor 1992, 148).

Job Structures

The repeal of job reservation (1981 and 1987: Kane-Berman 1992), the abolition of controls on influx into the White cities, and the long-term improvement of educational opportunities for non-Whites have strongly stimulated migration into the cities of South Africa. The persons involved are primarily Blacks from rural areas and from the homelands, but also relatives joining already urbanized Blacks or migrant laborers (Yudelman and Jeeves 1986).

Although the economic power of Blacks increased considerably during the last two decades, the proportion of social "losers" and persons suffering from hunger is growing even faster. The migrant population consists predominantly of unqualified laborers who have great difficulties finding jobs in the city. The majority is unemployed and engaged primarily in informal activities with very low income (Crankshaw and Hart 1990). Compared to an overall population growth rate of 2.5 percent per annum, the employment rate is rising by only 0.2 percent. Annually around 300,000 to 400,000 new jobs would be needed merely to absorb the new workers coming onto the job market (Keet 1991, 37). In actuality, in the period from 1980 to 1987, only about 29,100 new jobs were created annually in the formal sector (*Citizen*, 25 May 1989). Up to 40 percent of the total unemployment among Blacks in the big cities involves the group of sixteen to twenty-four year olds (*Race Relations News*, April 1991, 17). Prognoses of the Bureau of Market Research for the year 2005 assume a figure of 7.3 to 11.6 million underqualified job seekers who will not be able to find a livelihood in the formal sector (*The Star*, 2 October 1991).

Those non-Whites who have profited from the abolition of apartheid are business people in both the formal and the informal sector, and white-collar and blue-collar employees (Fair 1989). They have succeeded in establishing themselves as elite "black yuppies" (Schimmeck and Mendel 1991); or as members of a modest lower-middle class, they have been able to buy property in the townships. Less due to their (inadequate) schooling than to job-training programs run by employers, this specialized and technically qualified labor force has become the avant-garde of non-White employees. The legacy of the financially underprivileged Bantu education and the political chaos and school boycotts in the townships will aggravate the lack of qualified workers, so that in the next years there will be a shortage of several thousand persons (SAIRR 1993, 184). The result is a scarcity of human economic resources that are needed to raise the gross national product to cover the costs of guaranteeing social peace in the postapartheid era (*Race Relations News*, 1991:14).

Processes of Ethnic Change, Selected Examples

In this section, we document the variety of ways in which societal changes are reflected spatially on the basis of three different types of examples from three different regions. We shall examine inner-city mixed-race residential areas in Johannesburg, informal housing areas in the greater Durban area, and a mixed-race neighborhood that has grown up in Country View, Midrand, which was formerly planned as an open area. These examples were deliberately chosen from the most rapidly changing urban agglomerations, Johannesburg and Durban. In other cities only the first traces of the process of transformation of the apartheid city are evident. Although the case studies are not entirely representative, they can serve to point toward possible developments in the postapartheid era.

Inner-City Mixed-Race Residential Areas in Johannesburg

The influx of non-Whites into White group areas in the center of Johannesburg since the mid-1970s (fig. 11.2) was the result of a housing shortage in the townships for Blacks, Coloreds, and Indians and a housing surplus in White residential areas. Within a period of approximately ten years, violations against the Group Areas Act in areas like Hillbrow and Joubert Park at the edge of the CBD increased to such a degree (table 11.4) that illegal non-Whites could only be punished arbitrarily and were as a rule tacitly accepted.

Depending on the type of housing available—detached houses or anonymous rental housing—and the political receptiveness or lethargy of the indigenous White population, the areas concerned have responded differently to their development into a mixed-race area. For example, Mayfair, at the western edge of the CBD (fig. 11.2), is considered an example of gentrification because of the influx of Indians who purchase detached and row houses, then remodel them. Garside (1993) cites a similar example in Cape Town.

In high- and middle-rise areas like Hillbrow and Yeoville, social assimilation of non-White migrants, who are usually renters, and White neighbors has occurred (Schlemmer and Stack 1990b; Jürgens 1991; see also figure 11.3). However, these housing areas are characterized by urban blight because under the Group Areas Act and the Rent Act, illegal inhabitants had no protection as renters, so that non-White persons were in some cases forced to pay exorbitant rents. This induced overcrowding, which led to deterioration of the buildings and put too much strain on services such as water and electricity (Sello and Kweyi 1989; Greenblo 1990). These problems have not disappeared with the repeal of the Group Areas Act because landlords are able to exploit the widespread housing shortage to their own advantage (New Nation 1992). In Hillbrow alone, it is estimated that approximately 100,000 persons live in overcrowded flats, automobiles, and backyards (New Nation, 13–19 November 1992).

To be sure, such run-down houses are the exception, but with their

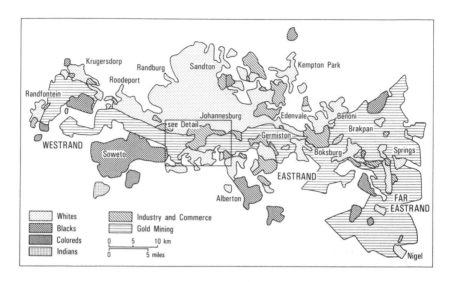

Whites
Blacks
Coloreds
Indians

Industry and Commerce
Gold Mining

0   5   10 km
0   5 miles

Krugersdorp Randburg Sandton Kempton Park
Roodeport
Randfontein
Johannesburg Edenvale Benoni
see Detail Germiston Brakpan
WESTRAND Soweto Boksburg Springs
EASTRAND
Alberton FAR
EASTRAND
Nigel

Detail

HOUGHTON
PARKTOWN
YEOVILLE
HILLBROW BEREA
BRIXTON BEZ VALLEY
PAGEVIEW BERTRAMS
JOHANNESBURG
MAYFAIR MALVERN
FORDSBURG

Gold Mining and   Industrial Area

0   1   2 km
0   1 mile

LA ROCHELLE
TURFFONTEIN
ROSETTENVILLE

——— Boundary of suburbs   ▓ 'Grey areas'   ▨ Living area of Indians   ① Joubert Park

Fig. 11.2   Zones of Work and Residence in the Witwatersrand Area (Urban
Foundation 1991a)

Table 11.4 Central Part of Johannesburg: Black Population in White Group Areas

Area	Year	Population group	Number or percentage of population
Jhbg. White group areas	1979	Blacks	c. 1,000 families
Jhbg. White group areas	1983	Blacks	12,000–15,000
Jhbg. White group areas	1988	Blacks	up to 100,000
Hillbrow-Berea	1986	Blacks	20,000 (c. 27%)
		Coloreds	9,000
		Asians	6,500
		Blacks	4,500
Hillbrow-Joubert Park	1988	Blacks	c. 40%
Hillbrow-Joubert Park	1988	Blacks	c. 50%
			c. 70%
Hillbrow-Joubert Park	1992	Coloreds	21%
		Asians	14%
		Blacks	46%

Source: Jürgens 1991,96; HSRC 1992.

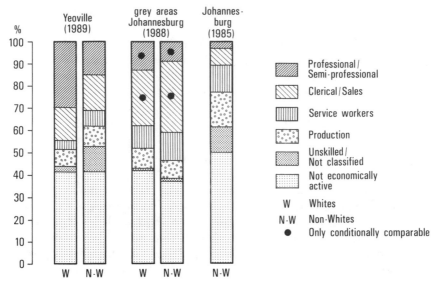

Fig. 11.3   Occupation in Yeoville and Grey Areas of Johannesburg (Jürgens 1991; Schlemmer and Stack 1990a; Republic of South Africa 1986a)

enormous publicity in the press they have contributed greatly to the loss of prestige of the surrounding housing areas. The decline in status, character- ized by high criminality and "Africanization" of the sidewalks due to hobos, street children, street traders, and prostitutes has led to White flight. The numerical decrease in the White population is not entirely the result of people moving out because they are dissatisfied with living in a mixed-race area. There are additional factors such as (1) the natural decline of the White population and (2) the growing impoverishment of White households who are losing their homes or having to move in with family members who previously lived separately because rents have become unaffordable (*International Herald Tribune*, 15 October 1991).

White flight is thus essentially a passive "thinning out" process in which White persons move out, leaving vacant flats and so-called trapped immobile Whites (*The Star* 1989). Few Whites replace them. Non-Whites have taken advantage of this gap to flee the remoteness and the hardship of township life. The first persons to move in, the "pioneers," created with their choice of housing a port of entry for other interested persons from the same ethnic group (Hart 1989). The social pressure to adapt in the "White city" was less intense in the residential atmosphere of shared interests and shared problems such as illegal housing status. The result was the formation of ethnic clusters and an attendant "block-by-block total transition" (Schlemmer and Stack 1990a).

The racial discrimination encountered when looking for a flat, opening a bank account (*The Star*, 20 March 1991), or having a line of credit granted has not disappeared, however, with the abolition of the Group Areas Act (*The Star*, 1993; *Weekly Mail & Guardian*, 5–11 November 1993). Landlords' fears of overcrowding in their apartments and rent boycotts help to keep "silent apartheid" alive (*Sowetan*, 3 February 1992). Otherwise, landlords still enforce the abolished Group Areas Act by using fly-by-night security companies to extort and terrorize residents (*The Star*, 13 April 1992). Changing neighborhood compositions due to an influx of Blacks could upset the current price levels for rents and real estate. White families fear considerable losses when they sell their houses. An example was seized upon by the *Sunday Times* of Johannesburg on 1 March 1992: In a previously White residential area in the southern part of Johannesburg with houses in a price range between R 200,000 and R 300,000 (not including land), a Black bank employee built a matchbox house for R 43,000 on a lot of comparable size, leading to misgivings that the entire neighborhood might suffer a loss of prestige.

Not only the composition of the population of inner-city residential areas has changed rapidly. There is a danger that the politicalization of the townships, which is reflected in the violent struggle for power between the African National Congress (ANC) and Inkatha, will spread to the downtown parts of Johannesburg. There are indications that house owners prefer supposedly conservative Inkatha members as renters (Gunning 1991), to form a counterweight to ACTSTOP, an association representing renters' interests that is connected with the ANC. The latter has frequently called rent boycotts and has also clashed violently with landlords (*Sunday Star* 26 August 1990). This development will probably cause more Whites to leave the regions concerned and contribute to the development of inner-city Black ghettos.

Informal Housing Areas in Greater Durban

The influx of non-Whites into erstwhile White residential areas has attracted a lot of attention in the South African public, but quantitatively it has been small so far. This is not likely to change in the near future, because only a few hundred thousand people can afford to live there. Much more important for the present and future city structure is the large-scale spread of squatter settlements and other informal housing structures. Because of the socioeconomic antagonism between non-Whites and Whites, the squatter phenomenon is more or less restricted to the Black population group.

In the Durban region alone, almost half of the three million inhabitants (Ndwandwe 1990, 31), or 69.2 percent of the Black population (*The Star* 12 November 1992), live in squatter settlements. The number of shacks increased by 3,600 per year in the 1980s (Urban Foundation 1991b, 14). In May 1991, Durban was identified as the fastest-growing city in the Southern Hemisphere (SAIRR 1992, 336). The number of people facing hunger, unemployment, lack of educational opportunities, and a climate of violence, both everyday and political, is growing (Hughes 1987; Booth and Biyela 1988). They are the target group of so-called warlords or shacklords, who pursue their own interests in a vacuum of unenforceable state power (see Ndwandwe 1990 on Durban; Kockott 1990 on the situation in Pietermaritzburg). The basis of power of these shacklords is vigilante groups, which are employed to fight local crime or which undertake politically motivated campaigns against other settlements. The groups are financed by a tribute (shack or household tax), paid by the squatters to the local strongman (Minnaar 1992, 40).

Under apartheid, the squatter camps could often be separated out of White South Africa by shrewdly drawn boundaries and put under the supervision of individual homelands (in this case KwaZulu) (fig. 11.4). The abolition of the homelands and a self-confident Black majority government will not allow the problems of social peace and social justice in squatter communities to continue to be marginalized and White interests to dominate political activity. Ndwandwe (1990, 31) stated: "out of a total budget of R 1.7 billion a year, R 98 million allocated to the uplifting of the beach front area . . . R 1.2 million reserved for the development of the squatter area."

Government antisquatter legislation has attempted since the end of the 1980s to direct uncontrolled settlement and building activity by setting up site-and-service schemes and transit camps, creating legalized squatter settlements (SAIRR 1992, 334ff.). Squatting is no longer spreading only in the areas at the edge of the city and peri-urban areas, but also on free areas in formally built-up regions. An example of this development in Durban is Cato Manor, an area near the city center that is partially grown over with shrub (*Natal Mercury*, 7 January 1992). Where in October 1990 there were around 145 shacks there, by May 1991 the number had increased to more than 600 (*Daily News*, 29 May 1991). The area is now subject to police observation to stop further influx of squatters (*Daily News*, 28 May 1991), partly because the White middle-income neighbors made furious petitions and demonstrations against this development. They perceive the danger that their house prices will decrease. Government agencies are striving for a negotiated solution with an officially accepted and registered number of squatters, with the aim of relocating the inhabitants in a site-and-service

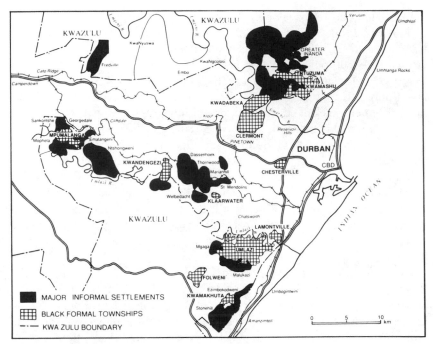

Fig. 11.4   Informal Settlement in the Durban Functional Region (Urban Foundation 1991b)

project (Personal Communication, G. Seneque, CMRA, March 1992). The ultimate goal is to create multiracial formal living space for as many as 180,000 persons (*Sunday Tribune*, 1 March 1992). However, if the social differences between the new neighbors are too high, racist debates can come again on the public agenda in the future.

Population and the Racial Composition of a Former Free-Settlement Area: Country View, Midrand

Under the provisions of the Group Areas Act, free settlement areas, in which persons of different skin colors were permitted to live together, were proclaimed all over the country. They enjoyed this legal status for a brief episode lasting around two years. In some cases, existing grey areas were proclaimed free-settlement areas. For the most part, however, they were newly laid out housing areas, especially in the surroundings of great metropolitan regions. The development of the latter type is interesting because it can give us an idea to what extent mixed-race areas will really develop after all legal restrictions have been lifted, and especially to what extent Whites will make a conscious decision in favor of a mixed-race residential area. In contrast, Whites already live in the grey areas of the inner cities and non-Whites are moving in. Over the medium term, Whites are being replaced by the new population group in a process of infiltration-succession.

The following analysis is based on empirical investigations carried out by the authors in the upper-market housing area of Country View, which was newly opened up and proclaimed a free-settlement area. Country View is part of the so-called Midrand, which is situated at the northern edge of the Witwatersrand conurbation with a total population of over nine million, including the Johannesburg metropolitan area as the core. The distance to the city center of Johannesburg is 37.5 km. Because of the very good infrastructure including the motorway system, the economic potentials of Midrand area are growing very rapidly. Job opportunities have increased because it is a very attractive location for high-tech industries and tertiary activities (for example BMW, National Panasonic, Nashua, and Development Bank of Southern Africa). To investigate the development and the racial composition of Country View, the authors mapped the area and analyzed the real estate sales registered in the Records of Transfers. The breakdown by race of purchasers and sellers was based on family name. In doubtful cases the names were classified in the residual category "unknown."

In the first phase of real estate sales, 50 percent of the purchasers were Indians (table 11.5), predominantly from Laudium, the Indian township of Pretoria (*The Star*, 4 December 1989). In addition, only a few Coloreds, some mixed-race families, some Blacks, and some Whites appeared as purchasers, the latter initially and mainly for purposes of speculation. Later, the racial composition of the purchasers changed considerably to include more Blacks who were doctors, insurance agents, lawyers, and employees in public administration. The Development Company for Country View explains the delay of Black interest in purchasing real estate, compared with Indians, by the fact that advertising started late in so-called Black papers. After the abolition of the Group Areas Act, a variety of other opportunities for acquiring land or houses opened up for well-to-do Indians, who are more easily accepted in a White neighborhood. This gap was filled by interested Blacks. A marked clustering of Black and Indian households in parts of Country View (fig. 11.5) underlines the hypothesis that people consciously seek the vicinity of neighbors of the same skin color, experience, and cultural background. The influx of Blacks also influences the adjoining Noordwyk. Of the seventy-nine new owners registered in the title deeds between July and December 1991, at least twenty-eight were Blacks and five were Indians. Country View can therefore be described as an Indian-Black township, with

Table 11.5 Country View, Midrand: Purchasers of Plots by Race Group

Period	Blacks %	Indians %	Whites/Coloreds/ unknown %	Not yet sold	Total N
5/90 - 7/90	20.4	51.0	28.6		49
8/90 - 10/90	31.5	51.9	16.7		54
11/90 - 1/91	43.2	38.6	18.2		44
2/91 - 4/91	52.4	28.6	19.0		21
5/91 - 7/91	58.3	33.3	8.3		24
8/91 - 10/91	82.1	7.1	10.7		28
11/91 - 1/92	75.0	5.0	20.0		20
2/92 - 4/92	85.7	14.3	0		14
5/92 - 7/92	83.3	8.3	8.3		12
8/92 - 10/92	66.7	6.7	26.7		15
11/92 - 12/92	0	50.0	50.0		2
Total	49.8	32.5	17.7		283
Development phase 1/92					
1	19.4	50.0	21.8	8.9	124
2	45.0	16.0	9.0	30.0	100
3	19.1	4.9	2.2	73.8	183
Development phase 12/92					
1	24.2	48.4	20.2	7.3	124
2	47.2	17.0	9.0	27.0	100
3	27.9	4.4	2.2	65.6	183

Sources: Record of Transfers 1990-1992; personal information of Sage Land Holdings; mapping by the authors in February/March 1992.

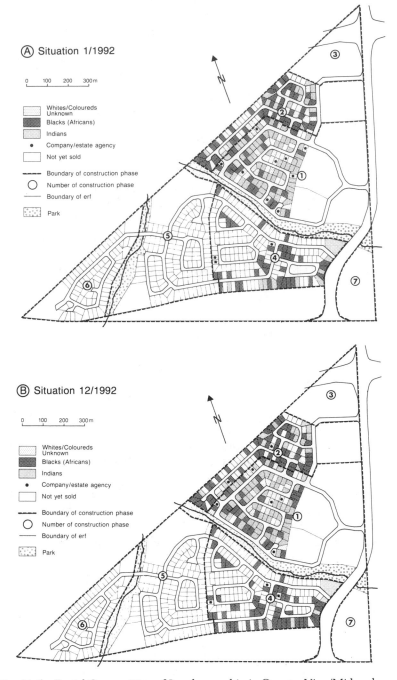

Fig. 11.5   Racial Composition of Landownership in Country View/Midrand
(Record of Transfers 1990–1992)

the trend pointing to small-scale concentrations of Indians and Blacks in parts of the suburb. There is also a trend toward succession, signaled by sales of houses or lots by Indians to Blacks.

Recent information provided by the Sage Land Holding in February 1993 indicates that Country View has increasingly lost its attractiveness for the Black population group as well. Houses stand vacant and no buyer can be found for them. The envisioned two-phase development of new lots has therefore been dropped and plans for shops or a school are likewise no longer being pursued. Because the former White market is now open to all interested persons, since 1992 well-to-do Blacks increasingly prefer established residential areas with intact services and a known level of prestige. There banks are more likely to grant credit lines and mortgages. Nevertheless, not all White areas are attracting the same interest, especially when the suburbs are perceived as conservative or when yuppie influx has inflated prices (*The Star*, 21 October 1992).

The Postapartheid Phase

Population, residential, and job structures are intimately interrelated and have been subject to basic changes in the past two decades. These processes, which we have demonstrated with examples from Johannesburg and Durban, should intensify in the future and should affect the spatial development of cities and the ethnic composition of both entire cities and individual city districts. The postapartheid city will be characterized by new spatial structures such as mixed-race areas and much larger squatter camps than ever existed previously. Many structures that developed during apartheid will likewise continue to exist, because legal equality for all population groups does not automatically mean economic equality, and laws alone cannot put an end to the open discrimination against Blacks.

The persistence of the apartheid city will be most evident in the White middle- and upper-class suburbs. Here apartheid can still be bought, because few Blacks can afford flats in these areas. Those who can do so often choose not to because they find it difficult to sell property they already own in the townships, because they consider the poor public transportation facilities a disadvantage, or (particularly for Indians) because religious facilities are lacking in the vicinity. So far the former White housing market has not experienced a boom due to increased purchases by Blacks.

In the zones adjoining the inner city, however, the invasion of non-Whites, and especially Blacks, will continue. The processes that we have observed primarily in Johannesburg and Durban will probably spread to other towns after a certain time lag. Because institutional and private discrimination continues to exist in the housing market, this invasion of Blacks is occurring only partially in the open, as initial evidence after the repeal of the Group Areas Act shows. To some extent, it is still taking place behind the facade of White nominees (*Daily News* 22 October 1991). Especially in densely populated high-rise areas, this invasion will be associated with a considerable concentration of population and a deterioration of the buildings, predestining these areas to become Black ghettos.

These changes will also have a decisive influence on the future development of the inner city in its function as location of shops and high-class services. It will lose more and more of its attractiveness for the White population, and large shopping malls in the suburbs will take its place for the most part. Even in the service sector, there is a noticeable shift toward the periphery of the city. For the inner city, this means that the mass of customers will eventually be non-Whites. The quality of the goods offered will increasingly be tailored to the needs of poorer population strata and there will be more informal street trading. Already today, many Whites see this as the beginning of a third world takeover.

The majority of the Black population, however, will not be able to afford a flat in the (former) White city, nor will they be able to buy or rent houses in the townships. Informal forms of living (people on the pavement) and house construction will thus gain in importance. The result will be, for one thing, a socioeconomic differentiation within the townships, which were originally divided more or less according to ethnolinguistic points of view. This is becoming apparent in the growing number of residential areas for higher income classes. At the same time, people are crowding into existing settlements of matchbox houses by building backyard shacks and outbuildings, and the authorities are proclaiming and financing new site-and-service schemes. Illegal squatter camps, which are at best tacitly accepted, are spreading rapidly.

This does not preclude the possibility of racial violence in the suburbs at the periphery of the city, where squatter camps are growing toward the White suburbs (*The Star*, 1992). The only realistic solution for the housing shortage, especially of the Black population, is informal housing construction. The choice of locations for such official squatter areas should not neglect the aspect of social tolerance between these and adjacent residential areas, but should not return to the buffer zones of the apartheid phase.

References

Bähr, Jürgen, and Ulrich Jürgens. 1990. "Auflösung der Apartheid-Stadt? Fallbeispiele aus Johannesburg, Durban und Port Elizabeth." *Erdkunde* 44(4):297–312.

Bernstein, Ann. 1989. "South Africa's New City Builders." *Optima* 37(1):18–23.

Boaden, Bruce. 1990. "The Myths and the Realities of Shack Upgrading." *Urban Forum* 1(1):75–84.

Boaden, Bruce, and Rob Taylor. 1992. "Informal Settlement: Theory Versus Practice in KwaZulu/Natal." In *The Apartheid City and Beyond*, ed. David M. Smith. London, New York and Johannesburg: Routledge.

Booth, Douglas, and Mlandu Biyela. 1988. "Exploring the Spatial Dimensions of Black Resistance and Political Violence in South Africa: The Case of Durban." *Urban Geography* 9(6):629–53.

Contreras, Joseph. 1991. "A Town Transformed—Once Johannesburg Was a City of Gold, then of White—And Now of Brown." *Newsweek* 7 Jan. 1991,16–21.

Crankshaw, Owen, and Timothy Hart. 1990. "The Roots of Homelessness: Causes of Squatting in the Vlakfontein Settlement South of Johannesburg." *South African Geographical Journal* 72(2):65–70.

Development Bank of Southern Africa, ed. 1991. A *Regional Profile of the Southern African Population and its Urban and Non-Urban Distribution, 1970–1990*. Halfway House: Development Bank of Southern Africa.

Fair, T. J. Denis 1989. "Black Advancement and the Metropolitan Core." *Social Dynamics* 15(1):108–10.

Garside, Jayne. 1993. "Inner City Gentrification in South Africa: The Case of Woodstock, Cape Town." *GeoJournal* 30(1):29–35.

Greenblo, Allan 1990. "Let Joburg Go Ahead." *Finance Week* 30 Aug.– 5 Sept. 1990, 3.

Gunning, Eugene 1991. "Inkatha-huurders kry voorkeur." *Finansies & Tegniek* 15 Mar. 1991, 56.

Hart, Graeme H. T. 1989. "On Grey Areas." *South African Geographical Journal* 71(2):81–88.

Hattingh, Phillip S. 1988. "Public Policy and Mobility: Recent Trends in a Changing South Africa." Paper presented at the IGU Commission on Population Geography Conference on "Planning for Population Change," 16–20 Aug. 1988, Sydney.

Hughes, Heather. 1987. "Violence in Inanda, August 1985." *Journal of Southern African Studies* 13(3):331–54.

Jürgens, Ulrich. 1991. *Gemischtrassige Wohngebiete in südafrikanischen Städten*. Kieler Geographische Schriften 82. Kiel: Selbstverlag des Geographischen Instituts der Universität Kiel.

Kane-Berman, John. 1992. *Südafrikas verschwiegener Wandel*. Zürich and Osnabrück: Edition Interfrom.

Karcher, Günther L. 1990. "Anatomie der Gewalt in den Townships Südafrikas." *KAS-Auslandsinformationen* 6(12):34–45.

Keenan, J. 1988. "Reforming Poverty: A Socio-Economic Profile of Soweto Households During the 'Reform' Era—1978–1986." *African Studies* 47(1):35–46.

Keet, Dot. 1991. "Unemployment." *South African Labour Bulletin* 16(2):37–41.

Kockott, Fred. 1990. "Pietermaritzburg: The Anatomy of Anarchy." *Cross Times* October, 34–37.

Minnaar, Anthony. 1992. *Squatters, Violence and the Future of the Informal Settlements in the Greater Durban Region*. Pretoria: HSRC.

Ndwandwe, Musa. 1990. "Durban: Tourist Heaven, Squatter Hell." *Cross Times* October: 30–33.

New Nation. 1992. "City Flats Resemble Slums." 27 November–3 December.

Park, Robert E., Ernest W. Burgess, and Roderick D. McKenzie. 1925. *The City*. Chicago, Ill.: University of Chicago Press.

Pickard-Cambridge, Claire. 1988. *The Greying of Johannesburg*. Johannesburg: SAIRR.

Praechter, Volkmar. 1961. *Durban—Siedlungsgeographische Untersuchung einer Hafenstadt*. Hamburg: Cram, De Gruyter & Co.

Race Relations News. 1991. "Down with Apartheid, Up with Violence, Blackmail, and Crime." July/August: 14.

Record of Transfers, ed. 1990–1992. *Record of Transfers of Stands and Properties in the Witwatersrand Area, Johannesburg*. (Pty.) Ltd. Johannesburg (monthly).

Republic of South Africa. 1986a. *Geographical Distribution of the Population with a Review for 1960–1985*. Report No. 02–85–01. Pretoria: Central Statistical Office.

———. 1986b. *Population Census: Selected Statistical Region—Durban/Pinetown/Inanda*. Report No. 02–85–11. Pretoria: Central Statistical Office.

———. 1989. *Official Yearbook of the Republic of South Africa*. Pretoria: Bureau for Information.

————. 1990. *South African Statistics 1990*. Pretoria: Central Statistical Service.

————. 1992a. *Population Census: Selected Statistical Region—Durban/ Pinetown/Inanda/Chatsworth*. Report No. 03–01–14. Pretoria: Central Statistical Office.

————. 1992b. *Population Census: Selected Statistical Region— Johannesburg/Randburg: Part I—Social Characteristics*. Report No. 03– 01–16. Pretoria: Central Statistical Office.

————. 1992c. *Summarised Results After Adjustment for Undercount*. Report No. 03–01–01 (1991). Pretoria: Central Statistical Office.

Rule, Stephen P. 1989. "The Emergence of a Racially Mixed Residential Suburb in Johannesburg: Demise of the Apartheid City?" *Geographical Journal* 155(2):196–203.

SAIRR (South African Institute of Race Relations), ed. 1992. *Race Relations Survey 1991/92*. Johannesburg: SAIRR.

————. 1993. *Race Relations Survey 1992/93*. Johannesburg: SAIRR.

Schimmeck, Tom, and Gideon Mendel. 1991. "Die schwarzen Yuppies von Johannesburg." *Süddeutsche Zeitung Magazin* 40:11–15.

Schlemmer, Lawrence, and S. Louise Stack. 1990a. *Black, White and Shades of Grey—A Study of Responses to Residential Segregation in the Pretoria-Witwatersrand Region*. University of the Witwatersrand Johannesburg—Centre for Policy Studies. Research Report No. 9.

————. 1990b. "The Elusive Ideal—International Experiences of Desegregation." In *Opening the Cities—Comparative Perspectives on Desegregation. Indicator SA Issue Focus* September: 15–22.

Schneider, Karl-Günther, and Bernd Wiese. 1983. *Die Städte des südlichen Afrika*. Urbanisierung der Erde 2. Berlin: Borntraeger.

Sello, Sekola, and Ronnie Kweyi. 1989. "Hillbrow—Future Slumland." *Drum*, May, 7–9.

Shevky, Eshref, and Wendell Bell. 1955. *Social Area Analysis. Theory, Illustrative Application and Computational Procedures*. Stanford, Calif.: Stanford University Press.

Shill, Louis. 1993. "The Housing Backlog: Solutions." *RSA Policy Review* 6(8):1–14.

The Star, ed. 1987. *The Star—Like It Was 1887–1987*. Johannesburg: Argus.

————. 1989. "Hillbrow Frightens the Aged." 16 November.

————. 1992. "Anti-Squatting Groups Mobilise." 5 June.

————. 1993. "Flat-hunter Runs into Racism." 22 February.

Urban Foundation. 1991a. *Population Trends.* Johannesburg: Urban Foundation.

————. 1991b. *Informal Housing. Part 1: The Current Situation.* Johannesburg: Urban Foundation.

Van den Berghe, Pierre L. 1971. "Durban, urbanisation et apartheid." *Revue française d'études politiques africaines* 67(July):40–53.

Van Niekerk, P. 1991. "Gleichheit in Armut?" *der überblick—Zeitschrift für ökumenische Begegnung und internationale Zusammenarbeit* 27(4):72–73.

Yudelman, David, and Alan Jeeves. 1986. "New Labour Frontiers for Old: Black Migrants to the South African Gold Mines, 1920–85." *Journal of Southern African Studies* 13(1):101–24.

Newspapers

Cape Times, Cape Town; *Citizen,* Johannesburg; *Daily News,* Durban; *Frontline,* Johannesburg; *International Herald Tribune,* Paris; *Natal Mercury,* Durban; *Natal Witness,* Durban; *New Nation,* Johannesburg; *Die Patriot,* Pretoria; *Sowetan,* Johannesburg; *The Star,* Johannesburg; *Sunday Star,* Johannesburg; *Sunday Times,* Johannesburg; *Sunday Tribune,* Durban; *Weekly Mail/Weekly Mail & Guardian,* Johannesburg

Chapter 12

Singapore: Ethnic Diversity in an Interventionist Milieu*

Warwick Neville

Issues deriving from ethnic differentiation have become increasingly prominent and contentious in recent years. Common responses have been either
to attempt to play down the ethnic dimension of social issues or to promote
the separation of ethnic groups territorially. In contrast, Singapore has chosen
to feature ethnicity as the main official basis for social classification (Clammer
1982), and most residents accept this as appropriate (Siddique 1990). Indeed,
the government of independent Singapore has attempted neither to minimize
the differences between ethnic groups nor to play down their significance,
but rather to recognize these features and to use them for its own ends while
maintaining the established proportional balance among the three main
ethnic groups of approximately ten Chinese to two Malays to one Indian,
with a small but diverse sprinkling of other groups.

   Like ethnic groups everywhere, the broad categories adopted may be
subdivided—and generally divide spontaneously—into minority communities defining themselves by diverse criteria that mostly, but not invariably,
place them unambiguously within the officially recognized ethnic groups. In
Singapore, these minorities are legion, frequently not discerned by official
administrative procedures (such as the census), but self identified by such
factors as place of origin, language, religion, occupation, class, and caste.

*The author gratefully acknowledges the assistance of Jan Kelley, Department of
Geography, University of Auckland, in the preparation of this chapter's figures and the
Institute of Southeast Asian Studies, Singapore, for the provision of research facilities.

251

Ethnicity as discussed in this chapter and as perceived by Singapore's bureaucracy refers then to a particular level of resolution, a middle order between "being Singaporean" and belonging to a specific minority community. This is important both because a small number of broad ethnic groups can more readily be defined, identified, and managed, and because at this level cultural differences can deliberately and officially be consolidated, enhanced, and even promoted while at other levels national unity and harmony are actively fostered.

Singaporeans are here viewed as a population with multiple identities that promote or inhibit intergroup relationships. Bureaucratization is the linchpin articulating two levels of institutionalization: individual identity is determined (or at least confirmed) by conventions of descent, language affinity, and other ascriptive characteristics. The state manipulates group identity as well, to ensure the perpetuation of the accepted conventions and to stabilize intergroup relations through the process of ethnic management.

This top-down perspective on ethnicity accords more closely with the corporatist view of the operation of the state than with the individual's bottom-up search for identity. Government intervention at many levels has been a major feature of independent Singapore's economic and social achievements (Rodan 1989; Neville 1993); and ethnicity has not been exempt but has constituted a major parameter for the control of people, thus exerting a sectional discipline and group commitment that infiltrates most phases of human endeavor.

This chapter establishes the broad parameters of ethnicity in Singapore and then attempts to identify some of the major instruments of ethnic management adopted by government as part of its overall strategy of development. It is organized into sections on demographic characteristics and social impacts, describing the ethnic mosaic and providing an interpretation of the interventionist processes in operation. The demographic sections address population dynamics (fertility, mortality, migration), structure (ethnicity, age, sex, labor force), and spatial distribution. The social impact sections assess the nature and significance of language, education, religion, marriage, and households, areas in which ethnicity assumes primary significance.

Population Dynamics

Fertility

Singapore is one of the growing group of industrializing countries experiencing a substantial decline in fertility. Following a period of high post–

Second World War birth rates, a sustained decline began as early as the mid-1950s. Direct government participation in family planning promotion began in the mid-1960s and by 1975 the falling total fertility rate (TFR) had reached replacement level (fig. 12.1). The three major ethnic groups followed rather different paths, with Malay rates generally moving down more slowly from higher levels (which were matched by high infant mortality rates) and the Chinese rates mainly lower than those of the Malays and Indians until the early 1970s. During that period, there was a shift in age-specific birth rates among the Malay and Indian populations as women postponed childbearing to the peak childbearing ages already adopted by the Chinese.

The spontaneous regulation of fertility, reinforced by a series of forceful, antinatalist, government incentives encouraging parents to "stop at two," had the effect of continuing to reduce fertility by 1985 to a TFR of 1.5 children per woman. Official concern at this low rate and its implications, especially for the increasingly acute shortage of labor, which (contrary to earlier expectations) was becoming chronic, induced a major policy reversal in 1987. The new pronatalist policy adopted the slogan, "have three, or more if you can afford it," and a package of incentives to induce higher fertility. The change in policy was timely for the predominant Chinese ethnic group since 1988 was the Year of the Dragon in the lunar twelve-year animal cycle—a

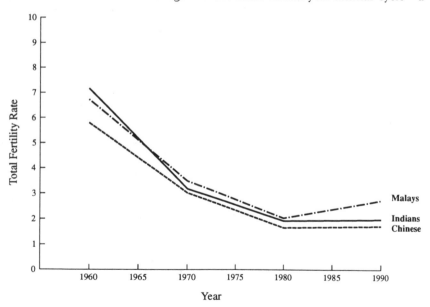

Fig. 12.1   Fertility Rates, by Ethnic Group, for Years ending in 0, 1960–1990 (Saw, 1970, 1990; Department of Statistics 1991)

year regarded as auspicious for the birth of a child (Goodkind 1991). Whatever the motivation, there was a marked upsurge in Chinese birth numbers (26 percent on the previous year), which did not occur in the other groups (fig. 12.2). A concurrent debate on population "quality" in relation to fertility has also persisted for more than two decades in both Singapore and Malaysia instigated by their respective prime ministers (although only the Malaysian case was explicitly ethnic in its connotations) and still not wholly laid to rest in the 1987 policy changes (Chee and Chan 1984).

The cumulative experience of all married women (based on census statistics) demonstrates the similarity in mean number of children born in 1990 to Chinese (2.9) and Indian (2.8) women, and the distinctly larger family size (3.4) of Malay women (fig. 12.3). Annual birth registrations during the 1980s indicate that the Malay population maintained the birth rate at a little above replacement level with the Indian rate slightly below replacement and the Chinese more than 30 percent below replacement (Saw 1990). Given the high level of awareness of the proportions in each ethnic group and the widely accepted assumption that this distribution should be maintained, it is not surprising that incentives, not only for childbearing but also for marriage, should be aimed particularly at the Chinese. The TFR for

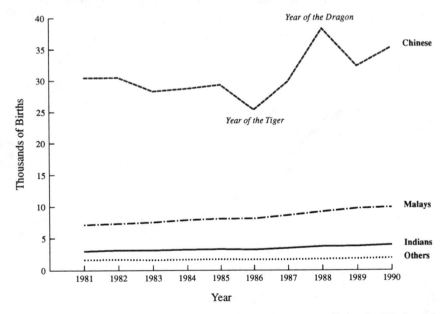

Fig. 12.2   Live Births by Ethnic Group, 1981–1990 (Registrar-General of Births and Deaths 1990)

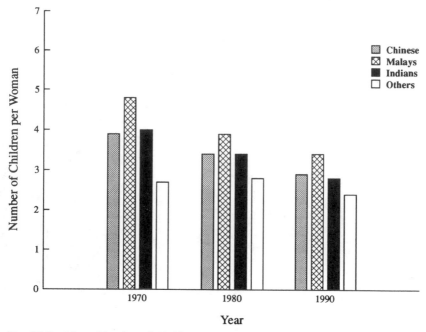

Fig. 12.3   Mean Number of Children Born Alive per Ever-Married Woman, by Ethnic Group, 1970–1990 (Department of Statistics 1973, 1991)

1990 suggests that the Malay rate has risen quite markedly following the policy change whereas the Chinese and Indian rates appear relatively stable (fig. 12.1).

Mortality

Mortality, like fertility, has assumed convergent rates among ethnic groups as causes of death have changed and life expectancy has increased. Infant mortality illustrates the substantial differences in rates that existed between groups prior to and during the fertility decline of the late 1950s and 1960s (fig. 12.4). This was a period when a strong association still persisted between customary practices (in antenatal care, preferred attendant at birth, and locality of confinement) and infant mortality rates. Increasingly comprehensive mother and child care, changing attitudes toward hospitalization and medical supervision, and rising levels of living have been concomitants of low and relatively stable levels of infant mortality in all groups. The overall improvement in mortality rates is reflected in the rising life expectancy rates over the last thirty years (table 12.1).

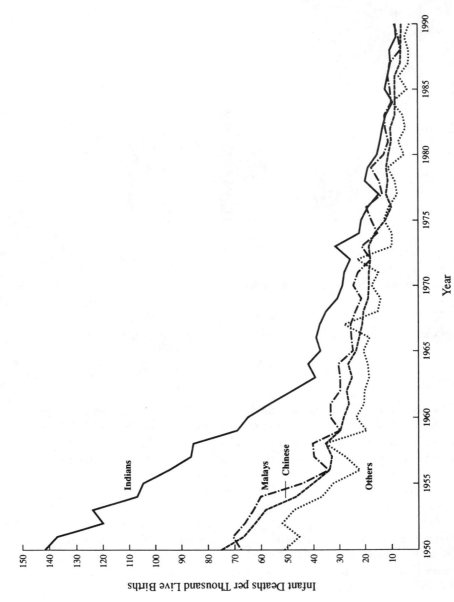

Fig. 12.4   Infant Mortality Rates, by Ethnic Group, 1950–1990 (Registrar-General of Births and Deaths 1990)

Table 12.1 Singapore: Life Expectancy at Birth and Age 40, by Ethnic Group and Sex, 1957–1990

No. of Years

		Chinese		Malays		Indians	
		0	40	0	40	0	40
1957	male	60.9	26.9	56.9	27.9	62.7	28.7
	female	67.9	33.2	58.7	29.3	61.4	27.6
1962	male	63.2	27.8	62.1	29.3	65.6	30.6
	female	70.6	34.4	63.2	29.8	65.3	29.4
1970	male	65.4	28.9	64.6	29.1	63.9	27.9
	female	70.8	33.4	65.6	29.4	65.5	28.7
1980	male	69.3	31.7	68.5	31.9	65.1	28.7
	female	74.7	36.8	70.3	32.6	69.6	31.9
1990	male	73.5	35.0	71.3	33.4	72.4	34.9
	female	78.3	39.5	73.8	35.2	74.7	36.5

Sources: Saw 1970; Department of Statistics 1973, 1980; Ministry of Health, Population Planning Unit 1990.

Migration

Modern Singapore is a creation of migrants, the majority of whom converged on the city-state during the nineteenth and first half of the twentieth centuries from southern China, south India, peninsular Malaya, the Dutch East Indies (subsequently Indonesia), and Britain.

Among the resident population (that is, excluding foreign workers, transient professionals and foreign students), 15 percent were foreign born in 1990, down only slightly from 17.5 percent in 1980. Although the proportion of foreign-born declined, actual numbers increased by 3.6 percent from 398,300 in 1980 to 412,500 in 1990, still substantially fewer than the 531,000 in the 1970 population, but reflecting a modest resurgence in the significance of migration to population growth during the decade. Cumulatively, the largest single group of foreign born is from Malaysia (47.2 percent in 1990), with a further large proportion from China, Hong Kong, and Taiwan (36.4 percent) and small proportions from South Asia (8.5 percent) and Indonesia (5.2 percent). The Malaysian share rose by ten percentage points 1980–90, whereas the other main groups (and especially the East Asian cluster) all had a smaller share of the total foreign-born in 1990 than they had in 1980.

The net outcome for the main ethnic groups of migration of foreign-born to Singapore is that by 1990, the Indian population still had the largest component of foreign-born (25.3 percent of the resident population), ahead of the Chinese (15.2 percent) and Malays (10.0 percent). The modest resurgence in the foreign-born contribution to the resident population reflects both the predominantly adult nature of recent movements and the longer term impact of earlier immigration, as demonstrated in the distinctive age structure of the foreign-born population, which is the product of survivors of immigration over many decades.

As early as 1968, there was some relaxation of the strict immigration policy, permitting access for substantial numbers of unskilled temporary workers mainly from Johor (Pang and Lim 1982; Stahl 1986) and since that time, because of an increasing labor shortage, the influx of foreign workers has escalated, and countries of recruitment have become increasingly diverse.

By 1973, work permit holders reportedly numbered over 100,000 or about an eighth of the total workforce (Pang and Lim 1982); and despite the negative impact of world recessions on economic growth and the reluctance of Singapore authorities to permit expansion of the foreign worker component of the labor force, indications were that they comprised over 10 percent of workers (perhaps 170,000) through the 1980s (Stahl 1991; Appleyard 1992). These workers were drawn not only from established sources such as Malaysia and India, but also from Bangladesh, Sri Lanka, Thailand, Indonesia, and the Philippines. Unskilled laborers are subject to strict control and worker rotation but even in Singapore, where monitoring is very efficient, problems of illegal immigrant workers occur (Sullivan, Gunasekaran, and Siengthai 1992; Pang 1992).

In 1990, the nonresident population in Singapore numbered 311,300 (10.3 percent of the total population); 48 percent are Chinese, 8 percent Malays, nearly 13 percent Indians, and 31 percent Others. Nationalities, ethnicity, and work status cannot be more precisely established from the census statistics published so far (Bangladeshis and Sri Lankans are listed as Indians; many Chinese and Malays are undifferentiated among Malaysians). For the most part, the nonresidential population comprises foreign workers (work permit holders, few of whom are accompanied by dependents), transient professionals and their dependents (employment, social, and dependent pass holders), and foreign students.

The census information released to date appears broadly to confirm the relative proportions of the estimates made by Skeldon (1992) of unskilled laborers, domestic maids, and professional and skilled workers as a ratio of 5:2:1 with additional numbers of dependents attached to the latter group. The whole issue of foreign workers and foreign residents in multicultural Singapore is very sensitive, and data are generally made available only through press releases. Further detailed 1990 census statistics could well provide fuller information, but the structure of tabulations may preclude detailed analysis.

Population Structure

Ethnicity

The plural society emerged very early as people were drawn from three of the major culture blocs of Asia (China, Malaya-Indonesia, India) to the opportunities of the entrepôt and its auxiliary activities (Neville 1979). The Chinese predominated from an early stage but the precise proportions of each ethnic group varied considerably until the mid-twentieth century (table 12.2) when, with the enforcement of immigration legislation and substantial Indian emigration, a relatively stable distribution emerged. Together, the three main ethnic groups accounted for 95.8 percent of the total population of just over three million in 1990, a proportion significantly lower than the 97.9 percent of 1980 and 98.2 percent in 1970. However, if the nonpermanent population is excluded, the proportions in the main ethnic groups comprise 98.9 percent

Table 12.2   Singapore: Ethnic Distribution of the Population, 1901–1990

	Chinese %	Malays %	Indians %	Others %
1901	72.1	15.8	7.8	4.3
1911	72.4	13.8	9.1	4.7
1921	75.3	12.8	7.7	4.2
1931	75.1	11.6	9.1	10.2
1947	77.8	12.1	7.3	2.8
1957	75.4	13.6	9.0	2.0
1970	76.2	15.0	7.0	1.8
1970[a]	77.0	14.8	7.0	1.2
1980	76.9	14.6	6.4	2.1
1980[a]	78.3	14.4	6.3	1.0
1990	74.7	13.5	7.6	4.2
1990[a]	77.7	14.1	7.1	1.1

Sources: Census volumes.
[a]Singapore residents only

of the 2.7 million Singapore residents, a level little changed from the 99 percent of 1980. In recent decades the balance between the main ethnic groups has remained fairly stable—a characteristic that the government has been anxious to maintain.

Such generalized categories give a completely misleading impression of the complex and fragmented reality that comprises a mosaic of self-identified communities for whom language is a major identifying feature (table 12.3). The Chinese comprise a number of dialect groups that differ not only linguistically but also in other significant elements of culture and behavior. The greater Malay group includes people of Indonesian origin deriving from various islands of the archipelago, also with variations in culture and social structure. Probably the greatest diversity within any of the three major ethnic groups occurs among the Indian communities originating from South Asia (including not only India and Pakistan but also Bangladesh, Sri Lanka, Nepal, and Bhutan) for whom many cultural features, in addition to lan-

Table 12.3   Singapore: Specific Communities, 1990 (in thousands)

Chinese		Indians	
Hokkien	328	Tamil	45
Teochew	171	Malayalee	6
Cantonese	118	Sikh	5
Hakka	57	Hindustani	1
Hainanese	54	Sindhi	1
Foochow	13	Punjabi	1
Henghua	7	Urdu	1
Shanghainese	6	Gujarati	1
Hokchia	5	Sinhalese	1
Other	18	Other	9
Total	777	Total	71
Malays		Others	
Malay	96	Eurasian	5
Javanese	24	Arab	2
Boyanese	16	European	2
Bugis	1	Filipino	1
Other	4	Other	1
Total	141	Total	11

Source: Department of Statistics 1992.
Note: Figures are of resident population.

guage, constitute the basis of differentiation. Of the Others, the local Eurasian group is the largest, with people of Arab and European ancestry representing small groups that have had a sustained presence; Filipinos and slightly smaller communities such as Thai and Japanese are more recent arrivals in Singapore.

Age and Sex

The postwar upsurge in fertility substantially modified the preceding age-sex distribution, which had been strongly influenced by the sustained inflow of migrants and has remained a dominant feature since. The impact of both of these elements is seen most clearly in the Indian age structure for 1957 (fig. 12.5), which depicted, in a more subdued form than previously, the predominance of males of working age for whom sex ratios as high as 6,640

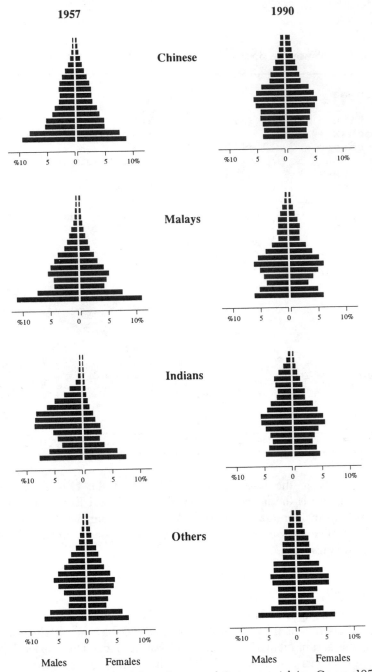

Fig. 12.5 Age Pyramids, by Ethnic Group and Quinquennial Age Group, 1957 (Total) and 1990 (Resident) Populations (Department of Statistics 1964, 1991)

males per thousand females (aged 45–49) were still prevalent. All four ethnic groups were strongly affected by the ten or more years of high birth rates up to 1957 and this had a major impact in rectifying existing imbalances in the overall sex ratios, especially for the Indian population.

The increases in the decade to 1990 in the child population then aged 0–9, have had a significant influence in slowing the overall aging of the Malay and Indian populations but the large numbers of working-age adults in all ethnic groups, the modest increases in Chinese child numbers, and the predominance of the Chinese generally in the total population perpetuates the country's secular trend toward an aging population. This is evidenced in the shift in the age-dependency ratio (0–14 plus 65 and over per thousand 15–64 years of age) between 1957 and 1990 from 859 to 398 people of dependent age per thousand working age adults for the Chinese, from 871 to 499 for the Malays, and from 529 to 415 for the Indians. The significance of this age structural shift is more explicitly illustrated by the change in the dependency component as exemplified by the ratio of the aged to children, 1957 to 1990: Chinese, from 55 to 287 elderly per thousand children, Malays from 32 to 149, and Indians from 26 to 239 (the latter influenced by the distinctive residual of older male migrants, which offsets the impact of recent increases in the child population).

Labor Force

The releases to date of 1990 census data preclude a detailed examination of the occurrence of niche occupations as attempted in earlier studies (Neville 1966) but differences in emphasis emerge even at the general occupation and industry group level. The presence of foreign workers is directly reflected in the Others' inflated representation in the 1990 labor force by 50 percent relative to their representation in the overall population (from 4.2 percent in the population generally to 6.6 percent of the workforce), which translates into high participation rates for Others, both male and female, and to a lesser degree for Indians (especially females; table 12.4).

The percentage distribution of each ethnic group across the activity spectrum indicates (fig. 12.6) that, while all ethnic groups are concentrated in the production process worker category, the Chinese are least so and are disproportionately represented in professional and administrative occupations (and clerical for females), whereas the Malays show up only in the clerical category for males (traditionally, in the civil service). Indians have the largest relative proportions in the professions after the Chinese, and for males are most likely to be in the sales group—a reflection of entrepreneurial interests.

The sectoral distribution of ethnic groups by industry reflects the predomi-

Table 12.4   Singapore: Labor Force Participation Rates, 1980 and 1990

	1980	1990
Chinese		
males	80.8	78.2
females	44.5	49.6
Malays		
males	83.2	76.6
females	44.6	45.1
Indians		
males	84.0	82.8
females	44.1	53.4
Others		
males	85.8	94.2
females	34.7	71.7

Source: Department of Statistics 1991.

nance of Chinese (both sexes) in the commercial sector, manufacturing (males), and financial services (females). Malays are strongly represented in manufacturing (especially females who have the highest proportions of any group in this sector and include a substantial element of work permit holders) and in other, mainly service, activities. Indian males are second only to Chinese in their proportions in commerce; to Others in construction (in which Bangladeshi and Sri Lankan foreign workers are important); and to Malays in other activities. Indian females are heavily concentrated in "other" activities, in this instance mainly Sri Lankans working as domestic maids.

Spatial Distribution

Soon after the settlement's foundation in 1819, certain areas were set aside for Europeans, Chinese, Bugis, Arabs, and Chuliahs. The designations were chiefly ethnic but also mentioned occupational and social status—merchants were to be treated more favorably than artisans and laborers, while the laboring classes were to be restricted to the western side of the town ("Notices of Singapore" 1854, 1855). Although considerably modified over the suc-

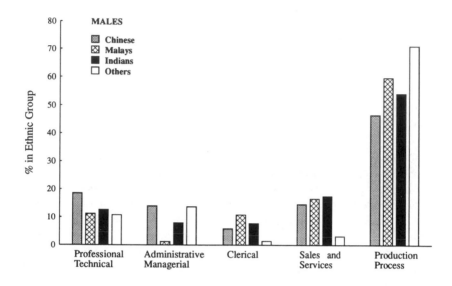

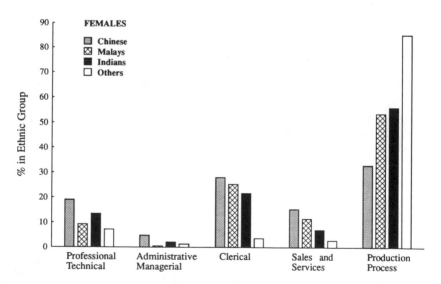

Fig. 12.6   Percentage Distribution of Occupation within Ethnic Groups, 1990
(Department of Statistics 1991)

ceeding century and a half as population numbers grew and settlement expanded (Hodder 1953), these core areas persisted and others emerged.

The years since independence have witnessed radical changes as a result of government policy preeminently in the matters of public housing and urban renewal (Humphrey n.d.). The significance of public housing to the ethnic groups and specific communities of Singapore lies in the consequential redistribution of population: dissolution of the largely spontaneous clustering of groups residentially by the mechanism of resettlement. Although the degree of choice of locality has gradually been liberalized, it is constrained by eligibility criteria and the availability of appropriate types and sizes of apartments. Ethnicity and community were never explicitly included among the criteria for eviction or for preference of location on resettlement (apartments are allocated on a lottery system that takes account of broad preferences), but from the earliest days of the program movement to public housing has had as one of its underlying motives avoidance of the creation of any latter-day Chinatowns or Malay settlements. Also, the selection of a particular area for redevelopment at any particular stage was likely to affect one group more than another because of the clustering that already existed; and the policy decision to abandon the bulk of agricultural production and resettle farmers from their smallholdings into HDB flats impacted almost entirely on the Chinese community (Neville 1992). Such impelled resettlement was a major source of resentment in the early stages not only socially as community ties were disrupted by dispersal but also economically through loss of clientele or proven creditworthiness (Hassan 1977), although it is less of an issue now that such large proportions of the population have been resettled.

In 1989, to counter any systematic shift toward ethnic clustering in neighborhoods or blocks of public housing, on the grounds that "to allow the races to regroup now would be to go back to the pre-1965 period when there were racial enclaves and racial riots" (Straits Times 1989), provisions were adopted to set limits on the proportions of the major ethnic groups allowed in every HDB neighborhood and individual block for both the allocation of new flats and the resale of existing flats. The limits for HDB neighborhoods (which average about fifty blocks providing some five thousand apartments) were set at levels several percentage points above the current HDB population's ethnic mix, which roughly parallelled the country's distribution: Chinese, 84.0 percent (76 percent in the HDB population); Malays, 22 percent (15.1 percent); Indians and Others, 10 percent (8.9 percent). The limits for specific blocks of apartments were set at three percentage points higher than for neighborhoods, but were not to be enforced strictly in low rise blocks with fewer than fifty housing units. At the time these regulations were promulgated (1 March, 1989), there were 35 neighborhoods (28 percent of all HDB neighborhoods) and 1,177 blocks (18 percent of the total) outside these neighborhoods in new towns and housing estates all over Singapore, which were immediately affected.

Social Impacts

Language

Language planning constituted a major plank of government policy right from the initial election to power of the Peoples Action Party (PAP) in 1959. Despite the numerical predominance of the Chinese and of Chinese dialects, and the established preeminence of English as the language of administration and international business, Malay was designated the national language. This choice was based on geopolitical considerations in the late 1950s and the aspirations of the PAP to merge with the Federation of Malaya in an enlarged political entity: "A lingua franca is necessary and moral, political, and practical considerations make Malay, rather than English, the obvious choice" (PAP Manifesto, cited in de Souza 1980,209). This provision is embedded in the constitution (Republic of Singapore Independence Act, 1965) and remains in force. In addition to the national language, in which for a number of years civil servants were required to achieve specified levels of proficiency to achieve advancement, four languages were designated as official languages substitutable in all transactions with the bureaucracy and appropriate for other public usage. These languages were selected on the basis of their links with the main ethnic groups for which they are deemed to be (in complete contrast to the technical sense of the term) the "mother tongue": Mandarin for the Chinese, Malay for the Malays, Tamil for the Indians, plus English mainly (in the early stages) for the continuity it would provide in administration. In fact, in the conventional sense of the term, neither Mandarin nor Tamil was (or is) the mother tongue of the majority of Chinese and Indians.

While these provisions have been highly influential in the subsequent development of language usage in Singapore, especially in education, day-to-day practice is much more complex. The majority of the population is multilingual in a variety of languages (including Chinese dialects) that are functionally differentiated. Malay, especially the pidgin variant of Bahasa Melayu, is used by people of different ethnicity in the markets and other traditional sectors although is increasingly being superseded by English among the younger generation; similarly, Hokkien is used by many Chinese in the markets and on festive occasions for interdialect group communication.

English, while still linked with earlier usage, is increasingly perceived as the language of technology and management, of modernity and international communication. Mandarin, which since 1979 has been actively promoted by the government's "Speak Mandarin not dialect" campaign among the Chinese population, parallels English in some areas of usage but tends to convey a more conservative image. English and Mandarin, like Malay, are both spoken with varying degrees of pidginization.

The census provides statistics that describe the change, 1980–90, in the language most frequently spoken at home (table 12.5). The general nature of the shift is quite clear: there has been an increased adoption of English, Mandarin and Malay (the three dominant official languages) by the ethnic groups for which they are important. In particular, home use of dialects among Chinese households has slipped from more than three-quarters to less than half, with Mandarin increasing to one-third and English to one-fifth of all Chinese households. Most significantly, Mandarin now exceeds in predominance the major dialect, Hokkien, which in 1980 was far more important as the primary medium of communication in Chinese households. The preference for Malay among Malay households has given way a little to English; and Tamil is no longer the choice of more than half of all Indian households, one-third of which now prefer English. Both Indian and Other ethnic groups recorded significant shifts to Malay.

Education

In many respects, the issues of education in Singapore are the issues of language. As one writer noted, "whenever major decisions on educational policy had to be taken these were expressed in terms of language rather than objectives or content" (Gopinathan 1980,175), and the major feature of the separate school systems that evolved in Singapore was the difference in media of instruction. This is hardly surprising since language has major consequences for the nature and extent of peoples' political and civic participation, issues of equity, social mobility, ethnic identity, interethnic relations, and personal competence to survive in a multilingual society. Consequently, medium of instruction largely determines the efficacy of educational experience in terms of relevance or acceptability to the labor market.

For all ethnic groups, educational attainment is partly a function of age and sex, as well as of attitudes to and opportunities for an extended education. At ages 60 and over, in 1990, only the Other ethnic group recorded significant proportions whose highest educational qualification was gradua-tion from secondary school or above, and for all groups those with "below

Table 12.5 Singapore: Language Most Frequently Spoken at Home, 1980 and 1990

Language	Chinese 1980 %	Chinese 1990 %	Malays 1980 %	Malays 1990 %	Indians 1980 %	Indians 1990 %	Others 1980 %	Others 1990 %
English	10.2	20.6	2.4	5.5	24.4	34.8	69.8	74.7
Mandarin	13.1	32.8	–	0.1	–	–	0.3	1.3
Chinese dialects	76.2	46.2	0.1	0.1	0.4	0.2	0.7	1.3
Hokkien	34.0	21.6	–	–	0.2	0.2	0.3	1.3
Teochew	16.8	10.0	–	–	0.1	–	0.2	–
Cantonese	16.8	10.6	–	–	0.1	–	0.2	–
Other	8.6	4.0	–	–	–	–	–	–
Malay	0.4	0.3	96.8	94.3	8.5	13.5	3.7	14.7
Tamil	–	–	0.1	–	52.1	43.6	–	–
Others	0.1	0.1	0.6	–	14.6	7.9	25.5	8.0
Total	100.0	100.0	100.0	100.0	100.0	100.0	100.0	100.0

Sources: Department of Statistics 1981, 1991.
Note: Figures are for persons aged 5 years and over in resident households (total households in 1980).

secondary" educational qualifications were predominantly female as the limited proportions who did go on to higher levels were mainly male (fig. 12.7). This pattern was essentially similar for people aged 40–59 except that notably larger proportions completed a secondary qualification.

At ages 25–39 the earlier pattern had been substantially modified. Much larger proportions graduated from secondary school and for Others this had become the most common level of attainment. For all three ethnic groups other than Chinese, the females recorded larger proportions than males with university qualifications. At ages 10–24, surprisingly large proportions especially of males left school with no formal qualifications. The male distribution is likely to change for these cohorts by the time they move into age groups over 25 as two to two and a half years national service largely precludes completion of university studies by age 24 whereas all the lower levels of attainment appear on the record since they are completed before national service. This requirement is frequently cited as an equity issue in which men are disadvantaged relative to women of the same age.

Government management of ethnic issues is an important concept in the context of education because in this area long-term influence can be exerted on the entire population, couched in terms of personal benefit and national aspirations, with less-direct confrontation of cultural values or community expectations than would be likely in most other contexts. For example, while government almost invariably discourages direct comparisons or disparaging comments of an ethnic group by others, it uses examination results at primary school leaving and high school graduation levels to spur on the groups achieving lesser results. Release to the press of information otherwise generally inaccessible (a highly developed practice of government in Singapore) enables publication of the examination results. The accompanying commentary takes a constructive approach in noting, for example, that "Malay students have chalked up better grades" at some levels than previously, but the basic message is clearly one of exhortation to do better: "in the long run, the interests of the community can only be served best by improving the educational performance of Malay students" the minister of state for education is quoted as saying (*Sunday Times* 1992). There are few other situations in Singapore where the singling out of a particular ethnic group for criticism, however indirect, would be acceptable either in the population at large or as a component of government management of ethnic issues.

Religion

For most groups in Singapore, to a greater or lesser degree ethnic differentiation has a religious dimension. On the basis of the 1990 census, 99.8

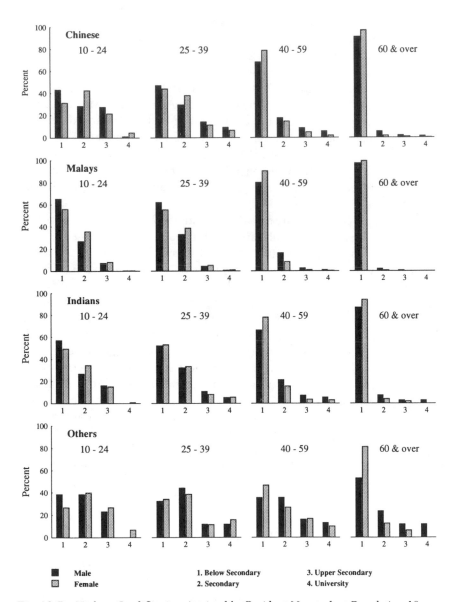

Fig. 12.7   Highest Qualification Attained by Resident Nonstudent Population 10 Years of Age and Over, by Sex, Ethnic, and Age Groups, as Percentage within Age Groups, 1990 (Department of Statistics 1991)

percent of Buddhists and Taoists are Chinese, 85.9 percent of Muslims are Malays, 99.8 percent of Hindus are Indians. The pattern becomes more complex, even for the undifferentiated major ethnic groups, when the breadth of religious affinities of each group is examined (table 12.6). Substantial proportions of Chinese are Christian and an even larger segment has recorded "no religion"—a far bigger component than for any other group. The Malays are virtually all Muslims but the Indian population is the most widely distributed with major proportions being Hindu and Muslim. Many important religious communities are subsumed under these broad headings and other major nuances are obscured: for example, Chinese Buddhists are part of the Mahayana tradition whereas Indian (mainly Sri Lankan) Buddhists are part of the Theravada tradition; and two-thirds of Chinese Christians are Protestant whereas a similar proportion of Indian Christians are Roman Catholic.

In a White Paper tabled in Parliament in 1989 to provide the basis for subsequent legislation (Maintenance of Religious Harmony Act, 1991), a paragraph addressing the notion of "fragility of religious harmony" asserts that, "two vital conditions must therefore be observed to maintain harmony. Firstly, followers of the different religions must exercise moderation and tolerance, and do nothing to cause religious enmity or hatred. Secondly, religion and politics must be kept rigorously separated" (Republic of Singapore 1989,4). In a "security perspective" annex to the White Paper, the government's concern is summarized in the conclusion: "Aggressive proselytization and exploitation of religion for political and subversive purposes pose serious threats to religious and racial harmony and public order. Unless all religious groups exercise moderation and tolerance in their efforts to win converts, and maintain a rigorous separation between religion and politics, there will be religious friction, communal strife and political instability in Singapore" (Republic of Singapore 1989,19).

In this context, the political attitude toward religion is instrumental, but this tendency for the state to appropriate to itself, for its own purposes, cultural manifestations falling outside the usual realm of politics is common in Singapore (Clammer 1991,16). There is also a sense in which the government's own development policies have impinged on these issues, notably in two major areas.

First, the introduction of religious studies in secondary schools in 1984 was perceived to be a measure aimed at offsetting the negative moral consequences of the materialism and economic competitiveness that are an integral part of the government's continuing drive toward greater economic development and a product of its own development policies. Whatever the

Table 12.6 Singapore: Religion, by Ethnic Group, 1990

	Chinese %	Malays %	Indians %	Others %
Buddhism/Taoism/Chinese traditional beliefs	68.0	—	0.7	6.6
Islam	0.2	99.7	26.3	24.6
Hinduism	—	—	53.2	0.9
Sikhism	—	—	6.1	—
Christianity	14.1	0.2	12.8	63.0
Other religions	0.1	—	0.1	0.9
No religion	17.6	0.1	0.8	4.0
Total	100.0	100.0	100.0	100.0

Source: Department of Statistics 1991.
Note: Figures are for resident population aged 10 years and over.

rationale, this measure has proved problematic and religious studies per se in secondary schools were discontinued at the end of the decade.

Second, urban redevelopment has resulted in widespread relocation of population through resettlement mainly in Housing and Development Board (HDB) estates. High levels of impelled geographic mobility and the policy (alluded to earlier) of mixing ethnic groups in housing estates as a preferred alternative to the spontaneous sorting of communities into more-or-less residentially segregated enclaves ("Chinatown," "Little India," the "Malay Settlement") has introduced a new degree of propinquity and constant contact, a trend acknowledged by the White Paper (Republic of Singapore 1989,4), and cited as part of the rationale for the introduction of measures aimed at ensuring religious harmony.

Marriage and Households

Marriage

Marriage, family, and kinship are at the heart of ethnic community life and along with language and religion are keenly guarded core elements of each culture. For the majority, endogamous marriage within the broad ethnic group is generally still encouraged although the stricter code of, for example, marrying within the same Chinese dialect group and out of the group of the same family name, are less often observed. Supporting this view are the provisions of two systems of family law that dichotomize society on the basis of religion into Muslims and non-Muslims (Wee 1976). The Syariah Court has jurisdiction in matters relating to Muslim marriage, divorce, and various aspects of the family, with marriages conducted under the Administration of Muslim Law Act, 1968. Non-Muslims are married under the provisions of the Women's Charter, 1961, which also provides safeguards for financial maintenance of divorced women, some of which also apply to Muslims.

This fundamental dichotomy precludes marriages between Muslims and non-Muslims, one of whom (usually the non-Muslim) must convert. There is a significant amount of intermarriage between ethnic groups within these two broad categories: in 1990, 16.5 percent of all Muslim marriages were interethnic, and 5.5 percent of non-Muslim marriages (table 12.7), a proportion that has been quite stable for many years. Over half of the interethnic marriages transacted under Muslim law were between Malays and Indians; marriages between Chinese and Malays were less common, but as for the Malay-Indian combination, more out-marriage occurred for Malay females

Table 12.7 Singapore: Interethnic Marriages, by Ethnic Group and Sex, 1990

Under the Women's Charter[a]

Males	Females					
	Chinese %	Malays %	Indians %	Eurasians %	Europeans %	Others %
Chinese	—	2.1	4.2	4.8	1.3	28.6
Malays	1.0	—	0	0.1	0	0.3
Indians	11.8	1.1	—	2.1	0.8	2.0
Eurasians	5.0	0.2	0.4	—	0.3	0.4
Europeans	16.0	1.2	3.0	1.2	—	2.4
Others	8.4	0.1	0.5	0.3	0.4	—

Under Muslim Law[b]

Males	Females					
	Chinese %	Malays %	Indians %	Eurasians %	Europeans %	Others %
Chinese	—	10.6	1.1	0	0	0.4
Malays	8.0	—	24.2	0.7	0.5	5.8
Indians	1.0	28.2	—	0.2	0.1	2.3
Eurasian	0	2.3	0.3	—	0	0
Europeans	0	2.8	0.4	0	—	0
Others	0.3	8.3	2.3	0.2	0	—

Source: Department of Statistics 1990.
[a]Total number: 1,046 = 100%
[b]Total number: 785 = 100%

than among Malay males. Of those married under the Women's Charter, one combination predominated: Chinese men marrying Other (Filipina and Thai) women. Significant numbers of European and Indian men also married Chinese women. Overall, however, the level of interethnic marriages remains fairly stable from year to year (Hassan and Bartholomew 1976).

Household Structure

Household size and structure show significant variations between ethnic groups with, in addition, notable shifts over the decade 1980–90. The general trend has been for a reduction in household size, which is primarily a function of reduced fertility. In addition, rules imposed by government regarding allocation of HDB apartments to nuclear families only (subsequently relaxed somewhat to permit a limited range of additional members such as elderly relatives or a lodger) have had a thirty-year impact in constraining expectations of family composition and living arrangements.

Despite the concentration of the majority of households of all major ethnic groups in the four-person size category (table 12.8) there are marked differences between groups in household size distribution although these have diminished since 1980. Chinese, Malays, and Indian groups all recorded a decline in mean size (minor in the Indian case). The Malays still have the largest proportions in households of five or more people; for them, as for the Chinese and Indian groups, households of six or more are relatively less common than before. For these three groups, the size categories that have expanded are households of two to five people, and especially those with four or five. The shift toward the modal household size was also marked by a reduction in the number of one-person households. One-person households are not favored by any of the major ethnic groups, and the waning in the impact of migrants in the resident population 1980–90 is reflected in the major reduction in Indian and Other one-person households.

Perpetuation of Pluralism

The perpetuation of pluralism in a wide range of manifestations is ensured in Singapore, guaranteed by the institutionalization of ethnic identity. In particular, the bureaucracy decrees that individuals have a declared, unambiguous, and unchanging ethnic identity, which is stated on personal identity cards and is required to be reiterated on most official forms and for most official procedures. The ethnic categories at this level of resolution are regarded as discrete and homogeneous, and institutional practice consolidates

Table 12.8 Singapore: Household Size by Ethnic Group, 1980 and 1990

Persons	Chinese 1980 %	Chinese 1990 %	Malays 1980 %	Malays 1990 %	Indians 1980 %	Indians 1990 %	Others 1980 %	Others 1990 %
1	7.2	4.5	6.5	1.8	19.0	7.6	17.7	6.3
2	10.2	12.9	7.4	8.5	10.3	12.6	19.6	17.5
3	14.1	16.9	13.5	15.7	12.8	16.9	18.6	21.2
4	19.5	26.1	17.6	24.1	16.7	24.6	24.4	23.7
5	17.2	20.9	14.6	22.3	14.4	19.1	10.4	18.8
6	12.3	10.7	11.7	14.0	9.9	9.8	4.6	7.5
7	8.0	4.6	9.0	6.6	6.8	4.6	2.3	2.5
8	5.0	1.9	6.8	3.6	4.2	2.2	0.9	2.5
9	2.8	0.8	4.9	1.8	2.4	1.3	0.7	0
10 and over	3.7	0.7	8.0	1.6	3.5	1.3	0.8	0
Mean size (numbers)	4.7	4.2	5.3	4.7	4.2	4.1	3.3	3.8

Sources: Department of Statistics 1981, 1991.
Note: Figures are for ethnic group of head of household, and for resident households (total households in 1980).

the status quo by enforcing ethnic boundaries and enhancing the appeal of group identity.

To some degree, such a strategy flies in the face of reality, first because many of the traditional markers of ethnicity are being eroded, at least partly because of policies operating at a higher level (as in education) that serve to reduce differences; and second because this system maintains a false "purity" of ethnic identity by allocating children to the ethnic group of their fathers even in the case of those who are the offspring of mixed marriages. In the context of an economy marked by a high order of dynamism and a society characterized by a large degree of pragmatism, adopting such a static approach to a major component of social organization creates an air of unreality. Yet the force of the institutionalization of ethnicity is such that it coexists with the informal (but powerful) clustering of the population in specific communities no matter how incomplete the correspondence between the two systems.

Such an approach is highly compatible with a policy of ethnic management as an integral component of the Singapore government's corporatist strategy of development. Despite the multiethnic character of society, the pervasive influence of the Confucianist ethic ensures the preeminence of the principle that the needs of society as a whole supersede the rights of any one group—a principle equally readily applied in Singapore to matters economic, political, or social. Consequently, the application of corporatist modes of control enables the establishment, implementation, and maintenance of the instruments necessary to ensure desired outcomes. This strategy may be considered successful on the grounds that neither the costs nor benefits of being Singaporean devolve inequitably on any one ethnic group; there is no ethnically based differentiation in access to the facilities and amenities of the infrastructure so that at least some features of inequality, such as niche occupations, are being progressively reduced; there has been no overt ethnic conflict since independence in 1965; and potential sources of discontent are reportedly not ethnic but concerned with economic, social, and political issues (Clammer 1982). If Singaporeans are willing to accept a corporatist approach involving extensive intervention in the social organization of their lives, which most appear to be, then ethnic management appears to have provided an important part of the social underpinning of economic development and an integrated nation-state.

References

Appleyard, Reginald T. 1992. "Migration and Development." *Asian and Pacific Migration Journal* 1(1):1–18.

Chee Heng Leng, and Chan Chee Khoon. 1984. *Designer Genes: IQ, Ideology & Biology.* Kuala Lumpur: Institute for Social Analysis.

Clammer, John. 1982. "The Institutionalization of Ethnicity: The Culture of Ethnicity in Singapore." *Ethnic and Racial Studies* 5(2):125–39.

———. 1991. *The Sociology of Singapore Religion.* Asia Pacific Monograph No.4. Singapore: Chopmen.

Department of Statistics. 1964. *Report on the Census of Population 1957.* Singapore.

———. 1973. *Report on the Census of Population 1970, Singapore,* Volume 1. Singapore.

———. 1980. *Life Tables 1980.* Singapore, unpublished.

———. 1981. *Census of Population 1980,* various volumes. Singapore.

———. 1990. *Statistics on Marriages and Divorces 1990.* Singapore.

———. 1991. *Census of Population 1990: Advance Data Release.* Singapore.

———. 1992. *Census of Population 1990: Statistical Release 1: Demographic Characteristics.* Singapore.

de Souza, Dudley. 1980. "The Politics of Language: Language Planning in Singapore." In *Language and Society in Singapore,* ed. Evangelos A. Afendras and Eddie C.Y. Kuo. Singapore: Singapore University Press.

Goodkind, Daniel M. 1991. "Creating New Traditions in Modern Chinese Populations: Aiming for Birth in the Year of the Dragon." *Population and Development Review* 17(4):663–86.

Gopinathan, S. 1980. "Language Policy in Education: A Singapore Perspective." In *Language and Society in Singapore,* ed. Evangelos A. Afendras and Eddie C. Y. Kuo. Singapore: Singapore University Press.

Hassan, Riaz. 1977. *Families in Flats: A Study of Low Income Families in Public Housing.* Singapore: Singapore University Press.

Hassan, Riaz, and Geoffrey Bartholomew. 1976. "Ethnic Outmarriage and Socio-Cultural Organization." In *Singapore: Society in Transition,* ed. Riaz Hassan. Kuala Lumpur: Oxford University Press.

Hodder, B. William. 1953. "Racial Groupings in Singapore." *Malayan Journal of Tropical Geography* 1:25–36.

Humphrey, John W. (n.d.). *Geographic Analysis of Singapore's Population.* Census Monograph No.5. Singapore: Department of Statistics.

Ministry of Health, Population Planning Unit. 1990. *Life Tables, 1990.* Singapore, unpublished.

Neville, Warwick. 1966. "Singapore: Ethnic Diversity and Its Implications." *Annals of the Association of American Geographers* 56(2):236–53; reprinted in *Population Geography: A Reader*, ed. George J. Demko, Harold M. Rose, and George A. Schnell. New York: McGraw-Hill.

―――. 1979. "Singapore: Urbanization and Demographic Change." In *Migration and Development in South-East Asia: A Demographic Perspective*, ed. Robin J. Pryor. Kuala Lumpur: Oxford University Press.

―――. 1992. "Agribusiness in Singapore: A Capital Intensive Service." *Journal of Rural Studies* 8(4):241–55.

―――. 1993. "The Impact of Economic Development on Land Functions in Singapore." *Geoforum* 24(2):143–63.

"Notices of Singapore." 1854. *Journal of the Indian Archipelago* 8:101–9; 1855. 9:453.

Pang Eng Fong. 1992. "Absorbing Temporary Foreign Workers: The Experience of Singapore." *Asian and Pacific Migration Journal* 1(3–4):495–509.

Pang Eng Fong, and Linda Lim. 1982. "Foreign Labor and Economic Development in Singapore." *International Migration Review* 16(3):548–76.

Registrar-General of Births and Deaths. 1990. *Report on the Registration of Births and Deaths 1990*. Singapore.

Republic of Singapore. 1989. *Maintenance of Religious Harmony*. Parliamentary White Paper Cmd. 21 of 1989. Singapore: Singapore National Printers, Ltd.

Rodan, Garry. 1989. *The Political Economy of Singapore's Industrialization: National State and International Capital*. London: Macmillan.

Saw Swee Hock. 1970. *Singapore: Population in Transition*. Philadelphia: University of Pennsylvania Press.

―――. 1990. *Changes in the Fertility Policy of Singapore*. Institute of Policy Studies. Singapore: Times Academic Press.

Siddique, Sharon. 1990. "The Phenomenology of Ethnicity: A Singapore Case-Study." *Sojourn* 5(1):35–62.

Skeldon, Ronald. 1992. "International Migration within and from the East and Southeast Asia Region: A Review Essay." *Asian and Pacific Migration Journal* 1(1):19–63.

Stahl, Charles W. 1986. *International Labor Migration: A Study of the ASEAN Countries*. New York: Center for Migration Studies.

―――. 1991. "South-North Migration in the Asia-Pacific Region." *International Migration* 29(2):163–93.

Straits Times. 1989, 14 December.

Sullivan, Gerard, S. Gunasekaran, and Sununta Siengthai. 1992. "Labour Migration and Policy Formation in a Newly Industrialized Country: A Case Study of Illegal Thai Workers in Singapore." *ASEAN Economic Bulletin* 9(1):66–84.

Sunday Times. 1992, 31 May.

Wee Kim Seng, K. 1976. *Family Law.* Singapore Law Monograph Series, No. 2, *Malaya Law Review.* Singapore: University of Singapore.

Chapter 13

Immigration and Ethnicity in the Urban Milieu

Frederick W. Boal

The second half of the twentieth century has been referred to as "The Age of Migration" (Castles and Miller 1993). Furthermore, a recent analysis by Brian Berry demonstrates that since 1950, 80 percent of transnational migration has been urbanward. Berry summarizes the effects of this flow (as far as high-income countries are concerned) as shoring up urbanization in those countries where urban growth has been least, while simultaneously accelerating the globalization of their urban populations (Berry 1993). "Globalization" of population emerges as a central theme for all the cities discussed in this volume.

Migration Models

When reviewing a range of case studies, one is tempted (perhaps, indeed, there is an imperative) to seek generalization—to scan the material in search of common themes, common processes, common consequences. At the same time, such an exploration must inevitably be sensitive to the variations that exist from place to place, in the timing and composition of the migration flows and in the nature of the receiving society. Additionally, case-study material is presented by each author in a way fundamentally shaped by her or his own perspective. All this makes life difficult for someone attempting an overview. It also turns such a challenge into an extremely interesting venture into both the variety of the urban migration experience and into the variety of ways that experience can be interpreted.

In their recent work, Castles and Miller (1993) suggest a fourfold model of the transnational migration process. First, there is what is intended to be (both by the migrants and by the receiving society) a temporary labor migration of young workers, with a strong orientation to their homeland, a concern to save for return thereto, and a wish to send remittances back to their families in their country of origin. This type of migration is frequently associated with the concept of "rotation," whereby temporary migration is encouraged, ensuring (it is hoped) that almost none of the migrant stream permanently settles. The second stage in the Castles and Miller model emerges when those who are supposed to be temporary migrant laborers begin to prolong their stay, develop social networks among those with the same ethnic origin, and secure thereby at least a modicum of mutual help. Once the immigrants prolong their stay, stage three begins to emerge, as family reunion is attempted and there is a growing consciousness of long-term settlement, now with a concomitant orientation toward the receiving society. Ethnic communities begin to emerge, equipped with their own institutions. The final stage of the Castles and Miller model is reached when settlement has become permanent. Here, however, two contrasting outcomes can be seen—one in which the migrants attain a secure legal status and eventual citizenship, the other in which permanent settlement occurs in an environment of political exclusion and socio-economic marginalization, creating a situation in which ethnic minorities emerge.

Castles and Miller claim that their four-stage model applies most readily to the large-scale migrations from the Mediterranean Basin to Western Europe and to Australia, and also to the flows from Latin America and Asia to North America. The migration from former colonies to the former colonial powers is also quite effectively handled. However, it is less appropriate for refugee movements, which cannot be explained by the dictates of capital accumulation theory (Miles 1993), nor for the increasing migratory volume of temporary, highly skilled personnel (Champion 1994). This latter situation also points to an increasing polarization of international migration into two components—a low-income, unskilled labor flow (which in turn contains a considerable volume of clandestine, undocumented, or illegal migrants) and a flow dominated by those with well-honed professional and managerial skills. This contrast is undoubtedly sharpened by the clandestine component of the labor flow, whose members are very vulnerable to superexploitation in the countries of immigration.

Immigration Policy

This volume focuses on the ways a range of immigrant groups have been received in the various cities examined, and on the ways those same groups have reacted to the environments they find themselves in. Here, again, Castles and Miller present us with a useful conceptual framework. In terms of immigration policies three groups of countries are distinguished. First, there are the classical countries of immigration—such as the United States, Canada, and Australia—encouraging permanent migration, treating most legal immigrants as future citizens, granting secure residence status, and permitting family reunion. Second, there are countries with histories of colonial possessions—such as France, the Netherlands, and Britain—who have given preferential treatment to the former colonials, many of whom, indeed, were already citizens of the mother country at their time of entry. Permanent entry has generally been granted and family reunion flows permitted. The third category belong to what Castles and Miller call rigid guestworker models, typified, above all, by Germany and Switzerland. Here labor market and civil rights are restricted, there is a belief in temporary sojourn, and family reunion is discouraged. Nonetheless, long stay does occur and families do reunite or even form in the new country.

Of course, the distinction between the three categories of immigrant country is not watertight, and the situation is dynamic, with former colonial powers becoming more restrictive and former guestworker countries less so.

Castles and Miller clearly differentiate between countries in terms of their policies toward immigrants. Fundamentally, the distinction is made between those where immigrants derive a sense of security in the knowledge that they can stay, and those where the migration is viewed as short term, both by the migrants themselves ("myth of return") and by the so-called host society. With the former, immigrants can put down roots, reconstitute their families in the new land and build communities with a concomitant array of ethnic institutions. With the latter, insecurity and instability are paramount, permanence is doubtful (even though many end up staying), ethnic group formation does occur, but the circumstances are ones of isolation, separation, and emphasis on difference.

Governments play crucial roles in their attempts both to regulate immigrant flows and to set conditions for residence, be it permanent or temporary. These roles find expression in the country-to-country differences demonstrated in the Castles and Miller categorization. However, social regulation by the state extends far beyond immediate issues of immigration policy. Most importantly, there are marked differences in the nature of welfare capitalism. To follow Esping-Andersen's analysis, we can distinguish countries from each other on the degree of "decommodification" that exists (Esping-Andersen 1991). Decommodification occurs when a service is rendered as a matter of right and when a person can maintain a livelihood without reliance on the market. Esping-Andersen lists three types of welfare state: (1) liberal, characterized by means-tested assistance and modest social insurance plans; (2) a cluster of countries where rights are attached to class and status and where there is a strong commitment to the preservation of traditional family values; and finally (3) a group of states where welfare is based on universalism, the objective being to promote an equality of the highest standards, not an equality of minimal needs.

It would be analytically tidy for our purposes if a close correspondence could be demonstrated between the two typologies presented above; that is, the typology of countries based on their immigration policies, on the one hand, and the typology of welfare states on the other. This is only partially so, however, although it is notable that Castles and Miller's classical countries of immigration do correspond with those Esping-Andersen recognizes as being low on the decommodification scale, the market being at its most dominant (United States, Canada, Australia). All in all, we have a fairly complex overlap of immigration and welfare policy, one that needs to be explicated specifically for each of the locations under examination in this volume. As far as immigrant experience is concerned, the crucial issue will be the degree and nature of government intervention in the housing and labor markets, and how such intervention impacts, directly and indirectly, on the members of the various ethnic groups present.

The central focus of the case studies offered in this book is on the imprint made on the respective cities by the various immigrant groups involved, and on how the receiving urban societies have responded to the immigrants. Most of the migration discussed is recent, much involving ethnic groups who are new to the cities concerned, while other streams are composed of people accumulating on foundations laid by fellow ethnics in years gone by. In the case of Blacks in the United States, however, it does not make sense to consider them immigrants. Rather, their situation is the product of forced migration long ago, where assimilation has still not worked its course. Beyond this, and not examined here, are situations of urban ethnicity where recent immigration is not paramount, but where ethnic relations are dominated by the copresence of ethnonational conflict.

Ethnic Emplacement Models

From a geographical perspective, a central issue, at the scale of individual cities, is the degree to which members of a particular ethnic group are residentially segregated from the rest of the population. This snapshot approach needs to be supplemented by an understanding of the dynamics underlying the spatial pattern—in what way has it evolved and what processes underlie it?

Just as general models can be offered in terms of the immigration process and of immigration policies, so with the actual patterns of residential segregation (or their lack). In all instances we are engaged in what William Cronon calls story-telling. Recently, Cronon published a paper entitled "A Place for Stories." In it he notes that all historians configure the events of the past into causal sequences—stories—that order and simplify events to give them new meanings (Cronon 1992). When we study ethnic segregation in cities, we construct stories in an attempt to obtain an ordered sense of what goes on. The most famous story of all is the model developed by Robert Park and his colleagues at the University of Chicago in the 1920s (Park 1926). Here, as we well know, the segregation of immigrant minorities was interpreted as a transitional stage en route to eventual social acceptance and economic parity. As Cater and Jones have put it: "The ethnic enclave is viewed as a transitional space within which immigrants may find protection from an alien society until such time as they are capable of affiliating to that society. Its main function is that of a social womb or chrysalis" (Cater and Jones 1989,142).

These immigrant ethnics are, for a time, segregated from the rest of society, but this is only a period of preparation for entry into the host society itself. The story may have a fairly rough beginning, but it has a happy ending as the immigrants (or at least their children) "make it." Segregation, in this case, is a temporary state and the enclave provides both haven and opportunity.

The assimilationist story seemed to make quite good sense as a description of the experience of European-origin immigrant ethnics in the United States. However, when I came to examine ethnic segregation in my own city of Belfast, the Chicago story was of little help. In Belfast, segregation did not seem to be a launching pad to anywhere. Indeed, evidence can be adduced for the existence of Catholic-Protestant segregation for the last two hundred years. Another story was called for.

The Chicago story is very much a consensus model—there are agreed notions concerning the nature of American society and routes into that society. For Belfast this would not do. Here a conflict model seemed more appropriate. Conflict situations in cities lead people to feel threatened. The perceived threat may materialize in the form of physical violence or may remain as a psychological threat. In both instances it is reasonable that the individuals or groups should attempt to cope with such a threat. Following the work of R. S. Lazarus (Lazarus 1969), I suggested a number of coping

strategies that would find their base in ethnic residential concentration:
physical defense, avoidance, and attack (Boal 1972).

The clustering together of a group within a city can provide the basis for
defense against external attack. By joining the cluster, members of a particular
group no longer find themselves residing in isolation, and the existence of
the group itself within a clearly defined area enables an organized defense to
be developed. Second, segregation promotes avoidance, where members of a
group may wish to reduce contact with the wider society. It also provides a
base for the development of cultural survival strategies. Finally, spatial
concentration of a particular group can provide it with a base for action in
the struggle of its members with society in general. This struggle may take a
peaceful form or may become violent. In terms of political action, spatial
concentration of a particular group may enable it to elect its own representatives who can then attempt to fight their group's battles in the political arena.
However, in a conflict environment, the significance of the group residential
concentration may extend beyond institutional politics. Such areas potentially provide the base for urban insurrection or guerrilla warfare—here, as
Mao Tse Tung would have it, the guerrilla is the fish and the people are
the sea.

It is worthwhile looking at the cultural survival dimension of this model
more closely for such may well be an important part of the conflict coping
strategy itself, in that the maintenance of a distinctive set of cultural attributes
can be highly instrumental in the group's struggles with the wider society.
Community solidarity is thus promoted, providing a base for other coping
strategies—defense and attack. At the same time, it should be acknowledged
that members of an ethnic group may *want* to retain aspects of their cultural
heritage simply for their own sake, the expressive dimension of ethnicity.
Whether motivation be expressive, instrumental, or both, ethnic spatial
concentration is certainly a necessary condition—promoting endogamy and
the effective intergenerational transmission of culture (as an aside it is worth
noting that the culture being transmitted may be as much or more a
product of current and recent circumstances as of historic, and often long-
distance, transfer).

In a sense, my Belfast story describes a kind of limbo; the groups concerned
are locked together separately in a situation where survival (physical and
cultural) is of the essence. Clearly, the sociopolitical conditions that contribute to this story would appear to be very different from those underpinning
the assimilationist tale.

As a coping strategy, residential segregation appears to be functional for
groups in conflict situations. This, indeed, will apply not only to specific
ethnic groups but to the wider, encompassing society as well. From the latter

point of view, the defensive function may be seen as one of containment. Avoidance may meet the prejudicial needs of the majority community enabling it to avoid sustained contact with "strange" ways of life, preservation may mean conservation of majority culture from dilution (pollution) due to ethnic influences, while external action may mean the manipulation of electoral geography so as to deny success to ethnic minority candidates or it may even mean, in the extreme, the availability of clearly defined target-population concentrations.

Both the Chicago and the Belfast stories tell of ethnic groups in interaction with encompassing societies. Both types of segregated situation provide haven: whether they both provide opportunity is another matter. The Chicago model defines the wider society as a relatively open, if grudgingly welcoming place: the Belfast model stresses group survival (both physical and cultural) rather than assimilation. The Chicago story is one of transition, the Belfast story one of permanence.

Does this suggest a simple twofold classification of ethnic segregation? Here we must raise the issue of choice. The Chicago transitional model has built into it the notion that it was the desire of the groups concerned to move from their early immigrant status to become in due course fully fledged members of the host society. Where segregation is of long duration can it also be said that the groups concerned have chosen to maintain their distinctiveness or is the segregated situation, in fact, a trap from which they have the greatest difficulty in escaping?

I suggest that we can find three subplots within the permanence story. The first is epitomized by the Jewish experience, where, in many Western cities at least, long-term segregation is a matter of choice, and a crucial mechanism for cultural survival. The second subplot refers to those situations where it is not clear which group is the dominant or host society. Here ethnicity provides the basis for national struggle (for instance in Jerusalem, Belfast, and Montreal) and separation is a distinctive feature, at least and until a clear winner emerges. Thus, under certain conditions, as Stanley Lieberson points out, political separatism offers a solution to disadvantaged groups in an ethnic stratification system that is not possible for groups disadvantaged on the basis of age, gender, or economic position (Lieberson 1972). In this case, segregation in the city is, in fact, the urban encapsulation of national conflict (Boal, Murray, and Poole 1976; Benvenisti 1983; Boal 1994).

The third subplot within the permanence story has been sharply defined by Susan Smith (1989). Here a process of racialization is taken to be at work where particular populations are identified by direct or indirect reference to their real or imagined phenotypical characteristics, and where these characteristics are taken to give meaning to the actions and attributes of the

290 Frederick W. Boal

populations concerned (Miles 1984). Smith's analysis focuses on Blacks in Britain. She rejects the use of the term ethnic as a description for immigrants from the West Indies and South Asia because, she claims, it has become a euphemism for race. She notes the existence of racial segregation in British cities and observes that "it may simply be a passing phase in the adjustment of markets and institutions to the needs and demands of a recently established Black population. On the other hand, residential differentiation in Britain may be an expression of entrenched racial inequalities that are politically and socially as well as economically inspired" (1989,17).

If the latter be the case, then significant (ritualized) populations are segregated, not from choice, but by the operation of barriers constructed by the wider society. At the same time, the defensive response of such groups tends itself to be segregationist, and the consequent separation perpetuates the view that Black people wish to remain segregated in the kinds of neighborhoods they currently occupy (Smith 1989).

What I am suggesting is that there are four basic stories to be told about ethnic residential segregation: as a transitional device on the road to assimilation, as a long-term situation selected by choice, as a prolonged phenomenon constituted by opposed nationalisms, and as an enclave that corrals unwilling people, probably again on a long-term basis.

Diverse stories, as discussed by William Cronon, may be different ways of looking at the same thing or they may be distinctive because they are tapping different realities. As far as ethnic residential segregation is concerned, I prefer the second interpretation. This being so we may well ask, why do some groups follow the assimilationist track while others opt for separation? Why do some become locked in situations of confronting nationalisms while others become ritualized and trapped? There are many stories to be told. In producing our narratives, however, we must remain vigilant to the fact that our interpretations "become covert exercises of power—sanctioning some voices while silencing others" (Cronon 1992, 1350).

Comparisons

What do the cities examined in this volume tell us, what is their story? In attempting an overview of a range of studies, a number of difficulties arise, some from the fact that different authors have somewhat varying approaches, some from differences in classification schemes, and some from problems of measurement.

No matter what the classification scheme employed, completeness of census enumeration must be a concern. Whether people are referred to as "undocumented," "clandestine," or "nonregistered," it is evident that a significant proportion of the "ethnic" population in any city remains un-counted. Thus, the geographies described are almost always based on those people who have reported their presence to officialdom, or who have been tracked down in some way. Consequently, undercounting not only mini-mizes immigrant/ethnic presence, it may well also distort description of the composition of the groups concerned. This is brought out very clearly in Madrid, where a regularization process was initiated in 1991 whereby those present in the city illegally could be "legitimized." This process demonstrated that the previous figures on foreign presence had been heavily biased toward highly qualified aliens from Western countries. Those who became newly regularized tended to be from Africa and East Asia and were engaged in low-qualification jobs. It is likely that a similar bias exists elsewhere.

A major focus of the case studies presented in this volume is on the degree to which the ethnic groups concerned are residentially segregated from each other and from what might be described, in some instances at least, as the host population. With some chapters, segregation description is of a general, verbal variety; with others, precise measurement is presented, through use of the index of dissimilarity (D). Even with the latter, however, difficulties of comparability arise because of the likely variability in the population size of the areal units employed in the D calculation. Thus comparison of segrega-tion levels for different groups within the same city can be made with some confidence, but intercity comparison is more problematic.

Most of the groups examined in this book are composed of immigrants and/or the descendants of immigrants. Overall, we are dealing with immi-grant ethnics, with ethnic groups that are multigenerational (though possibly having a significant immigrant component), with foreigners who will include an immigrant generation but who also may have one or more generations born in the country of immigration. We also find a number of groups that may be distinguished on ethnoracial grounds but where the designation "immigrant" is devoid of meaning, including Native Americans, and most Blacks in U.S. cities, Aborigines in Australian metropolitan areas, and South African Blacks. These groups, in many ways, are the product of power struggles over decades, indeed centuries. They cannot simply be treated analytically as immigrant groups.

Our case study cities demonstrate similarities in their experience of ethnic-ity, but each in its own unique fashion. While recent immigrant flows have been strikingly dominated by people from the non-European, predominantly less-developed realm, at the same time each individual city has its own unique immigrant combination, determined largely by the proximity of certain source areas and by historic colonial relationships. Thus, London,

Paris, and Amsterdam have a strong ethnic presence deriving from former colonial territories in the Caribbean, South, Southeast, and East Asia, and North Africa. Additionally, Paris, and, again, Amsterdam have other connections with the Mediterranean basin, shared this time with cities characterized by weak or nonexistent colonial connections (the Ruhr cities, Vienna, Milan, and Madrid), where Turkish and "former-Yugoslavian" immigrants become particularly important.

Los Angeles, Chicago, Sydney, and Melbourne all share what Castles and Miller call the "classic" features of immigrant reception. The populations of all of these have been fundamentally built on immigrant flows and their intergenerational consequences. All are based essentially on European origin flows, but are now in receipt of large influxes from their non-European neighbors—Latin Americans and East Asians in the case of the American cities, and Southeast Asians in the case of the Australian.

Singapore and the South African cities are special cases. Immigration to the former has always been Asian dominated, while Johannesburg and Durban have been in receipt of flows that are basically internal (like the movement of U.S. Blacks) and that have thrown up stark racial confrontation with dominant White populations—who, of course, in turn are of immigrant stock, albeit mostly of several generations back.

Immigrant flows from less-developed areas dominate discussion in the twelve case studies presented here. Fundamentally, these flows are seen as replacement labor. For instance, in Vienna the influx of workers from Turkey and from former Yugoslavia is aimed at "unattractive low wage jobs vacated by locals and post-war immigrants," where vulnerability to the business cycle and seasonal fluctuations in labor demand are high. Similarly, in the Ruhr conurbation, where immigrants from Mediterranean countries provide a workforce replacing Germans who have abandoned semi- and unskilled work niches. Exactly the same applies in London and Los Angeles. In addition, in these latter cities, as in Sydney, Melbourne, and Amsterdam, the immigrant inflow is seen not only as replacement labor but as replacement populations for areas of the cities increasingly abandoned by suburbanizing native-born peoples.

Although there is a similarity to all these migration streams, there are also important differences. Here the contrast is between those cities where the migrants are seen as permanent residents (some with citizenship rights deriving from former colonial connections—for example London and Amsterdam) and those where the intention was that the migrant labor should "rotate"—the *gastarbeiter* situations in the Ruhr and in Vienna providing the clearest examples. Situations of likely impermanence fundamentally affect the way the immigrant workers are treated in the host societies as well as shaping attitudes of the migrants themselves. This is demonstrated in the case of Vienna, where many labor migrants tolerate crowded housing conditions (subrenting), not only as a way of minimizing costs but so that savings thereby achieved may be channeled to the purchase of easily transportable consumer goods, or, indeed, to the building of new homes for themselves in their country of origin, pending their return—there is high poignancy in this for those from former Yugoslavia who have seen many of these selfsame houses destroyed or badly damaged in recent months (Ignatieff 1993).

Being replacement labor locates the groups concerned at the bottom of the socioeconomic hierarchy, with a consequent fundamental shaping of their spatial distributions within the recipient cities. The extent to which they are treated and, indeed, see themselves as permanent or temporary residents also affects their housing opportunities and aspirations. Migration of family members to join pioneering labor migrants, together with the increasing number of children born to the immigrants after they have settled in the recipient cities also reshape the migrant communities.

High-Status Migrants

All this paints a particular picture of the migrant streams entering and settling in the cities explored in this book—low-skill, low-income, high risk of unemployment, and, in some instances, uncertainty about length of stay. However, a second dimension to recent immigration gets emphasis as well. This is the increasingly significant presence in most cities of high-status, professionally qualified, high-income immigrants. For instance, Vienna reveals a West European and overseas migrant presence that contrasts sharply with what might be described as the traditional labor migrants. The former occupy top positions with companies that are using Vienna as a strategically located base from which to develop markets in East and Central Europe; they also work for a number of international organizations whose headquarters are sited in the city. Similarly with Madrid, where a demand for low-qualified labor in activities such as construction is contrasted with management and professional worker needs in the realms of finance and multinational corporations. In Sydney and Melbourne, a recent shift in the composition of the immigrant intake is noted, with skilled and business migrants making up a much greater proportion of the flow (for instance from Hong Kong and Malaysia). In Los Angeles, Asian Indians have generally entered the system with high levels of education and English language skills and, in some cases, with considerable wealth. Finally, we can note a shift from blue-collar to white-collar immigrants in Paris, with a growing proportion in management.

From the perspective of the detailed geography of ethnic presence in cities, these high-status immigrants inevitably generate a spatial pattern of residence that is very different from that of the low status.

Gender

When consideration is given to the composition of urban immigrant groups little attention has been paid to gender differences. However, one chapter in this volume, that on Milan, goes some way toward redressing this oversight. The point is made that many of the immigrant flows to Italy from third world countries are composed of female migrants arriving alone. These migrants tend to come from Catholic countries such as the Philippines and a number in Latin America. In contrast, migrants from Islamic countries tend to be almost exclusively male. Female immigrants, no matter what their skill levels, with few exceptions are incorporated in the domestic service sector. This has a very striking effect on their patterns of residence, not only in Milan but in many of the other cities examined in this volume. Within Milan, female immigrants are concentrated in the most prestigious zone of the city—the Centro Storico—where they work in households as nurses, assistants to the elderly, baby-sitters, cleaners and so on. Similarly with Los Angeles where live-in Latina maids and child-care providers in the affluent hill areas create residential distributions that appear quite counter to the expectation of concentration in low-income neighborhoods. In Madrid, housing conditions are better for immigrant women than for men because a large part of the former work as live-in maids and "enjoy a bedroom with good hygienic conditions." There is a price to be paid for this, however, in that the nature of their work prevents many women from living with their husbands and children, while their dispersal in Madrid means that they are more dependent than the men on their own social networks for assistance in time of need. The tendency for a portion of the immigrant women to be resident in wealthy districts is also found in Paris where, we are told, "the Portuguese . . . are well accepted by the French population (many Portuguese women work as cleaning ladies or caretakers in blocks of flats)." Finally, it can be noted that the isolation of immigrant women is reinforced by other factors such as occur in the Ruhr, where Turkish women have a very low labor force participation rate, while in Sydney there is a problem for older women of south Asian origin—initial isolation reduces the opportunity (indeed the need) to learn English, which in turn reinforces segregation. This is likely to be a recurrent problem in many urban immigrant situations.

Segregation

All the ethnic groups examined in this volume display some degree of residential segregation. However, segregation levels vary significantly from one city to another and from one group to another in the same city.

The benchmark segregation level in American cities is that between Blacks and Whites, and it tends to be high both for Los Angeles and Chicago. Of course, Blacks in this context are not in any meaningful sense immigrants, but their U.S. segregation levels tend to be used by some of the authors who write about non-American cities as a justification for claims that segregation in their cities is much lower than is the case in the United States. Despite measurement difficulties, however, there is a consistency in the reporting of segregation levels that does indicate that all the European cities studied display considerably lower ethnic segregation levels than is the case in the United States. With Paris, for instance, we are told that the foreign population, as a general rule, is largely dispersed: "the process of segregation here is in no way similar to that observed in many industrial nations, and particularly in North America." In Paris "it is undeniable that the segregation is weak compared to that observed in other European countries such as England or Germany." Similarly with Amsterdam "despite the rapidly rising numbers of foreign immigrants, it is an interesting fact that in [the city] . . . there is virtually no evidence of clear or increasing segregation of ethnic groups." Sydney and Melbourne do display distinctive immigrant segregation patterns but, once again, clearly not at the U.S. level. This difference is manifest in the criteria employed to designate segregation as being "high" or "low." In the case of the Australian cities, an index of less than .15 is taken to indicate low segregation, an index of .30 to indicate high; with Los Angeles and Chicago, however, low segregation is marked by an index of dissimilarity of less than .30, high segregation with an index of greater than .60. Finally, in Singapore ethnic segregation levels would appear to be low due to government efforts to cause the dissolution of the largely spontaneous clustering of groups. Sitting outside all of these are the South African cities, where it goes without saying that the white population is highly segregated from the Black.

Intercity variation in segregation is one aspect; the degree of segregation between groups in any one city is another. Some groups display high segregation levels, such as the Bangladeshis in London, Cambodians and Salvadorans in Los Angeles, and Vietnamese and Portuguese in Sydney. All these are recent arrivals. Whether or not they continue to display these high levels of residential segregation remains to be seen. However, recency of arrival does not always lead to high levels of segregation—witness the various groups in Paris and Amsterdam.

In sum, there are major contrasts in ethnic segregation levels between the various cities analyzed in this volume and between the various groups in each city. The United States seems to have the highest segregation levels, though Black segregation makes a powerfully unique contribution to this outcome, while London, Sydney, and Melbourne occupy an intermediate position. Relatively dispersed ethnic residential patterns characterize the other cities. Again, of course, the South African cities stand alone.

Perception

Whatever indices of dissimilarity tell us about ethnic concentration in cities, perception is also important. Indeed, with the mass of people, what matters is what the circumstances are *thought* to be rather than what objective measures tell us. As William I. Thomas once noted, "if men define situations as real, they are real in their consequences" (Thomas and Znaniecki 1920). A sense of the role of perception is powerfully provided in the Vienna discussion. It is worth repeating:

> With regard to the geographical origins of immigrants there is a wide gap between the public perception and empirical findings. Most Viennese would estimate the proportion of Turks, Romanians, and immigrants from former Yugoslavia to be much higher than it actually is. . . . [The presence of foreign labor migrants] is noticed particularly in public places like parks, playgrounds, schools, daily markets, and public transport. In conjunction with already existing fears and prejudices, this selective awareness leads to a collective dramatization of the actual extent of the phenomenon.

Likewise in Paris, where official statistics do "not always correspond to the French population's perception of the foreign presence mainly because of the change in the national origins of the foreign population, particularly the increase in the number of Africans and Asians, whose arrival is more visible." Finally, "visibility" has a major impact in Johannesburg where "at street level . . . downtown Johannesburg seems more like Abidjan than any European metropolis." This tendency to overemphasize ethnic presence is nothing new, resonating, as it does, with nineteenth-century Omaha, Nebraska, as analyzed by Howard Chudacoff (Chudacoff 1973).

Undoubtedly, in all the cities examined in this volume, there is some degree of ethnic segregation. However, the intensity of this segregation, as well as the degree of ethnic presence, tend to be inflated in the minds of many "nonscientific" observers. Beyond this, particularly with the contributions on European cities, there seems to be a twofold concern—first to stress the difference between what is taken to be the North American experience and that recorded in the European cities, and second to encourage action to prevent such circumstances from arising in the future. There is almost what one might describe as "a terror of the ghetto." The incomplete evidence available does suggest that European segregation levels are lower than those found in the United States, but I have a strong suspicion that the contrast being made is highly (though not solely) dependent on the strikingly high levels of Black segregation in the United States. It is fear of the possibility of the emergence of Black ghetto conditions that is at the root of European concerns. The underclass ghetto, a spatial and social construction redolent of racial connotations, lurks in the undergrowth of urban unease.

Whatever the reality, whether past or present, there is nonetheless a powerful concern among many of the authors of this volume that their particular cities should avoid circumstances that could possibly lead to increased ethnic segregation. Thus:

Paris: "This process [of segregation] can only be found for foreign groups that are markedly different from the French in physical aspect and especially in their education and level of qualification. Xenophobic attitudes are exceptional, but when they do arise, they particularly are directed toward Algerians, Moroccans, Turks, and Black Africans."

Vienna: "The slogan must be: social and spatial integration instead of ghetto-building."

Madrid: "Meanwhile, the majority of society waits. And the only way to avoid this majority from leaning toward the racist and xenophobic minority is to promote authentic public policies for immigration, policies that will avoid the formation of ghettos and will promote and facilitate means for raising the economic and cultural level of the immigrants."

Amsterdam: "Will the Dutch welfare state remain successful in avoiding polarization or will the result be an increase in segregation and polarization, and as a result, an exclusion of population categories from mainstream society?"

Finally, London: here the author of the chapter notes that in 1978 he argued that ghetto was already an appropriate label for minority quarters in Britain, as it was in America; he now admits that judgment to have been premature—"but for how long?"

Ghetto terror has its roots in a very negative view of the consequences of ethnic segregation. As the South African discussion in this volume notes, "as a rule the term 'segregation' has been associated with negative connotations" [probably nowhere more so than in South Africa!]. However there may be a danger that we will throw the baby out with the bath water—that is, the positive features associated with the residential concentration of ethnic groups may be ignored.

The strongest appeal for a reevaluation is found in the chapter on Sydney and Melbourne. Here Graeme Hugo, while acknowledging the contradictory nature of residential segregation, points to what he sees as a real need to get away from the negative stereotyping of ethnic concentration: "The conventional view of ethnic enclaves is a generally negative one . . . they tend to foster separation and delay and impede adjustment to the wider society. However, the research evidence does not support such a view; rather it tends to reflect the role of those enclaves in assisting the adjustment of new arrivals into the Australian economy and society by mediating that adjustment through the filter of day-to-day contact with and assistance from people of the same linguistic and cultural background" (see also Castles 1994).

Of course, Hugo does not necessarily favor segregation as a long-term condition for members of a group, because concentration can become an obstacle to effective assimilation (in the Australian case discouraging learning both English and the finer features of Australian bureaucratic procedures).

So the object here is not to paint a rosy picture of segregation as a counter to much of the negative stereotyping that exists. Rather, it is to suggest that we need a sensitive view of the topic—one that neither naively applauds segregation nor wishes to reduce or prevent it in all circumstances. It is interesting to note that in reform-Apartheid Johannesburg, Indians and Blacks, now able to buy into a new middle-class housing area, consciously sought "the vicinity of neighbors of the same skin color, experience, and cultural background."

Government Roles

While there is a need to reevaluate the nature and effects of segregation, there is also a concern to prevent the emergence of major ethnic residential concentrations. Sometimes this is attempted through direct government intervention in the housing system, as has happened in Singapore. In this case, policy objectives have never been made explicit, but the allocation of population to newly developed public housing has, nonetheless, been done in such a way as to dissolve the largely spontaneous closeting of groups and to avoid the creation of "any latter-day Chinatowns or Malay settlements." Indeed, upper limits have been set for each neighborhood and apartment block in terms of allowable proportions for the major ethnic groups—84 percent for Chinese residents of any given neighborhood, 22 percent for Malays, and 10 percent for Indians. At the other extreme of government intervention, we have had, until recently, the apartheid manipulations of urban South Africa under the Group Areas Act. Here, of course, the objective was not to prevent segregation, but to make it as complete as possible. Between these two extremes lie a number of other governmental strategies, ranging from the basic laissez-faire of the United States to indirect intervention through the welfare system, as in the case of the Netherlands.

In fact, the role of the state takes on crucial significance for any understanding of intercity variation in the economic, social, and spatial positions of recent immigrants and, indeed, of members of ethnic groups present for several generations.

First, at the level of immigration policy itself: how many people are to be admitted in any one year; are there any requirements regarding their skills and/or financial circumstances; are some origins favored over others; are preexisting linkages between sending and receiving countries important; are the immigrants viewed as temporary labor force (guestworkers) or as potential citizens? All these facets, variable from country to country and over time, affect the ways in which immigrants and their descendants are (or are not) integrated into the receiving societies.

The treatment of ethnic groups (immigrant or otherwise) varies considerably between the urban contexts examined here. Laissez-faire approaches contrast with direct intervention, while shades of indirect intervention lie between these two extremes. South Africa and Singapore have been highly interventionist. Intervention also occurs in the Netherlands, though in this case it is not directed at the prevention of ethnic segregation; rather, economic disadvantage, in part at least, is countered by the actions of the Dutch welfare state, including special arrangements regarding income redistribution, housing, social security subsidies, and a specific battle against poverty. Thus, in the Netherlands, in so far as ethnic segregation is caused by economic differences, so it is countered by social welfare redistribution. On the other hand, the apparent lack of such countervailing policies in Vienna has led to low-income immigrants being squeezed into a limited segment of the housing stock, a product, in part, of exclusion from the gentrifying city core and also from subsidized housing, the latter being the preserve of Austrian citizens. In contrast, general urban policies in Paris aimed at reducing inequalities produce a strong social mix in most of the communes; this in turn creates an intermingling of low-income immigrant households with the native French population.

Beyond the specific actions exemplified above, a number of authors in this volume call for recognition of the importance of certain philosophical positions that imbue state activity. In Singapore, there is the pervasive influence of a Confucianist ethic where "the needs of society as a whole supersede the rights of any one group." This means that clustering tendencies on the part of various ethnic groups have to be overridden by the activation of dispersal policies, as it is feared that such clustering would be detrimental to the communal well-being of the city-state. In another realm is Paris, where we are told that the low levels of segregation can be traced to the Age of Enlightenment and the French Revolution: "a universalist and egalitarian ideal has existed since then. The ideal vision of the nation is of a homogeneous country where juridical and territorial peculiarities are excluded, and where minorities do not exist." More modestly, many of the other countries discussed in this volume adhere to varying degrees of welfare-state provision. Critical, to adopt Esping-Andersen's term, is the degree of decommodification that exists. The Dutch, and specifically the Amsterdam case, illustrate the importance of this. Here welfare provision creates some uncoupling of income levels from housing, education, and participation in the labor market. At the other extreme lies the United States.

At this point it is tempting to see a relationship between the degree of decommodification, as measured by Esping-Andersen, and the tendency toward ethnic segregation. Thus, countries such as the United States and Australia are less decommodified but more highly segregated, while the Netherlands is one of the most decommodified and least segregated (Esping-Andersen 1990, table 2.2). Such an inverse relationship can only be offered as a hypothesis, because the degree and nature of housing-market intervention and precise and unambiguous measurement of residential segregation will be required before we can be clear as to its validity.

The issue of decommodification relates directly to the position in the economic order of the various ethnic/immigrant groups examined here. Basically, in so far as state intervention occurs, it has been aimed at ameliorating the economic positions of various groups in society. In so far as this translates to the spatial order, it should help modify tendencies toward segregation of ethnic groups from the rest of the urban population. In the case studies presented, there is a powerful sense that most of the immigrant/ethnic groups have their spatial dispositions substantially determined by their economic position—a position that, for many, is located toward the bottom of the economic order. For instance in Madrid "immigrants are located according to the economic means available to them and the standard of living in the district." In Paris "the segregation process is essentially of social and not of ethnic character. Assimilation will depend on the economy," while in Vienna many immigrants are squeezed into a limited segment of the housing market by their low income (as well as their exclusion from subsidized and public-sector housing). The same significance is attached to economic position in the Amsterdam case, but in this instance the process works in the opposite direction as "income redistribution . . . and provision of social housing has been highly effective in combating social segregation."

Prioritizing economic position as a key determinant of residential location is a dominant feature of many chapters in this book. Where immigrants are found is basically shaped by their economic position—low-income groups are found in low-income residential areas, high-income groups in high-income areas—but economic position does not explain the segregation that frequently exists *between* low-income ethnic groups. Here cultural factors undoubtedly come into play.

Varied Experiences

The immigration and ethnic presence experiences of the cities examined in these chapters are nothing if not varied. At the same time, they combine, in various ways, elements of general migration processes. Most migrants come to stay. Some assimilate rapidly; others remain distinct for generations, either through choice, through the exclusionary actions of receiving societies, or, indeed, some combination of these. All ethnics have been affected by government policies in the receiving countries—by immigrant selection, by desires for temporary or long-term stayers, by the welfare structures operative, particularly as they impact on accessibility to housing, and by attitudes toward the desirability, or otherwise, of residential segregation.

Strikingly, almost all the cities discussed here have experienced important changes in their immigrant source areas, particularly since World War II. In many instances, this has meant an increasing presence of peoples perceived to be markedly different from receiving populations—culturally and phenotypically. This, in turn, has sharpened problems of racism and has also contributed to perceptions of ethnic presence that frequently fail to correspond to reality.

Much immigrant urban ethnic entry has been as replacement for preexisting populations who have been striving to move upward in the job market and correspondingly outward to the suburbs. However, the exigencies of a globalizing world economy have not only drawn in labor supply at the lower end of the skills/income spectrum, they have also (and increasingly) attracted large flows of workers with managerial and professional qualifications. While low-income ethnics have been located in low-income residential districts, the higher income groups display geographies quite distinct from this. They are also less likely to operate ethnically and, indeed, are less likely to be treated as such by the host society. Gender distinctions are also important for their spatial manifestations. Many female immigrants find themselves in the anomalous position of occupying, at one and the same time, disadvantaged labor-market positions and apparently advantaged residential locations.

The contributions to this book offer a rich harvest both of similarity and of contrast in urban ethnic experience. Nonetheless, there is room for further comparative research on this topic. Such research should be encouraged. It should include a range of case studies, even broader than those presented here, encompassing cities where ethnonational conflict is a dominant feature, and also urban environments drawn from the burgeoning metropolises of Latin America, Africa, and southern and eastern Asia. It should also be based on a concerted effort at measurement standardization, so that the foundations for comparative conclusions may be appropriately strengthened.

References

Benvenisti, Meron. 1983. *Jerusalem: Study of a Polarized Community.* Jerusalem: West Bank Data Project.

Berry, Brian J. L. 1993. "Transnational Urbanward Migration 1830–1980." *Annals of the Association of American Geographers* 83(3):389–405.

Boal, Frederick W. 1972. "The Urban Residential Sub-Community: A Conflict Interpretation." *Area* 4(3):164–68.

———. 1994. "Encapsulation: Urban Dimensions of National Conflict." In *Managing Divided Cities*, ed. Seamus Dunn. Keele: Ryburn Press.

Boal, Frederick W., Russell C. Murray, and Michael A. Poole. 1976. "Belfast: The Urban Encapsulation of a National Conflict". In *Urban Ethnic Conflict: A Comparative Perspective*, ed. Susan E. Clarke and Jeffrey L. Abler. Chapel Hill, N.C.: University of North Carolina, Institute for Research in Social Science.

Castles, Stephen. 1994. "Population Distribution and Migration." In United Nations Expert Meeting on Population Distribution and Migration, Santa Cruz, Bolivia, Proceedings (ST/ESA/SER.R/133): 309–33.

Castles, Stephen, and Mark J. Miller. 1993. *The Age of Migration.* Basingstoke: Macmillan.

Cater, John, and Trevor Jones. 1989. *Social Geography.* London: Edward Arnold.

Champion, Anthony G. 1994. "International Migration and Demographic Change in the Developed World." *Urban Studies* 31(4):653–77.

Chudacoff, Howard P. 1973. "A New Look at Ethnic Neighborhoods: Residential Dispersion and the Concept of Visibility in a Medium Sized City." *Journal of American History* 60:76–93.

Cronon, William. 1992. "A Place for Stories: Nature, History and Narrative." *Journal of American History* 78(4):1347–76.

Esping-Andersen, Göspa. 1991. *The Three Worlds of Welfare Capitalism.* Cambridge: Polity Press.

Ignatieff, Michael. 1993. *Blood and Belonging: Journeys into the New Nationalism.* London: BBC Books.

Lazarus, Richard S. 1969. *Patterns of Adjustment and Human Effectiveness.* New York: McGraw-Hill.

Lieberson, Stanley. 1972. "Stratification and Ethnic Groups." In *Readings in Race and Ethnic Relations,* ed. Anthony H. Richmond. Oxford: Pergamon Press.

Miles, Robert. 1984. "Racialization." In *Dictionary of Race and Ethnic Relations,* ed. E. Ellis Cashmore. London: Routledge and Kegan Paul.

———. 1993. "Introduction—Europe 1993: The Significance of Changing Patterns of Migration." *Ethnic and Racial Studies* 16(3):459–66.

Park, Robert E. 1926. "The Urban Community as a Spatial Pattern and a Moral Order." In *The Urban Community,* ed. Eric W. Burgess. Chicago: University of Chicago Press:3–18.

Smith, Susan. 1989. *The Politics of 'Race' and Residence.* Cambridge: Polity Press.

Thomas, William I., and Florian Znaniecki. 1920. *The Polish Peasant in Europe and America.* Boston: Badger.

Index

Administration of Muslim Law Act, 1968 (Singapore), 274
Africanization, 237
age, 82, 261, 270; distribution, female, 151; structure, 207
apartheid, 224, 225–26, 233, 244
arbitrary threshold test, 41–42
assimilation, 1, 94, 150, 161, 180, 182, 185, 223, 289–90, 300
asylum: law, 143; political, 142; seekers, 146, 150, 171

barrio, 16
birth rate(s), 25, 169, 263. *See also* fertility
Bracero Program (United States), xix
brain drain, 23, 224
British Nationality Act, 98

Catholic Church immigrant assistance, 196
Chinatown, 16, 17–18, 38, 47, 88, 91, 266, 274, 298
citizenship, xxi, 143, 161, 213, 284. *See also* naturalization
Commonwealth Immigrants Act (United Kingdom), 99
concentration(s), residential: ethnic 13–18, 69–72, 288, 296, 298; foreigners, 78, 91; models of, 68–70. *See also* spatial distribution/pattern

Convention for a Democratic South Africa (CODESA), 224

decommodification, 285, 300
disadvantage, locational and multiple, 71
dissimilarity, index of, 18, 39, 42–44, 47, 61–62, 91, 128, 131, 291, 295–96. *See also* segregation index

education, 132, 157–59, 211, 268–70; foreign male and female, 270; foreign women's, 211; secondary, 134
employment, 155–56, 211, 233. *See also* labor
ethclass, 148
ethnic: change, impacts of, 23; change, processes of, 233; conflict, 288; diversity, 46, 73, 216; emplacement models, 286–87; enclaves, xxii, 72, 287, 290, 298; identity, xxii, 252, 278; management, 252, 278; mosaic, 25, 252
ethnic/immigrant/foreign groups (definition based on country of origin): Albanian, 188; Algerian/Algeria, 80, 82–84, 86–87, 91, 93, 192, 297; American, 83, 88, 206–7, 211; Argentina, 206, 213; Australian, 2; Austro-Hungarian, 166; Bangladeshi/Bangladesh, 99, 101–2, 108–9,

305

The Editors

Curtis C. Roseman is professor of geography at the University of Southern California. His teaching interests include population geography, migration, and ethnic geography. His published research includes work on internal migration processes and patterns, migration of ethnic groups, and the ethnic composition of urban and rural areas in the United States. He organized and chaired the 1992 International Geographical Union Population Symposium of Los Angeles from which this volume originates.

Hans Dieter Laux is professor in the Department of Geography, University of Bonn, Germany. His teaching interests are in urban, population, and social geography. His research specialties include population development in German cities since the Industrial Revolution. Together with Günter Thieme he is involved in a research project on Asian immigration to the United States and has published numerous articles on ethnic minorities and immigration issues in Germany and the United States.

Günter Thieme is professor in the Department of Geography at the University of Dortmund, Germany. His teaching interests are in population and social geography and in North American studies. His research specialities include regional disparities and the geography of social well-being in Germany. Many of his recent publications focus on ethnic minorities and immigration in the United States and Germany.

The Contributors

Mana J. Aguilera Arilla is associate professor at the Universidad Nacional de Educacíon a Distancia, Madrid, Spain.

James P. Allen is professor of geography at California State University, Northridge.

Jürgen Bähr is professor of geography at the University of Kiel, Germany.

Frederick Boal is professor of human geography at The Queen's University of Belfast, United Kingdom.

Heinz Fassmann is lecturer in geography at the University of Vienna, Austria, and director of the Institute of Urban and Regional Research of the Austrian Academy of Science.

Aurora Garcia Ballesteros is professor at the Universidad Complutense de Madrid, Spain.

M. Pilar Gonzalez Yanci is associate professor at the Universidad Nacional de Educacíon a Distancia, Madrid, Spain.

Michelle Guillon is affiliated with the Université de Paris, France.

Felicitas Hillmann is senior research fellow at Wissenschaftszentrum Berlin, Germany.

Erick Howenstine is associate professor of geography, Northeastern Illinois University, Chicago.

Graeme J. Hugo is professor of geography at the University of Adelaide, Australia.

Ulrich Jürgens is lecturer in geography at the University of Kiel, Germany.

David McEvoy is professor and director of the School of Social Science at Liverpool John Moores University, United Kingdom.

Rainer Münz is professor of demography at Humboldt University, Berlin, Germany.

Sako Musterd is lecturer in geography at the University of Amsterdam, the Netherlands.

Warwick Neville is professor of geography at the University of Auckland, New Zealand.

Daniel Noin is professor, Université de Paris, France, and president of the Commission on Population Geography, International Geographical Union.

Wim Ostendorf is lecturer in geography at the University of Amsterdam, the Netherlands.

P. Pumares Fernandez is assistant at the Universidad de Almeria, Spain.

Vincente Rodríguez Rodríguez is researcher at Consejo Superior de Investigaciones Cientificas, Madrid, Spain.

Eugene Turner is professor of geography at California State University, Northridge.